Feminism's Founding Fathers

The Men Who Fought for Women's Rights

Feminism's Founding Fathers

The Men Who Fought for Women's Rights

Kaevan Gazdar

zero books

Winchester, UK
Washington, USA

First published by Zero Books, 2016
Zero Books is an imprint of John Hunt Publishing Ltd., Laurel House, Station Approach,
Alresford, Hants, SO24 9JH, UK
office1@jhpbooks.net
www.johnhuntpublishing.com
www.zero-books.net

For distributor details and how to order please visit the 'Ordering' section on our website.

ISBN: 978 1 78099 160 3
Library of Congress Control Number: 2016934227

A CIP catalogue record for this book is available from the British Library.

Design: Stuart Davies

Printed and bound by CPI Group (UK) Ltd, Croydon, CR0 4YY, UK

CONTENTS

Prologue

Misogyny: A Question of Gender or of Character?

> *I am most anxious to enlist everyone who can speak or write to join in checking this mad, wicked folly of 'Women's Rights', with all its attendant horrors... Feminists ought to get a good whipping.*

A good whipping. Adding injury to insult, as if the list of contemptuous comments and crude value judgements on women was not long enough. A list that begins in antiquity and continues well into the 21st century. Aristotle contended that women embody natural deformities, while the poet Simonide generalised rather more strongly: "Women are the greatest evil that God has ever created." Both the Old and the New Testaments consider women to be men's inferiors. "Wives, be subject to your husbands, as to the Lord," writes St. Paul in his *Epistle to the Ephesians,* summing up the issue quite neatly.

In *Misogyny: The Male Malady,* the anthropologist David D. Gilmore traces woman-hating from the jungles of New Guinea to present-day American boardrooms. Philosophers and scientists have played a major role in justifying discrimination. "Man is born free; and everywhere he is in chains," proclaims Jean-Jacques Rousseau at the beginning of his impressive treatise *The Social Contract*. Nonetheless, in his philosophical novel *Emile: or, On Education,* he makes it perfectly clear that the upbringing of a free individual only makes sense for boys. Sophie, Emile's wife-to-be, needs just enough education to become a good wife and mother. Similarly, Kant thought the female sex to be strong on temperament and weak on character, while Hegel considered that women were incapable of "universal faculties."

Liberal philosophers on the other side of the Channel came to similar conclusions: John Locke considered husbands to be "abler and stronger" when making family decisions, thus justifying the exclusive right of males to own and dispose of property. David Hume took the elevated view in his essay *On the Immortality of the Soul* that "the inferiority of women's capacity is equally accounted for. Their domestic life requires no higher faculties either of mind or body."

Shades of Sexism

The profoundly influential ideas of Charles Darwin gave sexism a seemingly respectable scientific foundation. Darwinism's central principle was the survival of the fittest, and for various reasons, men were fitter than women, who, with their smaller brains, were "eternally primitive," beyond being "a real danger to contemporary civilisation." A whole generation of psychologists and sexologists, from Sigmund Freud to Havelock Ellis, subscribed to Darwin's ideas, with repercussions still echoing through today's society.

Since the advent of gender studies, a sizeable number of men from all epochs, including artists, scientists and above all writers, face charges of being sexist. Did not Milton emphasise Adam's superiority in *Paradise Lost*? Was Brecht a misogynist who exploited women in "sex for text" deals, as John Fuegi contends in his biography of the playwright? Sara Paretsky has called Raymond Chandler the most misogynist writer in America. It is fair to point out that he faces fierce competition from John Updike, widely criticised for prose that reduces women to sexual objects. Martin Amis could probably compete for the title of Britain's foremost sexist. His fellow writer Marina Warner once wrote, "I read him with a mongoose fascination for his unrepentant misogyny."

Which brings us to the question: who was responsible for the monstrous quote at the beginning of this chapter? At first sight, Nietzsche seems a likely suspect. In his philosophical novel *Thus*

Spake Zarathustra, one of the characters remarks, "Are you going to women? Do not forget the whip!" The German philosopher had a penchant for flip phrases like "Women are less than shallow." However, the same is true of his French colleague Pierre-Joseph Proudhon, who famously asserted that women could only be housewives or harlots. And wasn't the Swedish dramatist August Strindberg even more sexist, both in plays like *Miss Julie* and in his autobiography, where he declares that all women are born liars and traitors?

Alas, "Feminists ought to get a good whipping" was written by a woman, not by a man. To be more precise: by perhaps the most powerful woman of the 19th century. Writing to her confidant Sir Theodore Martin in 1870, Queen Victoria expressed her indignation at the fact that Lady Amberley had addressed a public meeting in support of female suffrage. Victoria (1819–1901) herself had quite a paradoxical character. On the one hand, after profusely mourning her dead husband, Prince Albert, she allowed herself a great degree of liberty with her Scottish personal servant John Brown, not to speak of her Indian servant-teacher Abdul Karim, with whom she shared a "deep friendship." On the other hand, she adamantly demanded that women keep to their roles as mothers and housewives.

Katharine Amberley (1842–74), the mother of Bertrand Russell, was a remarkably emancipated woman. With the consent of her husband, she had an affair with Bertrand's tutor, the biologist Douglas Spalding. Beyond being active in the suffrage movement, she supported birth control and equal pay for women. Victoria deeply disapproved.

"Person," not "Man"

Despite her views, Victoria profoundly admired Florence Nightingale, who had studied nursing in the face of intense disapproval on the part of her family and then gone on to memorable achievements in the Crimean War. "The Lady with the Lamp" had to overcome the opposition of doctors and officers, before she could improve sanitary conditions and save the lives of countless soldiers.

Though she spent most of her life in the company of women and had set off on her famous expedition to Balaclava in the company of 38 female voluntary nurses, Nightingale (1820–1910) was, to say the least, reticent as to women's rights, once remarking that she was "brutally indifferent to the wrongs or the rights of my sex." Some scholars argue that she had a feminist perspective despite her opposition to suffrage and other issues, but it seems more likely that she was a strong-willed woman with a mission, who adopted men as her role models, and often spoke of herself as "a man of action."

Disdaining other women was indeed standard practice during the Victorian era. The novelist Mrs Gaskell endorsed Nightingale's disapproval of women training to become doctors: "I would not trust a mouse to a woman if a man's judgement was to be had. Women have no judgement." Writers like Margaret Oliphant and Mrs Humphrey Ward expressed similar views.

1869. One year before Victoria's derogatory remarks on feminists, an essay found great public interest and stimulated enormous controversy. Why should the leading liberal thinker of the 19th century be lobbying so strongly for women's rights? What were his motives, and where was all this leading? *The Subjection of Women* was John Stuart Mill's cri de coeur, his rallying call to Victorian society, his appeal to reason and to humanity. He attacked the "legal subordination of one sex to the other" as morally wrong, and called for complete equality.

For his pains, Mill (1806–73) was satirised in the press as being the "women's member" of parliament; caricatures were drawn of him in a dress. He tried in vain to enlist Florence Nightingale's assistance for his great cause. The literary critic Anne Mozley even questioned his credentials as the self-appointed champion of women's rights, while Margaret Oliphant considered his criticism of the subjection of married women to be "a gloomy image conjured up in the philosopher's study." Many prominent women insisted that they were perfectly satisfied with the status quo.

Male reformers like John Stuart Mill, later followed by the activists of the suffragist-suffragette movement, thus fought a two-front battle: against a masculine establishment and a phalanx of female supporters of the powers-that-be.

Companions, Mentors, Soul- and Bed-mates

Since the beginnings of the emancipation movement, men have been friends and fellow travellers. Take Mary Wollstonecraft, generally considered to be *the* English feminist of the 18th century. As a girl, Wollstonecraft (1759–97) suffered extreme discrimination within her own family. Her brother received a formal education, later inheriting most of their grandfather's fortune, while Mary, despite a voracious reading appetite, had to make do with piecemeal education, later earning an uncertain living as governess and lady's companion. Early friendships with Jane Arden and Fanny Blood, with whom she opened a school that soon went bankrupt, sustained her.

However, during her adult life, a series of loyal male friends stood by her. They included the Reverend Richard Price, a prominent Dissenter, and the publisher Joseph Johnson, who provided both material and moral support through most of her insecure life.

Sadly, Wollstonecraft died at the age of 38 after the birth of her second daughter Mary Shelley, later known as the author of *Frankenstein*. Her bereaved husband William Godwin commemorated her memory by writing a biography of her that scandalised public opinion, because he freely narrated her love affairs and attempts at suicide. During her lifetime however, Wollstonecraft could rely on a greater degree of assistance from her male friends than from most of her female acquaintances.

She encountered men like Price, Johnson and Godwin on equal terms of mutual support.

Mentors, patrons, soulmates: the men in Louise Otto-Peters' life played similar roles. Germany's premier feminist was responsible for the country's first women's newspaper and association. Her father, a wealthy judge, enabled his daughters to obtain an excellent education with private tutors; he also urged them to develop their own opinions on social and political issues, including the rights of women. Louise (1819–95) became as much a socialist as a feminist, fighting for the rights of factory workers in her early years. One of her most important mentors was Robert Blum, the charismatic revolutionary tragically executed after the 1848 revolution failed.

Louise in her turn supported the revolutionaries. She married August Peters, who had been first sentenced to death and then pardoned, in gaol. Later, when the Prussian government banned her newspaper, August helped her to found a new publication and officiated as its editor. This kind of reciprocal backing is reminiscent of Wollstonecraft's relations with Price and Godwin.

Germany has the good fortune to possess an equal-rights constitutional provision that America's women have been denied. This is almost entirely the achievement of Elisabeth Selbert (1896–1986), a strong-willed lawyer, who quickly perceived that the voting rights accorded to German women in 1919 still left them discriminated against in family law, not to speak of the workplace.

Elisabeth's husband Adam Selbert had introduced her to politics, taking care of the children while she studied law. Elisabeth became a Social Democrat like her husband and was encouraged by Philipp Scheidemann, Lord Mayor of her hometown Kassel, and, for a brief period, Germany's Chancellor. This support proved vital for her later career.

Forgotten Pioneers

Throughout the fight for women's rights, some men have played positive roles as companions, mentors and even pioneers. The very word "feminism" for instance is by all accounts a male invention dating back to the year 1837. It is generally attributed to the utopian socialist Charles Fourier, though this claim has been variously disputed. Some scholars ascribe it to Alexandre Dumas, who used the term pejoratively as a way of stigmatising manly women.

Fourier (1772–1837), who coined a large number of terms, had grasped that female subordination to men had to end. His ideas strongly influenced Louise Otto-Peters in Germany. She once quoted his axiom, "By the position that women hold in a country, you can see whether the air is thick with dirty fog or free and clear." Judged by this standard, the whole of Europe was plagued by dark fog during most of the 19th century.

While Fourier's claim to a feminist pedestal is largely theoretical – far from supporting women personally, he indulged in a large number of sexual escapades during his life and never married, discovering at the age of 35 that he was particularly attracted to lesbians – Richard Pankhurst's is eminently practical. Without him, it is unclear when or how the suffragette movement would have started in Britain. Pankhurst (1834–98) was a brilliant lawyer who established the National Society for Women's Suffrage and drafted the first suffrage bill, characteristically called the Women's Disabilities Removal Bill. His lasting personal achievement was to infect his wife Emmeline and his daughters Christabel, Sylvia and Adela with his radically enlightened ideas.

At first sight, men's attitudes towards women and their rights seem to brand them as heroes or villains. Mill, Pankhurst, Peters versus Nietzsche, Hume and Martin Amis. At second sight, the greatly good are seldom without blemish, while the bad boys often have redeeming qualities. Mill for instance firmly believed that, given a choice, women would all opt to stay at home; thus, he was less strident than other reformers about improving working conditions for women.

Nietzsche's reputation as a woman-hater derives from his "Do not forget the whip" exhortation in *Zarathustra* and several other comments. According to feminist thinkers like Simone de Beauvoir and Judith Butler however, the whip metaphor was meant ironically as a rhetorical reflection on the Zeitgeist of the late 19th century. Nietzsche's admirer Ida von Miaskowski commented in her memoir that his behaviour towards women was "so sensitive, so natural and comradely," that she could not believe he despised women. Nietzsche's circle of friends included avowed feminists like Lou Andreas Salomé and Malwida von Meysenbug. Beyond this, during his term as professor at Basel University, he belonged to a minority that tried to get women admitted to do their doctorates.

Equally ironically, it proves difficult to find exonerating evidence for Queen Victoria's call for the whip. Theodore Martin reports that Her Majesty was furious when she wrote him her recommendation on dealing with feminists quoted at the beginning of this chapter and certainly meant what she said. On another occasion, she felt that women ought to be "what God intended, a helpmate for man, but with totally different duties and vocation."

The Queen's channels of communication with the Almighty remain her secret. However, other women in high positions echoed her verbal brutality. Lady Lilias Bathurst (1871–1965), who inherited the conservative newspaper *Morning Post* from her father, recommended the following: "When a suffragette has been convicted, first have her well birched (by a woman), then shave off her hair and finally depart her to New Zealand or Australia."

The term "women's rights" suggests a monolithic façade belied by reality. One could, like Mary Ward, firmly endorse higher education for women while denying the need for suffrage. One could, like Eliza Lynn Linton, lead a highly emancipated life and still become the voice of antifeminism during the Victorian era. Linton (1822–98) separated from her husband by mutual agreement and continued her successful career as a pioneer journalist and novelist. On the one hand, she criticised double sexual standards and called for a reform of the divorce laws, on the other, she constantly attacked the "New Woman."

The terms often used in books and essays to characterise antifeminist women, like "gender traitors," "Eve's renegades" etc. reveal a romantic belief in unified sisterhood. The conventional feminist vision of enlightened gender solidarity is however an illusion. Women, like men, are individuals with their own priorities. Collectivising them and implicitly expecting them to subscribe to the gender-justice cause often overestimates the role that sex affiliation plays in their lives.

The same applies to the male feminists, often called *Traitors to the Masculine Cause,* fighting *Against the Tide* or operating from *Inside the Citadel,* to quote the titles of three books on the subject. The implicit assumption being that they were and are almost inexplicably, and thus heroically, betraying their sex. This book concentrates on the role that personal experience on the one hand and liberalism, nationalism, humanism, eugenics and class-bias on the other have played in determining the attitudes of the men who fought for women's rights.

The characters and achievements of many male feminists figure neither in history nor in "her story." In *Dreamers of a New Day: Women who Invented the Twentieth Century,* Sheila Rowbotham heralds women who have been forgotten because they were not in power, nor were they heroic, glamorous figures. The same applies to feminism's "founding fathers." They had different backgrounds, varying motivations and divergent methods. One major reason why they have been overlooked is that they did not form a cohesive group. Beyond that, their very existence relativises the master narrative of female heroism in the face of male exploitation. This book tells some of their stories. It concentrates on developments in the U.S., Britain, France and Germany while also portraying personalities and discussing important issues in other European countries.

1

From Chivalry to Coherence: Pioneers

It is not biology but the experience of society which restricts each sex to those characteristics and activities defined as feminine or masculine within any one society or era.
Harry Christian, *The Making of Anti-Sexist Men*

How blinded by biology are men? A simple question, but the answer is often the key to men's attitudes and actions. Sex is a biological fact; gender by contrast is a complex construct involving social class, ethnic background, economic status, educational standards, early influences and adult experience among other things. Throughout history, reducing women to their sexual affiliation results in their being stereotyped and mostly maligned, though sometimes idealised. By men, and by women as well.

In many ways, the ancient world was the crucible for attitudes to and power used against women. Greece thoroughly subjugated women. They could not vote or own property. In fact, they were the property of their fathers and husbands, often married off at an early age.

Their greatest claim to prominence was as objects, whether as the addressees of love poetry or as protagonists in dramas written by men. At first sight, Aristophanes' *Lysistrata* has feminist undertones. The heroine ends the Peloponnesian War between Athens and Sparta by organising a sex strike. The women barricade themselves in the Acropolis and refuse sexual intercourse, while tempting the men by wearing attractive clothes. Ultimately, the men capitulate and the war ends.

Aristophanes (ca. 450–380 BC) in fact stereotyped women into their roles as seducers. Lysistrata gets the women to fight with their bodies, not their minds. The peacemakers exploit their roles as temptresses, though the heroine and her close allies are both intelligent and independent. Thus, the play suggests women have no social, cultural or political influence. Their primacy is purely sexual.

Plato's ethics, as expressed in *The Republic,* are more far-reaching. Education and ruling are considered desiderata for both sexes. In the ideal city, men and women are equally capable of being active guardians. The philosopher's own beliefs however belie these phantasies of an ideal state. Plato (ca. 428–348 BC) was frequently disparaging of women in general, emphasising their physical weakness and their proclivity to deceitfulness.

This indeed illustrates a central paradox in many men with feminist inclinations: the difference between principles and person, between professed convictions and actual actions. Plato goes as far as advocating that women should train naked in the gymnasium alongside the men, thus ensuring their fitness for military service. His statement that cowardly men are reborn as women strongly relativises his "proto-feminism." Similarly, Plutarch (ca. 46–122 AD) in his work *Virtue of Women* (*Mulierum Virtutes*) depicts both sexes with the same virtues. Women however have major roles as advisors and helpmates. Here again, a feminine stereotype, that of feminine docility, comes to the fore.

From Querelle des Femmes to Amorous Friends

These attitudes gradually change in the course of civilisation. While women are often portrayed as villains or shrews in need of being chastised, the Age of Chivalry leads to individual approaches marked by greater respect. Take Juan Rodríguez de la Cámara, a Spanish poet. His sentimental novels include *The Triumph of Women,* a work that posits female superiority.

Rodríguez (1390–1450) was responding to the misogyny in Alfonso Martinez de Toledo's *Corbacho,* a satire that ridiculed female vices such as jealousy and disobedience. Rodríguez reverses the arguments used by Martinez (ca. 1398–1470). His views belong to the subversive tradition of Spanish renaissance literature.

Emphasis on female superiority belonged to the "Querelle des femmes" debate, a genre that propounded the superiority of either the male or the female sex. Martin Le Franc (1410–61) was a highly educated priest whose major work is *Le champion des dames,* which recalls the nobility of famous women like Joan of Arc. Similarly, François de Billon (1522–66) constructed in his *Fort inexpugnable de l'honneur du sexe féminin* a kind of citadel for women to help them resist the calumnies of misogynists. These were often rhetorical exercises rather than real pleas for reform.

On the other side of the Channel, wit compensated for a certain lack of clear intention. Restoration poet William Walsh, a close friend of Pope and Dryden, wrote a *Dialogue concerning Women, being a Defence of the Sex,* this being gallant prose on the part of a man burdened with "an amorous heart." He dedicated he book to Eugenia, possibly his mistress.

Walsh (1662–1708) was a Restoration rake and the originator of a series of breezy bonmots. One example: He once pointed out that there was no folly he had failed to commit in his devotion to women, apart from marriage. Dryden praised his *Dialogue* for treating "so nice a subject with so much judgment," but the real message is that women are taken far less seriously at the end of the 17th century than they were during the lifetimes of Sir Thomas More and Sir Thomas Elyot more than a century earlier. The same applies to *A Present for the Ladies* written by the Irish Shakespeare-adapter and poet laureate Nahum Tate, who ended his life in a debtor's prison. Tate's (1652–1715) historical vindication of the female sex, though influenced by Ovid and Montaigne, lacks coherence.

Almost a hundred years later, Pierre Boudier de Lillemert (ca. 1722–?) achieved a rare feat: his book *The Ladies' Friend* became a bestseller in France when published in the late 1750s. Lillemert advocates better education for women, though not in abstract subjects, while criticising female passiveness and what he calls a sense of luxury. In the work's preface, he denies that it is a parody on women; however, his tone of voice clearly reflects Rousseau's influence in allotting women subordinated roles in society. The author in fact calls Rousseau an "excellent observer." Lillemert's avowed friendship to women seems in the final reckoning to be condescending, though he does point out to his fellow men: "We are born the friends of women and not their rivals, still less their tyrants."

Similarly imbued with good intentions: the *Essai* written by a prominent pre-revolutionary poet, Antoine Leonard Thomas. Thomas (1732–85) was famous for his eulogies on great men and won the prize for rhetoric of the French Academy five times. He was a great admirer of typically "feminine" qualities such as sensibility and virtue.

The *Essay on the character, manners and esprit of women during different centuries* published in 1772 is in fact a compendium of famous women. Thomas was a protégé of the salonière Madame Geoffrin, who awarded him a private pension. He was well acquainted with figures like Diderot, but lacked both originality and clarity in the development of his ideas.

Education is Everything

Demands for educational reform are far more concrete and date back to the 13th century. The Norman lawyer Pierre du Bois (ca. 1255–1322) developed a blueprint for cooperation between European princes and the pope in his Latin work *On the Recovery of the Holy Land*. Here he advocates equal education for boys and girls in all subjects. However, du Bois's ulterior motive was that the well-educated women could then serve as wives to the infidels, helping to convert them to the true faith.

By contrast, the great pedagogue John Amos Comenius had humanistic reasons for advocating universal education. Highly cosmopolitan in his views, the Czech educational reformer worked in various European countries. Apparently, John Winthrop putatively invited him to be President of Harvard College. As a Protestant bishop, Comenius (1592–1670) contended that barring women from learning constituted "a denial of the divine will and a waste of their proven capacity to learn." This openness extended not only to women but also to the poor and mentally retarded; Comenius firmly believed that all sections of the population were entitled to be educated.

Voices of reason developed in both Britain and France. Sir Thomas Elyot's *Defence of Good Women* is a humanistic plea that cardinal virtues are inherent in both sexes; better education improves women's suitability as wives and mothers. Elyot (ca. 1490–1546) was a landowner and a scholar during the reign of Henry VIII. He occupied high public positions such as clerk of the Privy Council and High Sheriff, and then served as an intermediary to the Emperor of the Holy Roman Empire, Charles V, trying to persuade the latter to take a lenient view of the king's divorce of Catherine of Aragon.

Though Elyot was loyal to the king, he supported Sir Thomas More's enlightened views on women's education. More (1478–1535) was perhaps the greatest Englishman of his time, a consummate lawyer and statesman; he was simultaneously a devout and inflexible Catholic luminary, who persecuted heretics and had Protestants burnt at the stake. More paid for his opposition to Henry VIII's marriage to Anne Boleyn with his life. In his famous novel *Utopia*, he envisions an ideal society, where men and women enjoy the same education. Impressively, More practised what he preached. He personally educated his first wife in areas like literature and music and gave his daughters the same high education that his son received. The Lord Chancellor delighted in the erudition of his eldest daughter Margaret, in particular her mastery of Greek and Latin. He once wrote that "rather than allowing my children to grow up ignorant and idle,

I would sacrifice all..."

André du Laurens, principal doctor of the French king Henri IV, mirrors More's mixture of idealism and realism. Laurens (1558–1609) took a dispassionate view of both sexes; he rejected contemporary notions of women as errors of nature and called these barbaric. He was an eminent anatomist, without however subscribing to biologistic speculation on women's physical inferiority. As Michael Stolberg points out in his essay *A Woman Down to Her Bones*, Laurens belonged to a group of physicians who were convinced of the "unique and purposeful features of the female skeleton and female genital organs..."

Who Is Superior to Whom? Gender Rankings Past and Present

Laurens' common sense was signally lacking in a broad variety of treatises on the equality of the female sex. In *Female Pre-eminence: or the Dignity and Excellency of that Sex, above the Male,* Agrippa von Nettesheim (1486–1535) exalts the "noble and delicate Feminine Race," seeing Eve as the paragon of creation. The German philosopher was a skilled dialectician, authoring both a comprehensive book on occult arts and a work attacking all fields of learning including the occult. He apparently had a profound knowledge of both alchemy and astrology.

Considering this, *Female Pre-eminence* is possibly a figment of Agrippa's heretic views and of his desire to shock public opinion. It was written in 1509, early in his career, and apparently aimed at gaining patronage from Margaret of Austria, Regent of the Netherlands, though it was presented to her 20 years later. The desire to please could well have inspired his fulsome praise of "the noble and delicate Feminine Race" in the preamble to the treatise. It also leads him to assert that menstrual blood has curative powers. Despite the clichés and the exaggerations, the worth of his diatribe lies in the argument that apparent feminine inferiority does not derive from any kind of "natural order," but rather from unjust treatment.

The same rhetorical sleight of hand is visible more than a century later in François Poullain de la Barre's *Equality of the Two Sexes,* published in 1673. Poullain (1647–1725), a fervent Cartesian, believed in the preeminence of reason and argued that male superiority was a figment of "master logic." For the sake of argument, he later published a pamphlet on the excellence of men, so the question remains whether or not his motives were purely rhetorical, attuned to showing off his dialectical skills.

However, Poullain did focus on the male interest in the status quo, revealing the power play involved in establishing male superiority. Like Elyot, Poullain pleads for better education and echoes Agrippa in his contention that women lacked opportunities and thus underachieved. Simone de Beauvoir quoted his famous maxim, "The mind has no sex," in her classic *The Second Sex.*

Claims of female superiority have echoed throughout the centuries; the modern versions generally have an anthropological basis. Ashley Montagu asserts in *The Natural Superiority of Women,* first published in 1952, that women, as the "mothers of humanity," are also embodiments of its true spirit.

Writing more than 50 years later, in 2015, fellow anthropologist Melvin Konner went even further: "Women are not equal to men; they are superior in many ways… It is a matter of chromosomes, genes, hormones, and nerve circuits." In *Women After All: Sex, Evolution, and the End of Male Supremacy,* he describes maleness as a birth defect. An odd mixture of biology and brave contentions like "glass ceilings are splintering into countless shards of light, and women are climbing male power pyramids in every domain of life," Konner's ideas can be considered a form of modern chivalry with both scientific and rhetorical flourishes. This kind of well-meaning determinism blithely ignores upbringing, social patterns and other gender determinants.

Mixed Legacy of the Enlightenment

Sexism of the conventional variety certainly plays a role in Europe's Enlightenment tradition. The French group of advanced philosophers generally entitled the Encyclopaedists, because many of them collaborated in the publication of the *Encyclopaedia,* opposed laws limiting women's rights as being against nature. This was particularly characteristic of the work's founder Denis Diderot. His views on women were highly paradoxical. While coming out for women's rights and calling for better education, Diderot (1713–84) simultaneously made no secret of his personal disdain for the female sex. In his essay *On Women*, he saw them as victims of their uterus, "an organ subject to terrible spasms, which rules her and rouses up in her phantoms of every sort." As a result, women tended to be cruel, unscrupulous and manipulative among other things.

The same dichotomy between "enlightened" general views and crude personal views applies to other major figures of the French Enlightenment. Charles de Secondat, Baron de Montesquieu (1689–1755), author of the famous book on the Spirit of the Laws, presents a good example. His novel *Persian Letters* is a heretical pamphlet with criticism of prejudice relating to race and class as well as gender. The author became a member of various salons, including one fittingly called the Libertines; Montesquieu was in fact more a libertine than a liberator. He believed neither in women's enfranchisement nor in their capacity for choice, pitying rather than respecting them.

The Scottish Enlightenment was more dispassionate. John Millar, one of Adam Smith's leading disciples, made the economic system responsible for social relations of all kinds, including gender relationships. In his major work, *The Origin of the Distinction of Ranks*, Millar (1735–1801) declared that authority gains legitimacy when used efficiently to satisfy needs. Consequently, brutality towards those in inferior positions has no place in a progressive society.

Millar sees the fact that women in barbarous societies have no right to property as proof of their servile situation. Implicitly, this made Britain a primitive society despite its economic proficiency. However, Millar stops short of any kind of normative comments on injustice; women's rights do not exist for him as a category. By contrast, his contemporary William Alexander employed a tyrant-slave dialectic when describing marital relations. Alexander (1742–88?), a doctor by profession, openly confronted negative value judgements and roundly asserted that women were equal to men in mental terms, while calling for educational improvements. His *History of Women: From the Earliest Antiquity to the Present Time* however also emphasises that education should be linked to usefulness and domesticity, while avoiding "more intense and severe studies."

In Spain, the Enlightenment faced strong opposition from religious and social traditionalists. Ironically, the country's preeminent feminist was a Benedictine monk of noble origin. Benito Jerónimo Feijóo y Mentenegro was an empiricist and as such an enemy of superstitions and traditional beliefs. This led Feijóo (1676–1764) to publish *An Essay on Woman*, which took issue with gender stereotypes of female inferiority.

Feijóo's arguments reflect the shift from women's supposed moral superiority to a more acute understanding of their intellectual equality. As Professor of Theology and Philosophy at the University of Oviedo, he was well acquainted with the ideas of Locke and Newton, but also with those of Descartes and Bayle.

Though the "Querelle" discussion resonates in his Essay, in intellectual terms, Feijóo ranges between Poulain and the Encyclopaedists. However, his motivation differs: the scholarly monk saw gender equality as a means of modernising Spain, by that time one of the more backward European countries. He praises French women for their erudition and lauds France for providing them with more opportunities to study.

France's Founding Father

Marie Jean Antoine Nicolas Caritat, Marquis de Condorcet is the great French feminist of the Epoch of the Enlightenment, unique in his idealism and his sense of justice. The Marquis saw women not only as rational, but also as equal beings with the clear right to vote and to take public office. Condorcet (1743–94) was a true humanist, as much against slavery as against sexism. His *Plea for the Citizenship of Women* of 1790 in which he advocates suffrage is perhaps the most impressive feminist document of the 18th century, surpassing Mary Wollstonecraft's *Vindication of the Rights of Women* in both radicalism and scope.

Condorcet is an anti-biologist: he makes education and socialisation, not nature, responsible for women's place in society. He even contends that true democracy can only exist if women participate. As a philosopher and mathematician, the politician had a broad intellectual background, which led him to illustrious positions such as Secretary of the Academy of Sciences and of the Legislative Assembly after the Revolution. Politically, he sided with the moderate Girondists. When the Jacobins overthrew them in 1793, Condorcet's position became untenable. Forced into hiding and then imprisoned, he apparently committed suicide.

Condorcet's feminism is a mixture of reason and passion. His arguments are clearly enunciated and yet, when one reads his famous pamphlet *Sur l'admission des femmes au droit de cité* (*Plea for Citizenship*), there is no denying his fervour when he calls for admitting women to the privileges of civil society.

This explains his influence on revolutionary women, most prominently on Olympe de Gouges. Like Condorcet, she was a passionate reformer, demanding more rights for slaves and illegitimate children as well as for women. Gouges (1748–93) attacked women's exclusion from political rights such as those to vote and modelled her *Declaration of the Rights of Woman and Citizens* on revolutionary France's *Declaration of the Rights of Man*. Her style of writing is more emotional than that of the Marquis;

in the introduction to her Declaration, she describes men as being "bizarre, blind, bloated with science and degenerated." However, the substance of her ideas on equality parallel those of Condorcet, who, together with the Dutch feminist Etta Palm d'Aelder, had called on the National Assembly to extend civil rights to women.

An unlikely ally of Condorcet was the aristocratic soldier and bisexual lecher Charles de Villette. A member of the landed gentry and heir to a large fortune, the Marquis fought in the Seven Years War and received the Saint-Louis cross for bravery in combat. Villette (1736–93) then became one of France's notorious debauchees, mixing freely with both men and with the celebrated lesbian Mademoiselle Raucourt. Through his mother, he became a great friend and admirer of Voltaire, who died at Villette's home.

His colourful lifestyle disguised the fact that the libertine was a great intellectual and a literary figure to boot; Voltaire admired Villette's brilliance, while appreciating his sense of humour and his general humanism.

Villette became an avowed revolutionary, publicly burning his patent of nobility. This did not prevent him from opposing the execution of Louis XVI and he himself was fortunate to have died a natural death. The same courage seems to have motivated him to demand active citizenship for women. In 1790, he called it a "revolting contradiction" that the French assemblies excluded a sex that other countries, including Britain and Russia, had raised to the throne. Beyond demanding civic rights for women in general, he pleaded for financial support of poor women.

Apart from Villette, Condorcet had a number of other allies. Among them were prominent priests. Abbé Sieyès, whose claim to lasting fame rests on his pamphlet *What is the Third Estate?*, called it a "bizarre contradiction" that women were barred from public life. Abbé Fauchet was active in the Cercle Social club and associated with feminist women like Palm d'Aelder. Abbé Grégoire affirmed women's intellectual equality and called for universal suffrage.

Other supporters of votes for women included Pierre-Marc Guyomar and Jean-Denis Lanjuinais. However, the victory of the Jacobins precluded any kind of progress and after the Directorate came to power, legislation became restrictive, most prominently in the context of the Code Napoléon.

Germany's Founding Father

The German Enlightenment thinkers matched the ambivalence of their French counterparts. Kant categorises women as children, who are thus unable to be citizens, their natural capacities being weaker than men's are. However, his deliberations on sexual objectification have influenced many feminists. The views of other thinkers like the dramatist and art critic Gotthold Ephraim Lessing are similarly biased.

Kant's friend Theodor Gottlieb von Hippel is the great German exception. Here, we have the rare case of a pioneer from the Establishment. Hippel (1741–96), a highly gifted lawyer, held a number of high positions including Head of Police and Lord Mayor of Königsberg, Prussia's second largest city. He also authored anonymous works of literature often attributed to Goethe.

A brother in spirit to Condorcet, his private life could hardly have differed more. The French thinker was happily married; his wife Sophie was both a prominent salon hostess who counted Olympe de Gouges among her guests and an intellectual in her own right, having translated both Adam Smith and Thomas Paine into French. She was also the author of *Letters on Sympathy*. Sophie influenced her husband's thinking on women's rights.

Hippel by contrast was a confirmed bachelor, who complained that his parents had neglected to teach him the facts of life. Frustrated after his courtship of a highly placed young woman he tutored failed because of his humble family background, his experiences with women were apparently limited to prostitutes. This makes him an improbable champion of women's rights; apparently, his personal history failed to warp his judgment.

The German thinker's signal achievement is his discovery of female individuality. Rather than categorising women and assigning them specific roles, Hippel sees them as persons. Like Condorcet, he demands citizenship for them with all attendant rights and duties. *On Improving the Status of Women*, published in 1792, two years after Condorcet's *Plea* and in the same year as Wollstonecraft's *Vindication*, is a landmark, a hundred years ahead of its time. "Why should a woman not be able to say I?" he demands. "Why should women not be persons?" Writing in 1882, the women's-rights activist Helene Druskowitz said of him: "Those who are a thousand steps ahead of their contemporaries will invariably fail to be heard."

Decades later, John Stuart Mill attempted to substitute the word "men" by "persons" in the electoral register of the reform bill. Hippel wanted women to enter all professions, including his own. He called for them to become judges and legislators.

Hippel accused the French revolution of betraying its own egalitarian principles and berated men for having constructed "artificial cobwebs" to relegate women to "eternal tutelage." The Lord Mayor was 50 years old when he wrote these words. He was a man of the world, a pillar of society, and at the same time a tortured soul. As a judge, earlier in his career, he enforced the law by condemning women guilty of infanticide to death. As an anonymous journalist, he wrote articles criticising the inhumanity of the law. Could he have been more courageous? Perhaps he could, but the storm of protest that he faced when a friend betrayed his confidence by publicly identifying Hippel as the author of feminist literature displayed the difficulty of his position.

An avowed Jacobin, Hippel was however proud of belonging to the nobility and had the family title, which had relapsed, renewed. As a man, he was full of contradictions, an odd mixture of great rationality mixed with superstition and sensibility. His belief in complete equality did not extend to sexuality: "If a man is guilty of infidelity, this is unjust; if however a woman philanders, it's unnatural and ungodly." Despite this, Hippel was remarkably enlightened in a pragmatic, worldly way.

America's Sexist Founding Fathers

The situation in America at the time was dispiriting. The Founding Fathers were mostly confirmed patriarchs and the same applied to a broad cross-section of the U.S. revolutionaries, notwithstanding the fact that luminaries like Washington, Jefferson and Franklin had strong friendships with individual women on a very egalitarian basis. However, their support for women's rights was lukewarm at best. When Abigail Adams wrote her famous letter to her husband John in 1776, the year of the Declaration of Independence, requesting him to "remember the ladies and be more generous and favourable to them than your ancestors," the future U.S. President responded with scorn, calling her suggestion "saucy."

The same applies to political thinkers. Thomas Paine for instance bemoans injustice to women in *An Occasional Letter on the Female Sex*. His ideas on how women are invariably "adored and oppressed" however lack substantial evidence and follow the general logic of the Age of Reason. Here he is in tune with the French Encyclopaedists, possibly influenced by both his Quaker upbringing and John Locke's ideas of natural rights. Paine (1737–1809), the celebrated author of *Common Sense*, emphasises the differences between men and women rather than rejecting or relativising them, as Condorcet and Hippel do. He sees them primarily as wives and mothers. Published in 1774, the *Occasional Letter* precedes his major works and is not followed up by more coherent ideas, though the English revolutionary collaborated with Condorcet on drafting a new French constitution and must have been acquainted with the latter's *Plea for the Citizenship of Women*.

By contrast, Charles Brockden Brown, one of the country's first literary figures, was receptive to the ideas of Mary Wollstonecraft and William Godwin, while also displaying an affinity to German romanticism. Like Paine, he had a Quaker upbringing; unlike Paine, Brown (1771–1810) faced the issues at stake with clarity and courage.

Alcuin comprises a fictional dialogue between the eponymous schoolmaster and Mrs Carter, a wise widow from Philadelphia. The American Revolution serves as a crucible for the prime emancipation issue: autonomy versus protection. Alcuin plays a typical Enlightenment role: he praises the women as belonging to the superior sex while questioning their rights to enter public life. "Pray, Madam, are you a federalist?" he asks her and she responds by posing the rhetorical question: "What in the name of decency have we women to do with politics?"

Mrs Carter then exposes the gap between the Declaration of Independence's rhetoric and the reality of laws that bar women and other discriminated groups like blacks, immigrants, men under the age of 21, from voting. Her further arguments expose "decency" as a ploy to trap women into set roles. *Alcuin* serves as a sounding board for the ideas of a bluestocking that culminate in Mrs Carter's refusal "to smile at their tyranny, or receive as my gospel, a code built upon such atrocious maxims." She then concludes: "No, I am no federalist."

Brown skilfully uses the dialogue mechanism to explore the parameters of the "woman question." This indeed is a seminal discussion of the issues at stake and, as Anita M. Vickers points out, "Ultimately, *Alcuin* provides a vehicle for Brown's emphatic support for women's rights within a republican society."

Utopians and Marxists

In the 19th century, the Age of Ideologies, women's rights received a growing degree of attention and became a greater part of public discourse. Charles Fourier contributed to this. The utopian's ideas of universal harmony pivot round the "Phalansterium," an ideal society organised in phalanxes composed of representatives of 810 personality types. His phalanx colonies developed in France and the U.S., but did not stand the test of time.

Fourier (1772–1837) saw both sexes as equally capable in both arts and sciences. Like Hippel before him, Fourier had woeful personal experiences with women and later developed a liking for lesbians. Since he never laughed, people later called him the Buster Keaton of Utopia in France.

The utopian considered himself a genius of social interaction on the lines of Isaac Newton, but society scorned him as a scientific pariah. In Fourier's eccentric universe, monogamy did not exist; each woman could have four husbands simultaneously.

Fourier's ideas of universal harmony were well-meaning but highly impractical. However, he was a perceptive observer. His observations on alienation were influential for Marxist thought; equally, his contention that the treatment of women indicated how civilised a country was, impressed women's-rights activists in both France and Germany.

Claude Henri de Saint-Simon was to a certain extent more realistic. His vision was that of an egalitarian meritocracy. A fervent admirer of the United States, Count Saint-Simon (1760–1825) gave industrialists a leading role in society. His vision of technocratic socialism proved influential for both Marxists and positivists, though his projects, including connecting the Atlantic and Pacific oceans through a canal, invariably failed to materialise. After his marriage dissolved, he lived the rest of his life in poverty.

According to Saint-Simon, men and women were both social individuals with equal rights. Despite this, feminism is a peripheral aspect of Saint-Simon's world-view and only entered centre-stage through his disciple Barthélemy Prosper Enfantin. Enfantin (1796–1864) was a strange personality: as a self-styled father figure, he focused strongly on sexual liberation, while manipulating and marginalising the movement's female activists.

Scandals involving single mothers and the suicides of two female followers of Saint-Simon led to Enfantin's arrest and the decline of the movement. However, the women who were at the forefront of Saint-Simonianism like Claire Bazard, Eugénie Niboyet and others constitute France's early feminists. The debates within the movement and the conflicts with Enfantin proved to be a valuable accelerator of feminist consciousness.

Robert Owen had one tremendous advantage over Fourier and Saint-Simon. They were eccentric theorists; he by contrast was a successful industrialist with a large following and illustrious visitors, including the later Tsar of Russia. Forced to leave school and to become an apprentice at the age of ten, Owen (1771–1858) rapidly made a career as a manager of cotton mills and then became the owner of the New Lanark mill in Scotland, marrying the former proprietor's daughter.

New Lanark became the symbol of a humane enterprise: shorter working days and workers' access to a village store with food and alcohol provided at fair prices. Their children were cared for in a nursery and day school.

Owen later put his ideas on community into practice in New Harmony in Indiana. Equal rights for women was a fundament: "They will be equal in education, rights, privileges and personal liberty," he proclaimed in his *Book of the New Moral World*. Owen regarded the institution of marriage as a "pure, unadulterated system of moral evil" and saw communal living as a way to achieve social harmony.

However, Owen's brand of Utopian Socialism proved impracticable; he was forced out of his own factory in New Lanark and the New Harmony experiment was a signal failure, though it triggered off a great deal of reflection on the antagonisms and contradictions of capitalistic competition and how these were linked with the exploitation of women. Owenite communities however displayed the gap between idealistic theories and mundane practice. In theory, all work was shared equitably; in practice, men were exempt from housework and women were strongly underrepresented in higher positions.

Karl Marx and his followers were far more in tune with the economy and society of the 19th century than the French Utopians, though they lacked Robert Owen's practical experience. Their interest in women's rights proved to be both doctrinaire and self-serving.

In *The Origin of the Family, Private Property and the State,* Marx's collaborator Friedrich Engels presents a historic overview culminating in the monogamous family. Engels (1820–95) considers bourgeois marriage to be "crassest prostitution," since it is a marriage of convenience governed by the class positions of husband and wife. Here, his views coincided with those of Owen, whom he however disdained. The Owenites, often called the first British socialists, were considered tame, peaceable and indeed "dogmatic and utterly hopeless," guilty of "crude theories" and "grand fantasies."

Engels sees the legal inequality of married women as the result of economic oppression. The woman "only differs from the ordinary courtesan in that she does not let out her body on piece-work as a wage-worker, but sells it once and for all into slavery." The husband is in this logic a bourgeois, while the wife belongs to the proletariat. Only proletarians without property can have equal relationships.

The rich industrialist was in his private life a carefree hedonist, having relationships with a number of working-class women and openly enjoying the services of prostitutes. His relationship with Mary Burns, a mill-worker and Engels' long-time mistress, illustrates his libertine sentiments, though he mourned her early death. The founder of Marxist feminism believed that women were domestic creatures; in his early writings, he however showed far more empathy for the plight of female and child workers. Indeed, Engels made no secret of his dislike of self-willed women. Tristram Hunt sums up: "Engels was the intellectual architect of socialist feminism and an old-fashioned sexist."

Materialism apparently precluded true sympathy for women. The women's-rights issue was reduced to class inequality; Marxists took the naïve view that the socialist revolution would solve all problems.

Quest for Justice: Theory Belied by Practice

In general, Marxism linked with feminism proved an "unhappy marriage," as Rosalynd A. Sydie points out. It was also a cruel burden to female Marxists, forced to preach the gospel. Eleanor Marx proclaimed that her female comrades had to organise as proletarians, not as women. The German feminist Clara Zetkin followed suit by emphasising that "women's petty interests" should not enter the foreground. Dogma isolated Marxist thinkers of both sexes from the feminist mainstream.

By contrast, Fourier as well as Marx influenced the leader of Germany's Social Democratic Party (SPD). August Bebel's bestseller *Woman and Socialism* begins with the contention that women and workers share the same fate of repression since ancient times. Bebel (1840–1913) was by no means a feminist and his book is full of patronising and insulting remarks. Despite this, it gives a graphic description of women's historic repression, in the same mould as Engels' famous study *The Condition of the Working Class in England*. Thus, it provided valuable ammunition for feminists of all persuasions.

Bebel also resembled Engels in his personal dislike of intelligent, articulate women. His derogatory comments on Rosa

Luxemburg ("too much a woman and too little a comrade") and Clara Zetkin ("too little sense for facts") display his fear of "Furies." He was in the final reckoning a respectable patriarch with an intact family, often called Kaiser Bebel because of his undisputed supremacy in the SPD.

Worlds separated Guiseppe Mazzini from both Engels and Bebel. Though Bebel's wife Julie had supported her husband during the period when he was imprisoned and had run his business successfully, she remained firmly in the background. The Italian revolutionary's wife by contrast was his true comrade until her premature death. Mazzini (1805–72) embodied the spirit of Risorgimento, the movement for the unification and independence of Italy, to a greater degree than Garibaldi and Cavour. Together, they form the trinity of Italy's independence heroes.

While Germany's unification was a "blood and iron" affair dominated by Prussia, the Italian road to independence involved a greater deal of idealism, notwithstanding the fact that Camille Cavour's astute alliances played a major role in eliminating Austrian and French dominance. For Mazzini, democracy and national self-determination were equally important goals; women's rights were an integral part of his vision of an ideal society. In a speech to Italian workers on men's duties (Doveri dell'uomo) held in 1860, he called for an end to the social and legal subordination of women.

Mazzini had strong emotional bonds to women and by all accounts valued them more than the men with whom he dealt. He was very close to his mother and considered his female disciples to be "loving sisters." Writing to a prominent fellow feminist Salvatore Morelli, Mazzini asserted that men and women were variants of the same type of human nature. In Milan, he consorted with aristocratic ladies and urged them not to overlook the exploitation of working-class women. Like Bebel, he believed that the emancipation of women and workers were linked.

Needless to say, Mazzini and Marx shared a mutual dislike. Mazzini described him as being "a destructive spirit whose heart was filled with hatred rather than love of mankind." Marx treated with disdain the Italian's high-flown ideas of a "middle-class republic" and certainly did not appreciate his devout belief in God.

Utilitarian Pragmatism

Utilitarian pragmatism was by contrast to the Utopians and Marxists a breath of fresh air. The intellectually banal principle of the "greatest happiness of the greatest number" automatically amplifies the radius of reform and puts the accent on doing, rather than theorising. Consequentialism focuses on results rather than sheer ideas, on outcomes rather than intentions. Here, quite clearly, are the germs of social activism that led to reform.

For Utilitarianism's guiding spirit Jeremy Bentham, equal rights for women were part of his liberal-hedonistic doctrine. His radical blueprint for an enlightened world included the legalisation of homosexuality, the right to divorce and abolition of the death penalty. Bentham's demands became reality in most Western countries during the course of the 20th century. The pragmatic humanism of this reclusive eccentric manifestly prevailed over the visions and dogmas of the Utopians and the Marxists.

Bentham (1748–1832) considered women to be equally entitled to happiness. By contrast, he considered them "commonly inferior" in mental terms, though morally superior. This is a surprisingly conventional viewpoint for someone arguing for women's suffrage, participation in government and the right to divorce. Indeed, it seems that the great reformer demanded the right things for the wrong reasons.

Bentham's secretary and collaborator James Mill was less hedonistic; as a Presbyterian, he was also closer to the Scottish

Enlightenment. His version of radical individualism called for a wide voting franchise while excluding women and men under 40. Women were best represented by their husbands.

Thus, Mill (1773–1836) contradicted his own contention that each person is the best judge of his or her own interest. It also goes against the logic of his *History of British India*, which equates social progress with women's status in society, thus recalling Fourier's standpoint.

Bentham and Mill both embody the logic of feminism, though they shrink back from the consequences of their own rationalisations. Bentham believed that men lacked the maturity to work effectively with women and thus justified the exclusion of the latter from the political process. It was James Mill's celebrated son, one of feminism's most remarkable Founding Fathers, who took the step over the Rubicon.

2

Battle for the Ballot Box: Suffragists and Suffragettes

> *Those only are happy who have their minds fixed on some object other than their own happiness: on the happiness of others, on the improvement of mankind, even on some art or pursuit followed not as a means, but as itself an ideal end. Aiming at something else, they find happiness by the way.*
>
> John Stuart Mill

Happiness was a core concept of the Enlightenment in both Britain and the United States. Francis Hutcheson's famous dictum, "That action is best which procures the greatest happiness," is mirrored in the American Declaration of Independence, which elevates "life, liberty and the pursuit of happiness" to the unalienable rights that provided the new nation with its raison d'être.

The utilitarian viewpoint, as expressed by Jeremy Bentham among others, is a kind of individualistic collectivism. It postulates that the well-being of a community is the sum of individual pleasure. Later, neoclassical economists equated happiness with utility, the homo oeconomicus functioning as the rational protagonist of utility.

Mill's credo is more sophisticated; he recognises the various layers of pleasure. The 19th century's great liberal thinker was more for idealism than for egotism: mental pleasure was certainly of a higher order than base physical pleasure. Mill's fight for suffrage seems indeed to be "a pursuit followed not as a means, but as itself an ideal end."

Founding Father of Liberal Feminism

John Stuart Mill is the rare case of a man of letters who was simultaneously a man of action. Mill (1806–73) started as a child prodigy under his father's tutelage. He learned Greek from the age of three and had read most of the Greek and Latin classics by the age of 14, by which time he had already mastered the basics of mathematics and economic theory. Behind the facade of the genius, who would come to write *On Liberty*, one of liberalism's sacred texts, was a highly sensitive individual, who suffered from a severe depression at the age of 20. Three years before that, Mill's visceral sense of justice got him arrested for distributing information on birth control after he found a dead infant in one of the London parks.

After rising through the ranks at the East India Company, finally becoming Chief Examiner, Mill entered politics and gained a seat in the House of Commons in 1865. Here he called for women's suffrage. Greeted with jeers, he persisted with his efforts, celebrating his 61st birthday by proposing that the word "man" in the Second Reform Act be changed to "person." This would have enabled women to vote, and after tenacious lobbying, Mill managed to get a quarter of the House – 73 votes – to support his motion. It was an honourable achievement; remarkably, the Tory leader Disraeli supported Mill, despite the fact that he had dared to say "that the Conservative Party was, by the law of its constitution, necessarily the stupidest party."

Mill cooperated closely with both male and female reformers; he was for instance President of the National Society for Women's Suffrage founded by Lydia Becker. No other male feminist has ever been as widely respected and highly acclaimed. His amendment, though defeated, earned serious debate. This alone represents great progress; in 1832, when the radical politician Henry Hunt (1773–1835) proposed universal suffrage in parliament, his fellow MPs simply laughed at the idea, refusing to discuss the issue.

Mill was profoundly humanistic, thus exposing the limitations of the Utilitarians, who doubtlessly influenced him. He refutes the ideas of his father James Mill and is more convinced of equality between the sexes than Jeremy Bentham, who in his Introduction to the *Principles of Morals and Legislation* contended that men were women's intellectual superiors, surpassing them also in "firmness of mind." JSM by contrast finds gender inequality socially harmful, its eradication vital for the improvement of humanity.

The Subjection of Women is a feminist classic, clearly argued, though slightly apologetic when dealing with clichés on women's minds. Mill faces a classic problem: he enunciates that sexual difference exists, while insisting that it derives from repression. In all his arguments, JSM was truly liberal: he believed his own rights were worthless if others did not have them. Thus, he was an idealistic feminist from the start.

Simultaneously, he was highly emotional. Emotionality certainly facilitated his remarkably egalitarian relationship with Harriet Taylor, with whom he fell in love in 1830. JSM treated her not only as his intellectual equal. He even considered her superior to him; some commentators chide him for exaggerating her contribution to his ideas. This might be partly true; it certainly testifies to rare generosity.

Mill differs from Taylor in his view that married women should not work, thus contradicting himself in terms of justice and ignoring the economic pressures on working-class women. Here, Taylor in *The Enfranchisement of Women*, which reflected her thoughts while published under his name, was definitely more progressive.

As an intellectual, JSM relates more to the mind rather than the body. In this respect, he seems somewhat Victorian, reflecting the general attitude towards sexuality as being something barbaric that needs to be controlled. However, his calls for the punishment of marital rape were at least as innovative as the suffrage campaign. Beyond that, he makes the connection between repression and sexual roles, pointing out in *Subjection of Women*: "Men hold women in subjection by representing to them meekness, submissiveness and resignation of all individual will into the hands of a man, as an essential part of sexual attractiveness."

Mill also presciently realised that universal men's rather than women's suffrage would privilege working-class men at the cost of women. This indeed proved later to be the case. However, he also pleaded for plural voting, which would have given educated voters stronger election rights than the British masses.

In his *Thoughts on Parliamentary Reform,* Mill goes as far as allotting different proportions of votes to members of various social classes. Unskilled labourers should have one, skilled workers two, while university graduates were entitled to six. Those who were illiterate or lived on the dole were barred from franchise. Here again, Mill relativises his own democratic convictions. The great man was in fact a bit of a prig and a bit of a snob, which probably makes him a typical Victorian. In no way does this detract from his massive achievements.

From Words to Action: New Zealand as Suffrage Trailbreaker

Mill's ideas led to concrete change in New Zealand, the first country in the world to grant universal female suffrage in 1893, only 14 years after the adoption of complete male suffrage. The liberal philosopher had a strong influence on both male and female suffragists. Mary Ann Muller, whose *Appeal to the Men of New Zealand* was published in 1869, the same year as *Subjection of Women,* was supported by Mill, who commended her on having made "an excellent beginning."

The Women's Christian Temperance Union (WCTU) was the backbone of the suffrage movement. The strong correlation between temperance and suffrage made the liquor lobby consequently the most vehement opponent of the women's vote. Alcohol producers rightly feared that women would vote for restrictions when given suffrage.

Temperance gave suffragists a respectability they lacked in other countries. WCTU leader Kate Sheppard (1847–1934), intelligent, well educated and with strong organisational skills, resembles Mill in her eloquence and likeability. Beyond canvassing for the women's vote, she was a dress reformer and one of the country's first women to ride a bicycle.

The suffrage cause in New Zealand demonstrates the importance of sociocultural factors. As a frontier country with a zest for experiments, it was more open to new ideas than Britain or for that matter other countries in Europe. Social mobility contrasted with the entrenched class system in British society.

Inclusiveness for women paralleled attempts to reconcile colonial settlement with the rights of local Maoris. Maori women duly gained voting rights together with white women. The temperance movement's high moral tone and propagation of "virtue" commanded respect and facilitated their demands for women's rights.

Parliamentarians like Alfred Saunders and Sir William Fox had proposed giving women the vote as early as 1843. Saunders (1820–1905) had in fact campaigned for both male and female suffrage; ironically, he lost his parliamentary seat in the 1881 general election, the first election with a universal male vote. Like Saunders, Fox (1812–93) was a temperance activist, thus close to the aims of WCTU. Beyond supporting women's suffrage, Fox, who was four times prime minister of New Zealand, also campaigned for a ban on women working in hotel bars.

It took until 1879 for women's suffrage bills to reach parliament. A succession of motions were either narrowly defeated, or passed in the House of Representatives and annulled by the Legislative Council (New Zealand's Upper

House). The Electors Bill of 1879 proposed giving female property owners the vote; suffragists wanting universal female franchise defeated it.

Parallel to this, the women's movement gleaned broad support from a cross-section of high-ranking politicians of both the Conservative and Liberal parties. The liberal Sir John Hall collaborated closely with WCTU and proposed the bill finally passed in 1893. However, he had reservations that enfranchised women would vote Conservative, the irony being that he himself had highly conservative views and only became a member of the new Liberal Party for opportunistic reasons. Hall (1824–1907) was apologetic about the apparent fact that women lacked the political education to vote responsibly, but contended that it was "a defect which will cure itself."

The Liberal Party founder and prime minister John Ballance was a more convinced supporter. As a newspaper editor, he had distinguished himself by criticising the government during a war against the Maori, showing liberal convictions that derived from his Quaker mother. Ballance prepared the ground for suffrage, but died prematurely in 1893, shortly before the bill passed parliament despite subversive attempts by his successor in office, Richard Seddon. Like Hall, Balance (1839–93) apprehended that women's votes would favour the Conservatives. For this reason, he delayed the implementation of the enfranchisement bill until after the 1893 election.

Ballance declared in parliament his belief in the "absolute equality of the sexes," influenced by both his colleague Julius Vogel and his feminist wife Ellen. Julius Vogel, a half-Jewish businessman and politician, had been subject to anti-Semitic attacks and was thus attuned to social discrimination. He saw female suffrage as a means of integrating women into society.

Vogel (1835–99), a paradoxical figure with imperialist views and liberal sentiments, was in and out of office for decades, including two terms as New Zealand's prime minister. Like

Ballance, he had owned a newspaper before entering politics. His final achievement is the futuristic feminist novel *Anno Domini 2000; or, Woman's Destiny*. Here women hold high positions in government; the book's heroine Hilda Richmond Fitzherbert is Under-Secretary of State at the age of 23.

Despite the country's pioneering role, political leadership for women developed slowly. Women gained the right to stand for election (passive franchise) as late as 1919. The first New Zealand female MP was elected in 1933; in Britain, by contrast, Lady Astor entered the House of Commons in 1919. Similarly, New Zealand's first female Prime Minister came to power in 1997, long after Margaret Thatcher's accession in 1979. This shows that suffrage alone does not guarantee upward political mobility.

Britain: The Men behind Suffragists and Suffragettes

Despite the support of a fair cross-section of politicians including Liberals and Conservatives, progress in Britain was painfully slow. Mill was a strong influence on both moderate and radical suffrage-seekers. However, only a small coterie of politically active men and women joined the struggle for suffrage.

One of Mill's greatest admirers was the parliamentarian Henry Fawcett, husband of the leading suffragist Millicent Garrett Fawcett. Having first qualified as a barrister, Fawcett (1833–84) then became a Professor of Political Economy in Cambridge, entering parliament in 1865. Though blinded at the age of 25 by an accidental shot from his father's gun while out hunting, Fawcett continued his public life and had both a wide range of interests and a strong sense of justice. When speaking in the House of Commons on suffrage, Fawcett cited his experience at Cambridge that women could hold their own with men while strengthening their characters. Like Mill, to whom he deferred on all issues, he insisted that they have the same opportunities as men.

Henry introduced his wife to politics, encouraged her writing career and her interest in women's-rights issues. Thus, he played an important background role in the foundation of the National Union of Women's Suffrage Societies (NUWSS). Millicent (1847–1929) doted on him and helped him greatly in his various activities, often being described as his amanuensis. She joined the Langham Place group and later took a leading role in the National Societies for Women's Suffrage.

As a member of the government, Fawcett clashed with the liberal Prime Minister William Gladstone on the latter's refusal to include franchise in the 1884 Reform Act. He used his official position as Postmaster General to employ female medical officers.

Fawcett was not alone in the Liberal Party; among his allies were his fellow Cambridge graduates Leonard Courtney and Charles Wentworth Dilke. Both saw votes for women as a way of achieving greater democracy. Baron Courtney of Penwith (1832–1918) had a career that paralleled Fawcett's: barrister, Professor of Political Economy at University College London, elected as a Liberal MP, later a member of Gladstone's cabinet. Courtney influenced his wife Catherine, elder sister of Fabian Society co-founder Beatrice Webb, towards suffrage activities. Baronet Dilke (1843–1911) was a more controversial personality. As a radical liberal, he had supported the law giving women municipal suffrage. For a time, he seemed predestined to reach the highest political office and had then to quit politics because of his questionable involvement in a divorce case.

The radical Richard Marsden Pankhurst was even more influential than Fawcett; his impact on the suffragette movement is in fact crucial. Pankhurst (1834–98) can best be characterised as a compulsive reformer in search of causes: free speech, abolition of the House of Lords, home rule for the Irish, independence for the Indians and votes for women. A brilliant lawyer, who won a gold medal when passing his LLD examinations, Pankhurst soon abandoned the confines of the Liberal Party, becoming one of the founders of the Independent Labour Party.

Universal suffrage was Pankhurst's lasting passion, one that he instilled as much in his wife Emmeline as in his daughters Christabel, Sylvia and Adela. The "Red Doctor," who twice ran unsuccessfully for a parliamentary seat, was a close friend of John Stuart Mill, collaborating with the great liberal thinker on various rights issues. In Manchester, where Pankhurst organised free evening tuition for workers, he was also responsible for a revolutionary amendment of the Municipal Franchise Act, which enabled propertied women to vote at local elections. Never before had women achieved the right to vote in Britain. Pankhurst literally sowed the radical suffrage seed; his wife and daughters were instrumental in drawing in the harvest.

When in 1879 Richard Pankhurst married Emmeline Gould, who was 22 years younger, she was diffident and shy. Under his guidance, she developed into the fearless public speaker and brilliant organiser who made Britain's suffragettes the world's most radical agitators for women's votes. Appalled by the tame approach of suffragists like Lydia Becker, Pankhurst held a meeting in his home and was so exasperated at the lack of progress that he hectored the women present: "Why don't you force us to give you the vote? Why don't you scratch our eyes out?" Unlike Becker, he demanded full suffrage for all women and refused to settle for less.

Pankhurst drafted a reading programme for his wife, made her a member of the Married Women's Property Act committee, and generally groomed her for her future role. After Richard's premature death in 1898, Labour leader Keir Hardie persuaded Emmeline to carry on her husband's work within the party. Later, the suffragette movement, consolidated as the Women's Social and Political Union (WSPU), became increasingly conservative and authoritarian; Sylvia quarrelled with her mother and sister about their disdain of working-class women, later acting in her father's spirit by endorsing a variety of causes, including the Russian Revolution and the Ethiopian resistance against the Italian invasion. She was duly ejected from WSPU.

Richard Pankhurst's achievements have still to be adequately honoured. In a tribute to him, the BBC acknowledged that Pankhurst's life now figures at best as a footnote to the suffragette narrative and came to the following conclusion: "However, was it not for his authorship of key parliamentary acts fuelled by a contagious enthusiasm for liberal politics, his family would almost certainly have trodden a less significant path."

Allies and Activists

Like Fawcett, Pankhurst had friends who shared his convictions and supported him. Jacob Bright, who introduced the suffrage bill to the House of Commons in 1870, belonged to his allies and shared the same radical views. Bright (1821–99) was a long-time MP for Manchester and had a supportive family: both his sister Priscilla and his wife Ursula campaigned for women's rights.

His brother John Bright by contrast, who served in two Liberal cabinets under Gladstone, was a thorough opponent of the women's vote. After John, an excellent orator, had spoken against suffrage in the House of Commons in 1876, Jacob attacked his brother in a public speech held in Manchester. John had asserted that women were well represented in parliament despite lacking voting rights, being privileged because they could sue for breach of promise, and that the Church in any case unduly influenced them. Jacob, caricatured by the magazine *Vanity Fair* as The Apostle of Women, responded by saying that the influence on male voters through landlords and mill owners was far more malignant.

Similarly, the businessman and parliamentarian William Woodall introduced several suffrage bills in the House of Commons. As Financial Secretary to the War Office, Woodall (1832–1901) annoyed Prime Minister Gladstone by refusing to withdraw his amendment to the 1884 Representation of the People Act; here there are clear parallels with Henry Fawcett.

Fawcett's successor in the House of Commons echoed his views. James Stuart was a highly qualified scientist, becoming Professor of Applied Mechanics at Cambridge University and serving as Lord Rector of the University of St. Andrews. Stuart (1843–1913), who also canvassed for women's education, was duly lampooned in *Vanity Fair* as being "many-sided and too enthusiastic. He champions Women's Suffrage because, being a student of Exact Science, he cannot understand Women." This was a common insult and one that female critics of John Stuart Mill had already levelled. Stuart tried to convince Prime Minister Gladstone's daughter Mary, a close friend, of the merits of suffrage, but does not seem to have been successful.

While Gladstone remained firmly opposed to allowing women to vote, his successors were more liberal. Sir Henry Campbell-Bannerman, Prime Minister between 1905 and 1908, was personally in favour of enfranchising women and even deplored the fact that the proposed Bill would only apply to single women and those of property. Campbell-Bannerman (1836–1908), Scottish-born and educated, like many male suffragists, at Trinity College Cambridge, apparently relied on the advice of his astute wife Charlotte.

Unfortunately, upon Campbell-Bannerman's death, his successor H.H. Asquith, who served two terms from 1908 to 1916, was of a Gladstonian persuasion. Despite this, in his cabinet were several ministers who made no secret of their sympathies for suffrage. This was preeminently the case with the Foreign Secretary Sir Edward Grey and with David Lloyd George, who succeeded Asquith in 1916.

Lloyd George (1863–1965) had initially professed support for the cause, but as a minister, he proved dilatory. Believing that women, when enfranchised, would vote Conservative, he opposed the extension of suffrage to those women who could already vote in local elections. Until he became Prime Minister, Lloyd George proved difficult to pin down and Christabel Pankhurst accused him of "always betraying us."

However, when an all-party coalition government came into place, the case for suffrage became undeniable. The WSPU had curtailed demonstrations and firmly supported the war efforts; the government responded accordingly. In a message read to Allied women war workers, the Prime Minister emphasised that women had proved during the Great War that they were fit for the vote.

Fredrick Pethick-Lawrence was one of the strongest supporters of WSPU. Educated in Eton and Cambridge, he became a barrister. Pethick-Lawrence (1871–1961) had an intense social conscience, working in the slums of East London, where he met the social worker Emmeline Pethick. She only consented to marry him when he converted to socialism. They both became fervent supporters of the suffragette cause. In the pamphlet *Women's Fight for the Vote*, published in 1911, Pethick-Lawrence argues that "forty years of ladylike methods" had not proved successful, thus necessitating "militant methods."

Pethick-Lawrence sacrificed his fortune for the WSPU and made his home the office of the movement. He represented suffragettes in court and provided bail for them. Beyond that, the Pethick-Lawrences agitated for the cause, duly going to prison and suffering forcible-feeding. When they expressed dismay at the illegal and violent WPSU methods, including the smashing of shop-windows, Emmeline and Christabel Pankhurst summarily dismissed them. Ironically, WSPU fought for democratic rights while being itself a highly authoritarian organisation.

Despite this or perhaps because of this, the suffragettes attracted men who not only shared the same convictions, but also participated in violent activities. Hugh Franklin (1889–1962) neglected his studies in Cambridge to organise meetings, sell newspapers and heckle speakers like Churchill. Franklin went to jail for trying to attack Churchill with a dog whip and for throwing a stone at his house. He endured force-feeding in prison more than a hundred times.

Henry Devenish Harben, who provided bail for Franklin, was a barrister and a prominent member of the Fabian Society. Harben (1874–1967) had resigned from the Liberal Party because of its hostility to WSPU, but later became a personal critic of Christabel Pankhurst, whom he accused of ignoring the problems faced by the movement's grass-roots supporters.

The Labour Party's pioneers advocated suffrage despite a distinct lack of working-class commitment to women's rights. James Keir Hardie, Philip Snowden and George Lansbury adhered to the strangely chivalrous idea that women would ennoble politics. All had strong Christian Socialist instincts.

Hardie (1856–1915), a great friend of Pethick-Lawrence, welcomed the Pankhursts and supported their heckling tactics at meetings, but was disturbed, like other Labour leaders, by violence. His *Plea for Women's Suffrage* of 1905 readily admits sexual differences, while attributing them to maltreatment.

His wife Ethel converted Viscount Snowden (1864–1937) to the cause; he allied with Hardie on the issue. Lansbury (1859–1940) risked his political prospects by supporting the suffragettes; when jailed, he went on a hunger strike. He later had a distinguished career in government and as the Leader of the Labour Party, motivated by the parallel injustices of gender and class. Arthur Henderson (1863–1935) played an important role in the final phase. As member of the wartime coalition government, he made women's suffrage a precondition of his consent to franchise extension.

In the Conservative Party, Prime Ministers Benjamin Disraeli and Lord Salisbury were sympathetic to the cause. However, they only paid lip service. The same applied to their colleague Arthur Balfour, who as prime minister supported the motion in 1892 to introduce franchise and warned of the consequences of ignoring the issue, but did little until, in Lloyd George's coalition government, he introduced the all-party bill in 1917.

Support of the Intelligentsia

A large number of progressive writers supported women's rights, in particular suffrage. Many of them belonged to the Men's League for Women's Suffrage, founded in 1907. Its members included Israel Zangwill and Laurence Housman. Both were converted by close relations: Zangwill by his wife, Housman by his sister.

Zangwill's claim to immortality rests on his play *The Melting Pot*, which has served as a metaphor for the society of the United States, and on various books that reflect his Jewish background. He had a gift for words and responded to the claim that suffragettes were unwomanly with the rejoinder that well-mannered methods were called for when there were gentlemen involved; however, the WSPU was dealing with politicians. He also prophetically pointed out in his speech *Old Fogeys and Old Bogeys* that the time was soon coming "when in no civilised country will be seen cars without electricity or women without votes."

Zangwill (1864–1926) was a critic of the violent methods and dictatorial structure of WSPU, though he generally supported the suffragettes. Together with his wife, he later founded the Jewish Suffrage League.

Housman (1865–1959), brother of the poet Alfred, founded the Suffrage Atelier with his sister Clemence. This arts-and-crafts society cooperated both with WSPU and with the non-violent Women's Freedom League. He often spoke at Hyde Park suffrage rallies. As a homosexual, Housman was an advocate of sexual freedom and tolerance; he travelled to Paris to pass funds to Oscar Wilde. His most prominent literary contribution was a play called *Alice in Ganderland*, an obvious parody of Lewis Carroll's celebrated *Alice in Wonderland*. Housman put Carroll's characters into political costumes: the March Hare represented Labour, while the Dormouse wore a Peer's robes and was an obvious Conservative. Alice herself wears the colours of the WSPU and in the end, she calls for representatives of the suffrage societies to invade the stage with their banners. The play, though well meant, was described as "feeble stuff, quite unworthy of Laurence Housman's reputation" by one critic and is mostly omitted in reviews of his work.

The journalistic members of the Men's League included Henry Nevinson and Henry Brailsford. Nevinson's wife Margaret and lover Evelyn Sharp both became members of the WSPU after leaving Fawcett's NUWSS. Nevinson (1856–1941) himself, a great womaniser, professed a romantic admiration for female militants. His progressive convictions collided with his conservative temperament. Later disillusioned by the WSPU, he supported Sylvia Pankurst's United Suffragists.

Brailsford (1873–1958) by contrast was hoping to rescue his marriage to a WSPU activist, Jane Malloch. His wife seems to have been neurotic and the marriage was apparently never consummated. She treated him with contempt and later had a nervous breakdown, followed by alcoholism. Brailsford was a gifted journalist who worked over a large period for the *Manchester Guardian*. Suffrage was an episode in a colourful life that led him across the world as a foreign correspondent.

The most prominent journalist in support of suffrage was the legendary *Manchester Guardian* editor C.P. Scott. Scott (1846–1932) had supported Jacob Bright's bill for suffrage and was more a supporter of Fawcett than of the Pankhursts, believing in rational debate rather than illegal actions. However, he condemned force-feeding as torture, torn between liberal convictions and humanistic sentiments.

Bertrand Russell was perhaps the most cerebral supporter of the woman's vote. Both his parents had been strong supporters of women's rights and the advanced ideas of Germany's Social

Democrats initially influenced him. In his superbly argued pamphlet *Anti-suffragist anxieties*, Russell (1872–1970) demolishes a succession of sexist prejudices including fears of "feminine emotion" and puts his finger on examples of male emotionalism, citing religious revivalism and imperialism.

Russell's goal was to eliminate the polarisation of the sexes. Personally, he considered the gulf between men and women to be "terrific" and deplored "natural antipathy" and "sex-patriotism." This made him a natural ally of Millicent Fawcett, who once said that she did not "believe in the possibility of a Sex War." Like Fawcett and Richard Pankhurst, Russell was a disciple of Mill, though he advocated adult suffrage for all women, not just for the propertied classes.

While strongly influenced by Margaret Llewelyn Davies, secretary of the Women's Cooperative Guild, Russell quickly lost sympathy with the WSPU because of its militancy. Other suffragist authors included H.G. Wells, G.B. Shaw, John Galsworthy, E.M. Forster, J.M. Barrie and G.K. Chesterton. The Men's League united an illustrious brotherhood of academics and writers, joined by ministers, lawyers and army officers. It is fair to say that a broad cross-section of the British intelligentsia supported suffrage. As Evelyn Sharp, Henry Nevinson's long-term lover, pointed out, their activities ensured that the suffrage cause was not a "sex war."

U.S.A.: Federal Weaknesses, Regional Strengths

The American movement for suffrage shows strong parallels to Britain's, particularly in the split between moderates like Susan B. Anthony's NWSA (later NAWSA) and radicals (Alice Paul's NWP). However, there were also important differences: the abolition-of-slavery issue drew a wedge through suffrage.

In the U.S., there was a strong connection between slavery-abolitionism and suffrage, comparable to the link between temperance and women's votes in New Zealand. The decisive moment occurred during the Anti-Slavery conference held in London in 1840, when women were barred from participation. The Anti-Slavery Society founder William Lloyd Garrison reacted by sitting with the women and not taking part in the proceedings. By contrast, the head of the American delegation, Wendell Phillips, strongly protested but then acquiesced with the decision to exclude women from the proceedings.

Garrison (1805–79) was a formative figure. He was actively involved in the seminal Seneca Falls convention in 1848 and convened other meetings, giving unwavering support for women's suffrage. Similar support came during the early years from Gerrit Smith (1797–1874), the presidential candidate of the Liberty Party and a cousin of suffragist Elizabeth Caddy Stanton. By contrast, Wendell Phillips considered black male suffrage more important.

The split between abolitionists and dyed-in-the-wool suffragists caused a deep rift within the movement. Stanton and Anthony went as far as opposing the passing of the 15th Amendment that enabled black men to vote. They even campaigned with dubious allies such as the Democrat politician George Francis Train, an open racist.

However, support also came from unimpeachable sources. The anti-slavery activist Parker Pillsbury sided with them on giving priority to female suffrage. Pillsbury (1809–98) memorably called the right of suffrage "as old, as sacred and as universal as the right to life, liberty and the pursuit of happiness," thus elevating it to the level of the universal rights proclaimed by the Declaration of Independence. Other supporters of the women's vote included intellectuals like Ralph Waldo Emerson and Henry David Thoreau.

Frederick Douglass arguably played the most impressive role in the early campaign. An escaped slave and highly eloquent on both issues, he played a decisive role in getting the suffrage resolution passed in Seneca Falls. Douglass (1818–95) supported the 15th Amendment and simultaneously campaigned for female suffrage.

Similarly, the black intellectual W.E.B. DuBois fought for Negro integration and woman's suffrage. Born a free citizen, DuBois (1868–1964) gained a doctorate from Harvard and wanted blacks to flourish in all occupations. As editor of the magazine *The Crisis* published by the African American Association NAACP, he called on black voters in 1915 to support women's suffrage and pointed out in this connection: "The statement that woman is weaker than man is sheer rot: It is the same sort of thing that we hear about 'darker races' and 'lower classes'." Interestingly, he did not believe that white women were in any way more intelligent or humane than men of the same colour. On the contrary, he expected Southern women in particular to be pettier and more prejudiced. Despite this, he very nobly supported suffrage for reasons of democracy and justice.

Men supported both the NAWSA and later the NWP. Agitation during World War One drew male support. Dudley Field Malone resigned his post of Collector of the Port of New York because of President Woodrow Wilson's hostile attitude to the vote, gave legal support to Alice Paul's picketing of the White House and managed to get activists released by intervening personally with the President. Malone (1882–1950) was later pressurised by the Wilson administration through Secret Service investigation of his activities into distancing himself from the movement.

Other prominent suffrage supporters included Louis Brandeis, America's first Jewish Supreme Court judge. Brandeis (1856–1941), known as the "Robin Hood of the law," saw suffrage in the broader context of social justice. Similarly, Rabbi Stephen S. Wise (1874–1949), later President of the World Jewish Congress and one of the NAACP's founders, saw suffrage as a milestone on the road to social justice: "The ballot is not the gateway to heavenly bliss, but it is the avenue to earthly opportunity."

There was a similar coterie of leftist intellectuals as in Britain though they proved to be less numerous. Max Forrester Eastman (1883–1969), a professor at Columbia University, belonged to the Greenwich Village radicals and published fiery articles in *The Masses*, the magazine he edited. Eastman's sister Crystal was closely associated with Alice Paul and he married Ida Rauh, a rich Jewish intellectual, who converted him to both socialism and suffrage. He also helped to organise the Men's League for Woman Suffrage together with Steven Wise and other prominent reformers like the philosopher John Dewey. Dewey (1859–1952) saw suffrage as a means of deepening democracy and warned his fellow men not to judge women on purely biological grounds. Together with a large number of other League members, these men participated in the famous suffrage parade of 1912, braving mockery and abuse.

However, in terms of male activists, America lacked major national figures like John Stuart Mill or Richard Pankhurst. Many men became involved through familial or marital connections rather than through their own convictions. On the other hand, full female suffrage came in 1920 with fewer compromises made at a later stage than in Britain, where fears that women would outnumber men after the carnage of World War One led to the initial restriction of voting rights to women over 30 and property owners. This restriction became obsolete in 1928.

One provincial legislator played a pivotal role in getting the 19th Amendment finally passed. After approval by Congress, ratification of female suffrage required the consent of 36 of 48 states. In summer 1920, 35 states had ratified. The motion then came to the Tennessee House of Representatives, with the vote evenly divided between proponents and opponents, which would have led to the motion's rejection. The 24-year-old Republican Harry T. Burn, influenced by his mother, changed his mind at the last moment and voted aye against the interests of his constituents. Burn (1895–1977) was the youngest member of the Tennessee state legislature and, touchingly, he explained his action by saying that his mother had taught him always to do as he was told. Febb Emsminger Burn was a remarkably self-willed and well-read widow with a firm grip on her son. Her "Don't forget to be a good boy" letter to him has become a historic document.

Individual American states were far more progressive than the federal government. This was particularly true of the Midwest states. Wyoming, which at the time was a territory, joining the Union in 1890, introduced suffrage as early as 1869. However, this was not the product of due parliamentary process as in New Zealand, but rather on the initiative of Democratic legislator William Bright, whose suffragist wife influenced him.

Bright (1826–1912) managed to manipulate both Democrats and Republicans into supporting the motion. His reasoning being that if blacks could vote, which he opposed, then women should certainly have the same right. Republican governor John Allen Campbell, instead of vetoing the parliamentary vote as expected, approved it immediately and played a vital role in overruling attempts at repeal two years later. Campbell vetoed the repeal motion and the legislative council failed by one vote to get a two-thirds majority to overthrow his veto. The "Equality State" soon became a Mecca for suffragists.

As in New Zealand, Wyoming's frontier culture favoured suffrage. Women played a variety of roles in public life, running ranches and hunting animals among other things. The male motive for supporting suffrage could well have been sheer loneliness. The state had a tiny population of less than 10,000, of which only about a thousand were women. However, the fact that other Midwest and Western states followed suit – Colorado in 1893, Utah and Idaho in 1896, Washington State in 1910, California 1911 – highlights the open attitudes of the frontier regions.

Germany: Socialists in the Forefront

The most significant difference between Germany and the Anglo-Saxon countries is easy to pinpoint: there was no liberal support for suffrage. Demands for women's votes developed hesitantly and later than in Britain and the U.S.

Historic irony lies in the fact that universal male suffrage was established as soon as Germany was unified in 1871, far earlier than in Britain. This in fact strengthened liberal and conservative opposition to female suffrage. Opponents of universal suffrage like the respected constitutional-law expert Robert Mohl sought to limit the "damage" already done.

Others however took a logical viewpoint. The historian Heinrich von Sybel expressed the opinion that if politically deficient men gained the vote, why should women be excluded. His reactionary conclusion however was that the electoral laws ought to restrict universal male participation. By contrast, Friedrich von Bülau, Professor of Economics at Leipzig University and a constitutional scholar, stated that women's mental capacities were equal or superior to those of men. Bülau (1805–59) also believed that women were at least as independent in their viewpoints as the great majority of the men and came to the resigned conclusion that their exclusion was because men made the laws.

The women's movement was divided. Feminist pioneer Theodor Gottlieb von Hippel's demands for complete civic rights seemed too extreme; early feminists were at best half-hearted in demanding the vote. Amalia Holst was afraid of its revolutionary consequences, while the founder of the German Women's Association Louise Otto-Peters had to shelve the subject because women were banned from tackling political issues in associations. Hedwig Dohm (1831-1919) was by far the most eloquent and consequent feminist of 19th-century Germany. Influenced by Mill, she called for suffrage in the 1870s, but remained an isolated figure.

The same applies to the eminent professor of law Franz von Holtzendorff, a reformer of legal process and an advocate of death-penalty abolition. As early as 1868, he vigorously demanded suffrage for women as an elementary right and pointed admiringly to developments in Britain and the U.S. Holtzendorff (1829–89) lacked followers; in a country marked by a tremendous number of guilds, charitable societies and associations, it is indeed significant that the German Association for Suffrage was founded as late as 1902.

The only coherent and consistent institutional support for suffrage came from the Social Democratic Party (SPD). August Bebel, the later party leader, tried to make the woman's vote part of the party programme in 1869, but failed. In 1875, the SPD agreed on a neutral formulation, whereby "all citizens" had the right to vote.

From 1891 onwards, the SPD officially endorsed suffrage. The party overcame reservations that women would vote conservative and generously endorsed a movement that would prove detrimental to their own electoral prospects.

Until shortly before the end of World War One, suffrage remained a secondary issue. As late as 1917, the other parties torpedoed a resolution proposed by the Social Democrats. After the overthrow of Kaiser Wilhelm in November 1918, the provisional government summarily proclaimed suffrage for all over the age of 20. The government took the nationalistic view that women, who had vigorously supported the war effort, deserved it; there was however no real recognition of the need for equal rights.

France: Conservatives in the Forefront

France differs diametrically from Germany: virulent opposition to suffrage came from Republicans and Socialists, who both feared the clerical influence on women's voting habits. A correspondingly positive attitude developed among Conservatives. In

Germany, whose citizens were mostly Lutherans, the Protestant women's organisation opposed suffrage until the bitter end; in France by contrast, a Catholic suffrage platform was launched in 1925.

The ideas of Condorcet were as neglected as those of Hippel in Germany. Napoleon's Code Civil codified the misogynist heritage of the Jacobins. A peculiarly French phenomenon is that those striving for social change were simultaneously the greatest detractors of women. Pierre-Joseph Proudhon is a good example. He combined socialist ideology with a demeaning view of women as being either housewives or prostitutes. Similarly, the influential historian Jules Michelet, a great interpreter of the French Revolution, preached democracy while confining women to a maternal role that precluded voting. He saw the "feminisation" of the French monarchy as being its major flaw.

Even male feminists shunned suffrage. Léon Richer, who founded the Women's Rights Association together with Maria Deraismes, fought against the discrimination of mothers and wives and managed to make Deraismes a freemason. He refused however to put suffrage on the agenda of the 1878 Women's Rights Conference and argued in his book *La femme libre* that suffrage would lead to most women obeying priests after confessionals. Deraismes seems to have shared his opinion; she did not push the issue.

During the 19th century, only marginal political figures like Victor Considerant and Pierre Leroux spoke up for the women's vote. As disciples of Fourier and Saint-Simon respectively, they saw women's freedom in the broader context of true democracy. Leroux in particular had the reputation of being a "romantic socialist"; both exercised virtually no influence on public opinion.

Prominent authors like Alexandre Dumas and Emil Zola were profound anti-feminists. This contrasts vividly with the large number of British intellectuals in favour of the vote.

Victor Hugo was a great exception. A major political and literary figure in 19th-century France, Hugo (1802–85) was a man of many convictions and pretensions, first a royalist, then a republican socialist. On the one hand, Hugo was a committed supporter of women's rights. The writer reaped mockery for his famous speech to the French parliament in May 1850 demanding suffrage for women. On the other hand, quotes like "God created man, so be it, the devil created woman" from *Ruy Blas* indicate a sexist viewpoint. Hugo was above all a great humanist, campaigning for the rights of slaves and proletarians. He was for free schooling and against capital punishment. His intervention for suffrage was an episode, not the leitmotif of his life.

Later, female suffragists, themselves deeply divided on many issues and less militant after the First World War than before it, gained the support of important parliamentarians. These included socialists like the short-term Prime Minister René Viviani (1863–1925) and the influential entrepreneur Jules Siegfried (1837–1922). The liberal deputy Paul Dussaussoy tried to get suffrage for women on a regional level in a bill proposed in 1909. The same year, radical socialist Ferdinand Buisson (1841–1932) authored the report of a parliamentary committee that supported Dussaussoy's proposition. Both were enlightened individuals: Dussaussoy (1860–1909) was a lawyer highly convinced that voting was a "necessary civic experience for all members of a democracy," while Buisson was a cosmopolitan pacifist who co-founded the League of Human Rights and was later awarded the Nobel Peace Prize.

Other politicians like the Radical Republican Georges Clemenceau made no secret of their strident animosity towards women. In a pamphlet published in 1907, Clemenceau (1841–1929), who was Prime Minster at the time, predicted that France would fall back into the Middle Ages if women were able to vote. Some parliamentarians supported suffrage on a pro forma basis, regularly relying on the Senate to reject the resolutions of the Chamber of Deputies. The entire parliamentary process was intransparent and manipulative. The writer Maurice Bedel fittingly commented: "The French State is a bachelor. It is to be hoped that he will soon be struck by a mid-life crisis and finally discover woman."

The bachelor remained single long after World War One. Buisson's report was discussed in 1919; among its supporters were the conservative deputy Pierre-Étienne Flandin and Jules Siegfried, who in the meanwhile had become the doyen of the National Assembly. The Senate however only dealt with the proposition three years later, continuing a dilatory policy that was prevalent in the pre-war years.

Suffrage support came from unlikely and dubious sources. Joseph Barthélemy, later Minister of Justice under the Vichy regime, was one of the first to take up the demands of France's first suffragette, Hubertine Auclert. In 1920, Barthélemy (1874–1945) had published a 600-page book, *Le Vote des femmes*, in which he concluded that suffrage was preferable, while hoping that women would retain their grace and charm. Responsible for the Anti-Jewish legislation of the Vichy regime, Barthélemy was arrested after the liberation of France and died in prison awaiting trial.

Flandin (1889–1958) was of equally equivocal convictions. Having held a number of ministerial positions in the inter-war years including that of Prime Minister, he endorsed appeasement and sent Hitler a fulsome message after the Munich Agreement of 1938, which enabled Nazi Germany to annex parts of Czechoslovakia. Hitler telegrammed him with thanks for the "collaboration," a word that would soon assume an ominous importance in France. For a period of five weeks, he was Foreign Minister of the Vichy regime, being then ousted from power. After France's liberation, Flandin suffered internment for two years and was then released. Other suffrage supporters from the Catholic right wing included the anti-Semite Charles Maurras

(1868–1952), who achieved notoriety as the philosopher of the crypto-fascist Action Française.

France's supposedly progressive Third Republic failed to pass a suffrage law during an epoch that lasted from 1871 to 1940. Militant suffragists like Louise Weiss gave a new impetus to the issue during the 1930s. Weiss (1893–1983), a redoubtable pacifist with feminist convictions, drew public attention by highly publicised demonstrations organised by the New Woman Association founded by her. On one occasion, the demonstration featured several female aviators.

However, France's defeat during the Second World War and the installation of a collaborative regime under President Pétain put a firm end to the ambitions of the suffragists. The Vichy regime stood for motherhood and sacrifice; it was as violently opposed to female self-determination as its Nazi masters were.

The vote ultimately came in 1944 through a decree passed in exile by the French Committee of National Liberation headed by General Charles de Gaulle. De Gaulle's strongly Catholic background at first sight explains his readiness to accord suffrage. However, the real reason was that women, including Louise Weiss, had played a prominent role in the French resistance movement and the provisional government in Algiers felt morally bound to reward their commitment.

A communist deputy of the Consultative Assembly called Fernand Grenier chaired a committee that advocated suffrage and the Assembly adopted the recommendation by 51 votes against 16. De Galle himself was indifferent to the issue, barely mentioning it in his memoirs.

As in Germany, suffrage came because of women's exemplary conduct during a period of crisis, not because of any true belief in the importance of the women's vote. Overall, the suffrage issue reflects poorly on the country responsible for the Declaration of Human Rights (or rather the Declaration of the Rights of Man and of the Citizen, a tighter translation of *Droits de l'homme et du citoyen*). Fittingly, France accorded universal male suffrage in 1848, earlier than Germany and Britain. The nation suffered under the dearth of key figures like Mill or Bebel and lacked well-organised suffragist and suffragette associations. It became a crudely partisan issue: when for instance Field Marshall Paul von Hindenburg was elected President of Germany in 1925, French observers interpreted this as a fatal result of female suffrage.

Italy: Isolated Individuals in the Forefront

In a number of ways, Italy resembles France. Suffrage came to the country after the Second World War, with women voting for the first time in 1946. Like France, the country lacked organised activism; unlike its Latin neighbour, Italy brought in male suffrage at a late stage. In 1882, men's voting rights still depended on their "capabilities," in particular literacy.

Thirty years later, suffrage was extended to all men over 30 and to those over 21 who had served in the armed forces. During the parliamentary debate in 1912, the Conservative Opposition Leader Sidney Sonnino declared himself in favour of a more radical reform that would have included votes for women. However, the government of Giovanni Giolitti did not take up the issue and later shelved it by appointing a commission that took an inordinate amount of time to come to a negative conclusion.

By this time, the women's movement had called, though not unanimously, for suffrage. Risorgimento philosopher Giovanni Mazzini's many female followers, some of whom published the magazine *La Donna* (*The Woman*), saw themselves as the advisors of their husbands, not as independent civic beings.

Courageous individuals pursued the issue on their own initiative. Anna Maria Mozzoni (1837–1920) had translated Mill's *Subjection of Women* into Italian and evolved from socialism in the Fourier mould to become a prominent liberal thinker. In her uncompromising attitude towards any kind of discrimination, she was certainly comparable to Hedwig Dohm and equally isolated in her own country, though well connected in the international women's movement.

By contrast, the Russian-born Jewish socialist Anna Kuliscioff (1855–1925) had a formative influence on the Italian Socialist Party PSI through her close working and personal relationship with one of the key party leaders Filippo Turati, who was both a lawyer and a poet. Turati (1857–1932) and Kuliscioff, who was strongly influenced by August Bebel's ideas, founded a journal that advocated universal suffrage. However, it was a side issue for Turati, a highly enlightened politician who firmly opposed Mussolini and fled the country during fascism.

The country's pioneer male feminist, a parliamentarian called Salvatore Morelli, reaped mockery for his efforts to improve women's lives. Morelli (1824–80) had been imprisoned under demeaning conditions during the campaign for Italian unification. In 1861, eight years before Mill's *Subjection of Women*, he published his major study on *Woman and Science*. It was translated into French and English and gained him recognition abroad. His circle of correspondents included Mill, Victor Hugo and above all Mazzini, who however urged him to concentrate on other issues.

Morelli criticised women's suppression by their husbands and their lack of civil liberties; he thus logically came to demand suffrage. In 1867 and on later occasions, Italy's parliament refused to consider his propositions for legalising divorce and making education a universal right. His fellow parliamentarians considered him an eccentric utopian. However, he did gain support from a number of leftist deputies in parliament including Berenini, Lanza, Nicotera and Depretis.

Roberto Mirabelli (1854–1922), a radical leftist closely connected to Anna Mozzoni, proposed a suffrage law in 1904. Mirabelli's efforts, unlike those of Morelli, were the subject of a parliamentary debate. Beyond this, a committee was appointed to investigate the issue; it however refrained from recommending suffrage for women.

In the final reckoning, Giolitti, the country's leading statesman during the pre-war years, torpedoed the initiative, pointing out that if female suffrage came into being, the Clerical Party would erect a monument to his honourable colleague Mirabelli. Giolitti (1842–1928) cleverly played on the widespread assumption that women were under the influence of the Catholic Church. Here, there are obvious parallels to the French anti-suffragists. Beyond that, the prime minister also, not unrightly, pointed out that the suffrage issue was only of interest for "some ladies" and not for the vast number of female peasants and workers.

After the First World War, the issue surfaced again. Initial attempts at electoral reform gained positive reactions. As in Germany, women's support for the war effort seemed to make suffrage inevitable. However, the fringe question of whether prostitutes should be excluded from the electoral rolls proved divisive and, ultimately, the Senate blocked the ratification of the law.

When a new resolution came up in 1922, the Fascists had come to power. Mussolini's attitude to suffrage was equivocal and thus far more enlightened than that of the National Socialists in Germany. He promised to introduce communal suffrage for literate women who were over the age of 25 and had distinguished themselves in public life. However, the proposed law, which would have only enfranchised a small minority of women, never came into being and democratic procedures rapidly disappeared. Beyond this, the falling birth rate led to the regime focusing entirely on women's roles as mothers. Thus, suffrage only came to Italy after the fall of fascism. Both the Christian Democrats under Alcide de Gasperi and the Communist Party led by Palmiro Togliatti were in favour of extending suffrage and in 1944, a decree enabled women to vote for the first time in a referendum held in 1946.

Switzerland: A Democratic Latecomer

Why did suffrage come to one of the world's oldest democracies as late as 1971? In the conservative canton of Appenzell, women could indeed vote only from 1990 onwards. The easy answer to the question being that the country's system of direct democracy makes referendums imperative. Thus, both houses of parliament approved women's suffrage in 1958; a year later, voters rejected it.

The Swiss Constitution of 1848 declared all human beings to be equal; the laws that followed equated human beings with men. This was by no means an extraordinary viewpoint: half a century before, the French revolutionaries had similarly propounded the Declaration of the Rights of Man. A women's-rights movement developed during the second half of the 19th century: Meta von Salis (1855–1929), one of Switzerland's foremost feminists, visited several cantons in 1894 to canvas for suffrage, being regularly heckled during her speeches.

Then, Carl Hilty, a renowned professor of constitutional law, published a highly acclaimed article contending that freedom involved participating in the process of justice. He concluded: "Thus, female suffrage is at the core of the female question."

Hilty (1833–1909) was a renaissance man: lay theologian, Head of the Military Justice Authority, Member of Parliament. He later became the Swiss delegate to the International Arbitration Court in The Hague. Like Mill, he believed that individual happiness is a core social goal; he also contended that women had a greater sense of justice and more idealism than men did.

The government shelved Hilty's proposed constitutional amendment; the initiatives of parliamentarians like Herman Greulich and Emil Göttisheim experienced the same dilatory treatment. The founder of the Swiss League for Human Rights,

Leonard Jenni, put the case to the Supreme Court in 1923 and 1928. His appeals failed, but public interest had been awakened. 170,000 women and 79,000 men signed a petition demanding suffrage.

The suffragists continued their efforts in the following years. Parliamentarian Emil Oprecht made a new attempt to achieve suffrage in 1944 and the year after, an Action Committee came into being. In 1955, Professor Werner Kägi made an expert assessment that focused on the importance of changing the Swiss constitution.

These actions provoked a backlash on the part of both male and female conservatives. The Catholic Women's Association distanced itself from the demand for the vote, and a Swiss League against Suffrage came into being. The League united men and women who considered suffrage to be an obnoxious foreign concept; some of them made racist comments on one of the country's leading feminist women, who had been born abroad. Then, an incident occurred that made headlines across the world.

In the tiny village of Unterbäch, deep in the mountains of the Valois, the local council headed by the village mayor Paul Zenhäusern (1917–2002) suddenly decided to allow women to register as voters. The Valois Council of State soon annulled this decision, but after intense arguments on the legal principles at stake, it did allow women to be registered separately from men. On March 3, 1957, a group of 33 women braved catcalls and stones to vote.

Everyone in Switzerland knew the identity of the mastermind behind this historic incident, the man who had instigated Zenhäusern's actions and forced the Valois Council to compromise. In a country full of conservative conformists, Peter von Roten (1916–91) was indeed a blithe spirit. A man of many parts, educated as a lawyer, officiating as prefect of a region, Roten also edited a newspaper called *Walliser Boten*. After doing a survey revealing that only 40.7 per cent of all women were for suffrage, he agitated for the cause both in the Valois assembly and in the national parliament.

Like Mill before him, Roten earned insults from all and sundry; unlike the English liberal thinker, the rich aristocrat was at heart a conservative, who started life firmly convinced that men and women had separate roles to play. Then, he encountered one of the country's foremost feminists, Iris Meyer, married her, converted to her viewpoints and became the most fervent campaigner for women's rights in the country.

Hilty, Greulich, Göttisheim, Jenni, Zenhäusern and Roten: anyone analysing the lives and characters of these "traitors to the men's cause" will find more differences than similarities. Hilty: an austere idealist; Greulich: of working-class origin, founder of the Swiss Social Democratic Party; Göttishem: judge and Liberal Democrat; Jenni: constitutional lawyer and prominent naturalist; Zenhäusern: primary school-teacher and communal official; Roten: aristocratic lawyer and journalist.

The Swiss microcosm also provides evidence of how men supporting women's rights are often wilfully ignored by women's organisations. In 1985, Unterbäch celebrated its suffrage coup with prominent guests, including Elisabeth Kopp, the first woman to become a minister in the federal government. Peter and Iris von Roten were in the audience; both were surprised that all the speeches heralded the achievements of the women who had voted, while ignoring his pivotal role. Conversely, when the Swiss Association for Women's Suffrage celebrated its 100th anniversary in 2009 with a commemorative publication honouring those who had fought for women's votes, the only man portrayed in the book was Roten.

Contrary Suffragettes: Traitors or Symptoms of Gender Complexity?

A major factor in Switzerland was not only the weakness of the suffrage movement, but also potent opposition emanating from men's and in particular women's groups. The Catholic Women's Association had distanced itself from suffrage in the 1920s and other pressure groups formed in reaction to suffrage activism. Some of them had mixed membership; others, like Margret Matti-Steudler's Action Committee against Women's Voting Rights, were exclusively female.

In 1958, an anti-suffrage Women's Committee crystallised under Matti-Steudler and successfully influenced the referendum of 1959. After a two-thirds majority rejected suffrage, the Committee continued its lobbying activities with new zest. The committee united mostly conservative, well-educated women from privileged circles, who feared that the social order would be upset through greater rights for poorer, "simpler" women. It was a highly militant and independent group; the women were by no means the stooges of male antisuffragists. They rationally pursued their own interests, disproving expectations of female solidarity. Their propaganda was both anti-socialist and nationalistic, highlighting the uniqueness of the Swiss mode of direct democracy while emphasising the separate roles played by men and women in everyday life. After suffrage came, the Committee reluctantly ceased functioning in 1971.

Similar tendencies emerged at a much earlier date in Britain. Antisuffragism was prevalent with male leaders in the 19th century, particularly with self-styled moralists like Gladstone. Among their female allies were prominent writers like Mrs Humphrey Ward and Marie Corelli, diplomats like Gertrude Bell and a number of aristocratic women. After signing a petition in 1899, they united to found the Women's National Anti-Suffrage League in 1908, later merging with the Men's National League.

This led to one of the most hilarious episodes in the history of gender struggle. Two of the most celebrated public figures of the age headed the Men's League: Lord Curzon, former viceroy of India, and Lord Cromer, who returned to Britain after having served as pro-consul in Egypt. Both were used to lording it over their fellowmen and were dismayed by the radicalism and resilience of their female allies. Cromer confided in Curzon at one stage: "I am physically incapable of doing eternal battle with all these rampaging women."

Julia Bush describes the infighting for hierarchic positions and the many feuds in her book *Women against the Vote*. Convinced that the suffrage war had been lost, Curzon resigned to reality in 1916 and refused to oppose suffrage in the House of Lords. The women he was supposedly leading thereupon attacked him as a coward.

The major motivation of the anti-vote women was the concept of separate spheres, of women's proper place at home. In an article on the *Humors of Anti-Suffrage*, Israel Zangwill highlighted the paradox of agitation in the service of domesticity: "The very notion of an Anti-Suffrage League is only fit for the pantomime season – for what can be more topsy-turvy than for women to rush into a political agitation to prove that woman's place is the home?"

Again, attempts to marginalise antisuffragists as "idle women" in the words of Frances Power Cobbe are beside the point. The antis included highly active and respected women. As in Switzerland, class interests were stronger than any kind of gender solidarity. Julia Bush points out: "Leading anti-suffrage women linked their views on women's social role to a positive concept of feminine gentility, and also to a profoundly negative fear of the ignorant masses."

The antis were no fools. A number of the leaders had been educated in Oxford and were both highly intelligent and extremely literate. Elizabeth Wordsworth was in fact principal of the Oxford University women's college Lady Margaret Hall. They did not agree with each other on all issues, their motivations differed, but they shared the same general convictions. Moreover, if their claim that the majority of women in Britain was against the vote is true, they mirrored the common mind.

The situation in the U.S. was largely similar. A network of highly placed East Coast women fought the "feminist disease," their motivation deriving from broadly the same mixture of the cult of domesticity and fear of lower-class women usurping their positions in society. Ladies of the Massachusetts and New York State Associations were often highly placed professionals in academia, journalism and even in social services.

In her study of the American anti-suffrage campaign, Susan E. Marshall highlights gendered class interests as the major focus. Women like Helen Kendrick Johnson (1844–1917) collaborated closely and on equal terms with men; they felt no need for voting rights, since they could assert themselves behind the scenes. Johnson and her husband Rossiter, a newspaper editor, both wrote pamphlets against suffrage; in *Woman and the Republic,* Helen argued that women could achieve legal and economic equality without having the vote. The naysayers, inspired by self-interest rather than maternal traditionalism, were thus excellent partners of the antisuffragist men.

More so than in Britain, the East Coast antisuffragists relied on cogent arguments, emphasising for instance that the vast majority of women polled in Massachusetts were indifferent to the vote. When the suffragists called these women unenlightened, the antis called this an insult rather than an explanation and questioned the legitimation of the suffragists to represent what "we women" wanted. Their agitation involved close cooperation with highly placed men: Ernest Birnbaum of Harvard University for instance edited a book of antisuffrage essays by women from Massachusetts.

Having lost the war against suffrage, conservative women were more successful in opposing the Equal Rights Amendment (ERA). With support from both Democrats and Republicans, the ERA gained the approval of both the House of Representatives and the Senate in 1971. However, it lacked ratification by the prescribed majority of states. Opposition crystallised in the Eagle

Forum led by Phylis S. Schlafly. The Forum asserted that ERA would have a negative effect on female privileges like alimony and would legitimise abortion. It also played on fears of women being drafted into the armed forces and their being forced to use unisex toilets.

The anti-rights agitators closely collaborated with right-wing groups like the Moral Majority and successfully torpedoed a consensus on the state level. The chances of ERA ever being passed seem slim, since the kind of bi-partisan Great Society consensus of the 1960s no longer exists in a country where right-wing groups like the Tea Party movement are radically opposed to any kind of social change.

Female anti-suffragism in the Anglo-Saxon countries was mostly, if not entirely, a conservative preserve. The same was true in Germany: the Conservative Party and the Agriculturists Association led the opposition. Both had women's organisations that supported the anti-cause. The contrary is to a great extent true for countries like France and Italy, where liberals, socialists and radicals have often feared that suffrage would help the Catholic Church get the upper hand in politics.

Spain is a special case. The Second Republic carried out an unusual electoral reform that gave women passive rather than active voting rights, meaning that they could not vote, but could be voted into parliament. Male voters to the Constituent Assembly duly elected four left-wing women in 1931.

When Clara Campoamor (1888–1972), one of the country's leading feminists, vigorously and successfully campaigned for giving women the right to vote, her colleagues from the radical left Margarita Nelken and Victoria Kent opposed her, assuming that enfranchised women would vote for the Catholic Conservatives. Indeed, in the next election in 1933, both Campoamor and Nelken lost their seats. Women's suffrage was later abolished by the Franco regime in 1939 and only restored after the dictator's death in 1975.

Subjective Preferences versus Gender Expectations

Antisuffrage is a prime example, but not the only example of how gender solidarity can prove flimsier than the power of vested interests or of ideology. Standpoint, rather than sex affiliation, is the decisive element in attitudes and decisions.

The context of women's activities cannot be collectivised. The phenomenologist Alfred Schütz propagated the concept of direct experience as opposed to indirect knowledge. Projected onto the suffrage issue, this explains why women's attitudes to suffrage diverge from objective expectations of their behaviour as collective members of a discriminated sex. Many women were personally content not to vote; beyond that, they believed in separate spheres, or, if they were Marxists, that the class question was more important than gender issues. When faced with the question whether or not they wanted to vote, their decisions reflected subjective preferences.

The implicit "we women" attitude of some feminists is thus an assumption that many women do not share. Similarly, the expectation that men should oppose women's suffrage because it would threaten their privileges is facile. Ben Griffin has analysed the attitudes of more than a thousand British parliamentarians to the issue, revealing the complexity of diverse masculinities, as well as fundamental differences in attitudes to the nature of political representation.

The idea that men embody an abstract world as opposed to the concrete female worlds of wives and mothers reduces both sexes to templates. Dualities such as the bifurcation of consciousness can be intellectually tempting; the suffrage issue illustrates however, that manifold shades of idealism, pragmatism and Machiavellism influence situative behaviour.

3

Women's Minds: Writers, Teachers, Entrepreneurs

It is a paltry Trick to deny Women the Cultivation of their mental Powers and I think it is partly a proof that we are afraid of them if we endeavour to keep them unarmed.
Dr Samuel Johnson

It is fittingly ironic that the term "bluestockings" first described a man, the botanist and poet Benjamin Stillingfleet. The story goes that Elizabeth Montagu invited him to participate in her salon. Stillingfleet (1702–71) was learned but impoverished; when asked to attend, he first declined, and then attended in everyday clothes, including blue worsted instead of black silk stockings. When absent, the conversation of the bluestocking was dearly missed.

The rich heiress Montagu's circle was then entitled the Blue Stockings Society or Club and was so well known that Thomas Rowlandson caricatured its dissolution in the early 1800s. The word was soon applied to learned women in general, often loathed as "the most odious character in society" (to quote Hazlitt) by intolerant or envious men.

Discussion circles led by talented women like Montagu (1718–1800), Frances Boscawen and Elizabeth Vesey were avidly attended by members of a masculine elite which ranged from literary figures like Oliver Goldsmith, Samuel Richardson and Walter Scott and historians of the stature of Edward Gibbon, to theatre celebrities like David Garrick and Richard Sheridan. The salons brought together personalities as distinct as the Archbishop of Canterbury and the economist Adam Smith. They levelled the playing fields of discussion for women otherwise expected to be decorative and reticent.

One prominent protagonist in bluestocking circles was the great lexicographer Dr Samuel Johnson. Dr Johnson (1709–84) was a typical split personality: on the one hand, he delighted in misogynistic turns of phrase such as comparing a woman preacher to a dog walking on its hind-legs. On the other hand, he insisted that it was "a paltry Trick to deny women the Cultivation of their mental Powers" and roundly declared: "No woman is the worse for sense and knowledge." Both Mary Wollstonecraft, who knew him personally, and Virginia Woolf wrote favourably about him.

Johnson supported literary friends like Charlotte Lennox by publicly praising them; he also introduced them to publishers. Andrew Millar, prominent bookseller and publisher of authors like Henry Fielding, brought out Lennox's *The Female Quixote*. Thomas Cadell, Millar's partner and successor, printed the works of Catharine Macaulay and Hannah More. He also published the novels of Charlotte Turner Smith until she wrote *Desmond*, which he rejected as being too radical. The Whig bookseller George Robinson eventually issued the novel, an early feminist work drawing parallels between the subjection of English women under common law in Britain and under the Ancien Régime in France.

Thomas Hookham published Smith as well as writers like Ann Radcliffe, Mary Robinson and Laetitia-Matilda Hawkins. He supported Hawkins despite making steady losses with her books, and was thus more a patron than a businessman. Similarly, Joseph Johnson published works by Mary Scott, as also Maria Edgeworth's plea for education. His most famous female writer was of course Mary Wollstonecraft. He issued both her *Vindication of the Rights of Men* and *of Woman*.

Publishers' motives differed. Hookham and Johnson played the role of mentors, while William Lane's intentions were mostly mercenary when recruiting women to write Gothic novels.

However, the publisher of the Minerva Press apparently also appreciated female talent when attempting to access funds in support of poverty-stricken authors like Eliza Norman.

A. From Sensitive to Sensible: Writers' Viewpoints

Writers' motives were equally divergent. Samuel Richardson for instance resembles a moralistic bluestocking. In his life and works, he was sympathetic to women's feelings and appreciative of their minds, while however bowing to traditional marriage and family norms. *Pamela* and *Clarissa,* heroines of the eponymous novels, are positively portrayed, in an odd mixture of sentimentality and close analysis. Whether Richardson (1689–1761) was an early feminist or, in fact, the supreme patriarch is subject to debate. His Christian convictions certainly forced his protagonists into tiresome corsets.

Conversely, Daniel Defoe's *Moll Flanders* was vastly closer to life, an outlaw profiting from rather than oppressed by marriage. Virginia Woolf considered Defoe (1660–1731) to be an empowered feminist; Moll exploits the system designed to confine her. Others disagree, emphasising Moll's use of her body for fortune-hunting. The same applies to his other famous novel *Roxana*. Defoe's feminist credentials are certainly improved by his essay *The Education of Women,* in which he calls the fact that women are denied education "one of the most barbarous customs in the world."

Defoe's appeal for education lacked an echo in the 18th century and he remained a controversial figure. Alfred Lord Tennyson (1809–92) on the other hand was as Poet Laureate a highly respected establishment figure during the Victorian era, his enduring fame deriving from fervent poems like *The Charge of the Light Brigade*. Tennyson called higher education for women one of England's two great social issues. This was in 1847, when Queen's College was founded.

Defoe explores the gutter in *Moll Flanders,* while Tennyson describes a heavenly world in his poem *The Princess*. His heroine disdains manly company and founds a women's university barred to men. Despite the conventional happy end, Tennyson's poem celebrates feminine independence and erudition to an intriguing degree, while it does include ignoble verse like "Man to command and women to obey; /All else confusion."

By contrast, Robert Browning's female protagonists like Pompilia in *The Ring and the Book* and the protagonists in *Porphyria's Lover* and *My Last Duchess,* are helpless victims of male cruelty. Browning (1812–89) condemns misogyny without however giving his female characters lives of their own.

Thomas Hardy's heroines are far more real as victims of social norms. This is particularly the case in rural areas like Wessex, the setting of his novels. Hardy (1840–1928) in fact shows a sense of affinity to his female protagonists without idealising them. He cogently criticises patriarchal norms by individualising female characters like *Tess of the d'Urbervilles,* who are far more of flesh and blood than Tennyson's princess or Browning's victims.

His fellow novelist George Meredith showed greater commitment to the cause of the New Woman. Influenced by Mill's *Subjection of Women,* he firmly believed in education as the key to women's advancement. Meredith (1828–1909) favoured good manners and orderly conduct; this led him to condemn suffragette militancy. His heroines like *Diana of the Crossways* are both intelligent and independently minded. He saw women as a crucial element in social evolution and actively supported charismatic women, though his relationship with his first wife Mary Ellen ended with her eloping. His second wife Marie was less intellectually demanding and apparently catered more to his ego.

Between Timidity and Licentiousness

British writers with feminist credentials have often tended to be either timid or licentious in their personal lives. William Butler Yeats and George Bernard Shaw belong to the first category, H.G. Wells and Oscar Wilde to the second.

Both Yeats and Shaw were passionate critics of bourgeois society, in particular the sexual roles assigned to men and women. Yeats' poetry celebrated interdependence between men and women. Despite his occult tendencies, Yeats (1865–1939) had coherent views on social reform and condemned sexual repression. The poet admired strong women, but often suffered personally under their dominance, most prominently under Olivia Shakespeare. Many of his female lovers suffered from depressions.

Shaw was luckier; he flirted with many prominent women like Ellen Terry, but had a platonic marriage with Charlotte Payne-Townshend, who looked after him like a mother. He criticised the exploitation of women in plays like *Lady Warren's Profession*; intriguingly, Shaw saw prostitution as an economic issue, not a moral one. In *Pygmalion*, later adapted into the popular film *My Fair Lady*, Shaw (1856–1950) created the remarkably forceful persona of Eliza Doolittle, who ultimately asserts herself against Henry Higgins' social and intellectual arrogance.

Feminist views on Shaw have varied from lavish praise (Lady Rhondda) to contempt (Germaine Greer). There is however no denying the playwright's affinity for strong women, including Major Barbara and St. Joan. Beyond that, Shaw propagated innovative ideas like the "coupled vote," which presaged the quotas for women in politics and the professions. Obviously, Shaw was a strong supporter of suffrage; his real contribution is however, in his own words, that of a "first class ladies tailor."

H.G. Wells was less serious in his intentions than Shaw was, but at gut level possibly closer to the feminine psyche. *Ann Veronica* created a scandal comparable to *Lady Chatterley's Lover* when published in 1909. The novel describes a young feminist woman who also happens to be very feminine and exploits the tension inherent in this mind-body conflict. Alone in her room, Ann Veronica "sobbed heavy tears of feminist heartbreak." Wells (1866–1946) gently makes fun of her, but reserves heavy sarcasm for philistine men unable to grasp why women want to be independent, study and vote. The protagonist's closeness to Amber Reeves, with whom Wells, a supreme rake, was having an affair, contributed to the scandal.

Shaw belonged to those who condemned the novel. Despite its noble intentions, *Ann Veronica* is actually mediocre literature. In *Parade's End*, Ford Madox Ford's massive tetralogy on the First World War, the author's heroine Valentine Wannop is far more a flesh-and-blood figure, a high-minded, high-spirited suffragette who also happened to be a pacifist.

Oscar Wilde ultimately became the victim of nasty prigs and of the Victorian norms condemning homosexuality. Behind his flippancy lurked an anarchic socialist and feminist. The Irish writer exalted women, evidently seeing them as his allies in his campaign against boring rationality and traditional masculinity. More importantly, Wilde (1854–1900) makes hilarious fun of the men, his epigrammatic wit at its best in *A Woman of No Importance,* in which Mrs Allonby contends that men "are horribly tedious when they are good husbands, and abominably conceited when they are not." The author speaks through Lady Windermere when she declares there being "the same world for all of us, and good and evil, sin and innocence…"

His friend and fellow homosexual Edward Carpenter was more discreet, though equally prominent as a co-founder of the Fabian Society and a valiant supporter of the Labour Party. Like August Bebel and other progressive leftists, Carpenter (1844–1929) believed that women would only attain true equality under socialism. He was a great advocate of sexual freedom for both men and women. Moreover, like Richard Pankhurst, he was a man of many causes, opposing the exploitation of the lower classes and of colonial people, while deploring environmental pollution.

Disappointing Indifference in the Salon Homeland

Though salons originated in 16th-century Italy, France is widely acknowledged as being the homeland of civilised gatherings organised by talented, charismatic women. The number of salons in Paris greatly exceeded those in London and served as models for Elizabeth Montagu and other hostesses. In terms of prominent guests, salonières like the Marquise du Deffand attracted a comparable number of big names: Voltaire, Montesquieu, d'Alembert, not to speak of her friend Horace Walpole.

However, in terms of the support and mutual encouragement that salon culture implied, French intellectuals proved to be largely indifferent. They profited both materially and socially through their contacts to the rich and influential ladies, but there seems to have been no reciprocal support for budding female writers.

During the long 19th century, intellectual support for women is generally hard to find in France. Victor Hugo is the great exception. He repeatedly asserted his support for women's rights. In 1875, he wrote to a women's association, "In our society, such as it has been made, woman suffers. She is right to claim a better fate." Together with Maria Deraismes, Hugo (1802–85) called on women to "enrol in the feminist army." In private life by contrast, Hugo was a great womaniser, maltreating both his wife and numerous lovers, seemingly indifferent to their fate.

Similarly, Gustave Flaubert was a notorious bisexual rake. Critics praise his famous novel *Madame Bovary* for highlighting the many restrictions on women, though Emma's machinations have also been criticised as being faux-feminism in the sense of her exploiting sex appeal to get further.

Alexandre Dumas the Younger showed sympathy for the plight of women and illegitimate children in novels like *The*

Illegitimate Son. On the other hand, he empathises with husbands who kill their unfaithful wives. Nor is his *La Dame aux Camélias* any more enlightened than *Madame Bovary*. Beyond this, Dumas (1824–95) voiced strong disapproval of women behaving like men in a pamphlet called *L'homme-femme*. In general, French intellectuals were revolted by any kind of seeming masculinity on the part of women.

The only real literary feminists in France were obscure figures like Jules Bois, who combined a whole-hearted endorsement of the New Woman with an odd taste for the occult, writing a book on *Satanism and Magic*. Bois (1868–1943) collaborated with feminists like Maria Deraismes; however, he is best remembered as the author of *L'Ève nouvelle,* a treatise published in 1896 that explores women's historic oppression by men.

Bois called men's reign anthropocentrism and spoke of the "profound, barbarous and tenebrous past" in which women were enslaved. He overdid the feminist case by grossly idealising women as miraculous beings: "My purest desire is to declare myself a man who shares the desire to be New; who has understood the New Woman's superiority, learned her sublime lessons, and who now inclines toward her, begging to be one of her soldiers." Bois represents an odd mixture between Christian mysticism and a naïve feminism that lived and died with him.

Equally obscure, but in a completely different vein, was the novel *La Garçonne,* a succès de scandale in the 1920s. Rather in the vein of H.G. Wells' *Ann Veronica,* but published 13 years later in the aftermath of the First World War, Victor Margueritte's heroine Monique Lerbier wears bobbed hair and a short skirt; she also has intercourse with both women and men. Here comes La Femme Nouvelle with a vengeance.

Unsurprisingly, the novel became a bestseller, though the author was subsequently divested of his Légion d'honneur medal. Marguerrite (1866–1942) has an intriguing personality. Together with his brother Paul, he was one of France's leading pacifists. Son of a famous general who died during the Sedan battle in 1870, Margueritte first served in the army, and then became a novelist and playwright, using his talents to support women's emancipation fervently.

La Garçonne was adapted for both the stage and the cinema, pioneering the androgynous novel while ruining the author's reputation in the process. Feminists were divided on the issue; some accused him of being titillating rather than liberational. Margueritte had already upset the mainstream of public opinion in France by attacking the "criminals" of all countries who had participated in World War One. After the defeat of France in the Second World War, he collaborated with the German occupiers for pacifist reasons, dying however before France was liberated.

Philosophical and Romantic Sympathies

Even more so than in France, German salons were mere meeting places for cultivated men and women. The famous Weimar salons such as those of Duchess Anna Amalia and of Johanna Schopenhauer, mother of the famous philosopher, were full of spirited discourse and included guests like Goethe.

However, in Germany, women were traditionally defined as wives and mothers. Salonières were not motivated to advance the interests of their sex. No supportive networks of men and women developed as in Britain. More significant was the free mixing of people of different religions and social standings, particularly in the salons hosted by Jewish hostesses like Rachel Varnhagen von Ense and Henriette Herz.

In a fragmented country full of principalities and lacking urban centres like Paris and London, women had less leeway. Beyond that, literary luminaries like Goethe and Schiller had condescending attitudes to women. Kant's famous dictum that the female sex was characterised more by temperament than by character resonated strongly. His "theory" of gender characters relegated women to being the beautiful sex. Fortunately, Kant's views did not go uncontested; however, his critics, including Johann Adam Bergk and August Ludwig Schlözer, were too obscure to change public perceptions.

Traditional gender roles persisted even when personal sympathies existed. Christoph Martin Wieland, the poet who laid the foundation to Weimar's fame as the country's cultural centre, had been engaged to Germany's pioneer female writer Sophie von La Roche and remained in close contact with her throughout his life. Despite the fact that Wieland (1733–1813) initially appreciated her intelligence and breadth of knowledge, Sophie later played the conventional role of muse, while he was her mentor and "artistic arbiter."

Similarly, the famous theologian Friedrich Schleiermacher had a high opinion of women's moral and religious status while resisting claims for women's education and advancement. He firmly excluded women from civil society, though they played an important role in the religious community.

The philosopher Karl Christian Friedrich Krause developed new ideas of human rights and social reforms. Ignored in Germany, he attracted an enormous following in the Spanish-speaking world, where Krausismo as an enlightened, anticlerical movement led to reforms in areas like women's education. However, even Krause (1781–1832) had traditional ideas of women's domestic roles.

By contrast, his students Heinrich Ahrens, Karl David August Röder and Hermann Karl von Leonhardi collaborated with 19th-century feminists in propagating women's rights. They were particularly active in legal reforms. Leonhardi invited representatives of the German Women's Union to a Philosophic Congress held in 1868 and treated them as intellectual equals. Röder spoke a year later at the General Meeting of the Women's Association and criticised women's discrimination.

While the German Krausianer favoured evolution, the German Romantics revolutionised sexual attitudes. This was particularly true of Friedrich Schlegel, who had an affair with Dorothea Veit, daughter of the Jewish philosopher Moses Mendelssohn. They later married and after converting to her husband's Protestant religion; Dorothea was then instrumental in their joint conversion to Catholicism. Their relationship profoundly influenced *Lucinde.* Less a tract than a sensualist manifest, Schlegel's novel caused an enormous scandal when published in 1799.

Schlegel (1772–1829) idealised women while emphasising the importance of exchanged roles and androgyny. Influenced by his highly intelligent wife, an author in her own right, he firmly believed in women's intellectual qualities. In a letter to her, Schlegel concluded that philosophy was vital knowledge for women. This was in clear opposition to the general norm that too much education was detrimental to female virtue.

Schlegel's ideas are considered to presage Judith Butler's gender theories. As a writer, he tried to undermine sexual clichés subversively. He is thus close to viewing gender as a social construction.

Russian Realism

Russia in the 19th century may have been very much on Europe's periphery. Despite this, it featured a remarkable number of intellectuals with feminist affinities. First and foremost was the revolutionary writer Nikolay Chernyshevsky, who influenced an entire generation, including Lenin, with his novel *What Is to Be Done*.

Chernyshevsky (1828–89) saw women's rights as parallel to the class struggle. His novel begins with the statement that his heroine's training "was very ordinary." He then describes the struggles of a woman yearning to emancipate herself both from her mother and from marital bonds. Vera Pavlovna was in fact a New Woman, not interested in looking good, but in being equal to men and economically independent. The author also rejects traditional ideas of possession; men and women are equally autonomous.

Influenced by Mill, Mikhail Larionovich Mikhailov advocated suffrage and education for women. A revolutionary like Chernyshevsky, Mkhailov (1829–65) translated Harriet Taylor Mill's *Enfranchisement of Women* into Russian and attacked the misogynistic ideas of Michelet and Proudhon.

The literary critic Dmitry Pisarev had comparably enlightened views. It was Pisarev (1840–68), who rejected the primary assumption of Kant and other philosophers that women are more capable of feeling rather than thinking. According to him, the goal of human education was quite simply to develop a person's full potential. He too was a formative influence on Lenin.

Pisarev supported figures like Valerian Krempin, founder of a journal for women called *Daybreak*. The cover of the first issue shows a girl awakened by a figure symbolising knowledge. In characteristically caustic fashion, Krempin called the journal "sugary, but all right."

From Universal Brotherhood to Bohemians

Salons were slow to develop in the U.S., though Anne Lynch Botta and Emma Embury attracted a large cross-section of the East Coast elite at their soirées. Botta's guests included luminaries like Edgar Allen Poe, Ralph Waldo Emerson, Horace Greeley and Andrew Carnegie.

Thomas Wentworth Higginson's life achievement lies in his championing of the poet Emily Dickinson. Like Greeley, Higginson (1823–1911) was a militant reformer. As an abolitionist, he participated in the anti-slavery movement and belonged to the Secret Six who supported John Brown, the activist executed for attempting to raid the federal armoury at Harpers Ferry.

Dickinson had responded to an article by Higginson in *The*

Atlantic Monthly with advice to young writers; he encouraged the poet to develop her originality further, though he was sometimes baffled by her style of writing. After her death, the activist-reformer edited and published her poems.

Higginson firmly supported higher education for women and came out for the vote, co-founding the Women's Suffrage Association. He systematically refuted Edward H. Clarke's influential diatribe *Sex in Education*, which contended that academic studies would inhibit women's capacities to be mothers. In his essay *Ought Women To Learn The Alphabet?*, Higginson ridicules a philosophy that accepts that "John is a fool; Jane is a genius: nevertheless, John, being a man, shall learn, lead, make laws, make money; Jane, being a woman, shall be ignorant, dependent, disfranchised, underpaid."

He also corrected the moralistic views of reformers like Frederic C. Howe, Immigration Commissioner of the Port of New York. Howe (1867–1940) believed that women should have the vote because they were morally superior and could thus redeem men from their sins. Higginson by contrast trenchantly pointed out: "It is a plausible and tempting argument to claim suffrage for women on the ground that she is an angel, but I think it will prove wiser, in the end, to claim it for her as being human…" For him, women were not men's better halves, but simply their other halves.

Male American writers rarely encouraged their female colleagues. Walt Whitman was a firm supporter of women's property rights and employment opportunities. His expansive poetry celebrated human bodies, famously in *Song of Myself*:

And I say it is as great to be a woman as to be a man,
And I say there is nothing greater than the mother of men.

Whitman's lyrical egalitarianism sees women as part of a universal brotherhood. Beyond this, the poet befriended prominent female suffragists and was a strong supporter of the women's vote, influenced here by the Scottish feminist Frances Wright.

Ironically, or perhaps typically, Whitman is reported to have taken a dim view of female poets. Here, he was surprisingly similar to authors with prejudiced views like Henry James and Mark Twain.

By contrast, Edgar Allan Poe portrayed women as passive creatures in his stories, as victims of marauding men, but firmly supported them as writers, reviewing their works and mingling with them at salons. Poe (1809–49) however led a dissolute life and was indeed guilty of paedophilia, in view of the fact that he married his 13-year-old cousin, Virginia.

John Neal is a far obscurer literary figure, though credited at the time as the first American writer to use colloquial expressions. He was a jack of many trades, ranging from clerk and travelling tutor to miniature artist and journalist. He firmly supported suffrage and made cogent remarks about women's education. One sample: "Feminine ignorance leads to scandal – to backbiting." Neal (1793–1876) asserted that women were enslaved; they were also taxed without representation, a clear allusion to the primary issue that had ignited the War of Independence.

Greeley and Neal were both moralists; their feminism derived from an old-fashioned sense of justice. In the early 20th century, the Greenwich Village bohemians were more against the puritanical hegemony of the American middle class and the Calvinistic separation of mind and body. Less ecstatic than Whitman, who strongly influenced them, they were equally radical in sexual terms.

The Bohemian writers include Floyd Dell and George Middleton. Dell (1887–1969) upturned conventional logic by calling for feminism as a way of making men free in his book *World Builders: Studies in Modern Feminism*. He points out: "Men want the sense of power more than they want the sense of freedom." In an excellent insight into the nature of contemporary marital relationships, Dell alluded to men acting as "sultans in little monogamic harems" and firmly supported birth control. He and his left-wing, libertine friends certainly could not be accused of monogamy.

George Middleton, a minor playwright, was also an ardent feminist. At the famous meeting in New York organised by the feminist Heterodoxy Club in 1914, Middleton (1880–1967) started by saying: "Feminism means trouble: trouble means agitation: agitation means movement: movement means life: life means adjustment and readjustment: so does feminism." This sentence reads like an elliptical summary of the road to sexual equality.

Middleton realised that suffrage was only one element of women's rights; he called it the "kindergarten" of feminism. The playwright joined the Men's League for Woman Suffrage co-founded by Max Eastman with prominent participants like Rabbi Stephen Wise and the philosopher John Dewey. Eastman (1883–1969) discounted arguments based on feminine virtue. Women would not improve politics, on the contrary: politics would develop women. Here, he is close to the logic employed by Higginson.

In the magazine he edited, *The Masses*, Eastman wrote a well-reasoned *Confession of a Suffrage Orator*. He also walked the talk by having a highly egalitarian relationship with his wife Ida Rauh.

B. From Educationists to Educators

Many writers, from Defoe to Pisarev, demanded full education for women. Educators faced the task of turning these thoughts into action.

Women's education in Britain reflects the strong influence of clerics and religiously inclined laymen. Sidney Smith is a prime example as an unconventional curate, highly intelligent and endowed with sceptical wit. In an article on Female Education, the curate refuses to accept "that there can be any just cause why a woman of forty should be more ignorant than a boy of twelve years."

Smith (1771–1845) was a great humanist, canvassing against slavery and for Catholic emancipation in addition to advocating women's education. His sermons attracted huge audiences. He accuses ignorant men of feeling jealousy and alarm at women's advancement, while drily reassuring them of a big stock of ignorant and foolish women. However, Smith's liberality had limits; he rejects the idea of women writing books or arguing arcane issues like the tomb of Achilles.

Across the ocean, the young American poet John Trumbull similarly made fun of the poor educational standards affecting both men and women. At the age of 22, he published a satirical poem, *The Progress of Dullness*, in which Tom Brainless, who gets a diploma without studying, and Dick Harebrain, a dissipated fop, who learns immorality from Hume and Voltaire and finally lands in jail, are paralleled by a flirtatious woman. Harriet Simper lacks sensible education, is seduced by Harebrain and ultimately settles down to dullness by marrying Brainless. Trumbull (1750–1831) attacks norms that prize beauty rather than wisdom in women. The poetic satire is a plea for rationality and seriousness. Trumbull perceives women as being different from men, but worthy of receiving an equal education adapted to their interests.

This mindset was signally lacking among the country's Founding Fathers. Their progressive views on universal liberty included retrogressive ideas on women's place in society. The famous lexicographer Noah Webster for instance was a snob and a ladies' man in his youth. He was also a fervent abolitionist and supporter of women's education. However, the utility of this education was restricted to feminine tasks such as supporting husbands and raising children. Reading novels was considered unnecessary. Shades of Rousseau. Nevertheless, Webster (1758–1843) did believe that women should be well educated to "extend their influence as far as possible over the other sex."

Specific views varied. Thomas Jefferson thought the ideal education for girls would include learning French, dancing, drawing and music. Benjamin Franklin by contrast saw women as business partners of their husbands; arithmetic, bookkeeping and letter-writing were in his opinion of central importance.

Of all the Founding Fathers, Benjamin Rush paid the greatest attention to the subject, well visible in his *Thoughts on Female Education*. By contrast to Webster, who went to Yale at a time when it consisted of three buildings and 40 students, Rush (1746–1813) studied both in Princeton and Edinburgh University, later opening a medical practice. The founder of Dickinson College promoted "Republican motherhood"; he expected women to uphold and advance public morality while raising their sons to become virtuous citizens.

In terms of curriculum, Rush wanted women to master English and to write properly; he also advocated the study of history, geography, astronomy and even philosophy. He was firmly against putting music and foreign languages, including Greek and Latin, onto the curriculum. Differing from the other founders of the nation, Rush felt passionately about the issue, attacking opposition to better education as stemming from "the prejudice of little minds."

In his *Thoughts*, Rush also envisions women as the "stewards and guardians of their husbands' property." Despite this, they remain subservient. In a letter to a woman friend, Rush advises her that "from the day you marry you must have no will of your own. The subordination of your sex to ours is enforced by nature, by reason, and revelation." He really believed this to be in women's best interests, continuing the letter with the sentence: "Of course it must produce the most happiness to both parties." Like Webster, Rush was a cultural nationalist, seeking to free the young nation from British norms. In the final reckoning, he was more a patriot than an advocate of women's rights.

Despite the views of the Founding Fathers, educational reforms in the American Republic empowered women and made them socially aware. The "pursuit of happiness" credo in the Declaration of Independence led to a certain degree of educational emancipation.

The views of the nation's founders corresponded to moderately enlightened views in Britain. The Scottish moralist John Gregory encouraged women in *A Father's Legacy to His Daughters* to expand their knowledge and cultivate their taste. Gregory (1724–73) was repeating his wife's views on education after her premature death. Simultaneously, he asked them to display "modest reserve" and "retiring delicacy." He also advised young women not to display their knowledge, as this might detract from their ability to attract a husband; Mary Wollstonecraft attacked him for leading women into deceit. By contrast, the bluestocking Elizabeth Montagu highly admired and liked him.

Gregory represented mainstream opinion. The officer and writer James Henry Lawrence by contrast made a tomboy the heroine of his novel *The Empire of the Nairs; or the Rights of Women*, first published in Germany and strongly praised by Wieland and Schiller. Lawrence (1773–1840) was a kindred soul of Wollstonecraft; he refers to a book on the vindication of women's rights written by a woman who was "an ornament to her sex." Camilla is not supposed to read the book, but receives it from her Etonian schoolboy friend. She yearns to study in Eton and join in the boys' pranks, runs away from home in boy's clothes and manages to enter Eton, helped by a scoundrel whom she bribed with her mother's jewels. She then studies at the University of Göttingen. Lawrence's utopian romance is a remarkable document of emancipated thought.

The Unitarian missionary Richard Wright can be located between Gregory and Lawrence. His *Letters on Women* assert that lack of education degraded women, rendering them incapable of proving themselves useful in society. Wright (1764–1836) wanted both men and women to receive a liberal education and attain public virtues. Like Sidney Smith, he used sarcasm to emphasise the fundamental equality of the sexes, pointing out that men were capable of the "same ignorance, weakness of mind, vanity and frivolousness." However, he did expect women to observe their duties as wives and mothers.

Paragons of Christian Virtue

The leading educational activists in 19th-century Britain were mostly Christian Socialists like Charles Kingsley, who excelled in various spheres, as Canon of Chester Cathedral, chaplain to Queen Victoria, Regius Professor of Modern History in Cambridge and author of *The Water-Babies*. Kingsley (1819–75) was a social reformer shocked by the social conditions in Victorian England and committed to improving both the lives and the educational standards of his parishioners.

His pamphlet *Health and Education* reveals a straight-laced attitude; women should certainly be educated on health issues, but by other women, so that nothing objectionable can be said or heard. He lauds a course on hygiene for ladies held by a Miss Chessar, which governesses can attend at half-fees. Similarly, Kingsley strongly supported secondary education for middle- and upper-class women, particularly in scientific subjects, though he was oddly afraid that chemistry might prove dangerous to young women.

Overall, the chaplain was more interested in preventing "dirt and drunkenness, disease and death" than in putting women on the same footing as men. He gives the impression of being scared of women, wanting them to be virtuous rather than intelligent. Thus in the first lines of his poem *A Farewell*, he writes, "Be good, sweet maid, and let who will be clever."

Kingsley believed in the fundamental difference between the

sexes. Thus, it comes as no surprise that he opposed female suffragists, while admiring Mill; men in his opinion should advance women's interests. Overall, he was a moderate modernist rather than a feminist.

Kingsley's signal achievement was his collaboration with F. D. Maurice, who founded both Queen's College and Working Women's College, putting his Christian Socialist convictions into practice. Maurice (1805–72) was curate, chaplain in a hospital, editor of the *Education Magazine* and Professor of history and divinity at King's College, London. Perhaps because of his strong theological views, various contemporaries considered him a great bore.

However, his credentials as a social reformer are unimpeachable. Together with other King's College colleagues, Maurice founded Queen's College as a finishing school for girls over the age of 12. The College's primary aim was to educate and improve the status of governesses. This led to a gentle approach to education, including no rewards or punishments for pupils. Since teachers were mostly male, aristocratic women acted as chaperones during classes.

Queen's College duly received a royal charter in 1853 as the first women's educational institution. Prominent pupils included Gertrude Bell and Katherine Mansfield. It was a typically Victorian institution: solid and narrow-minded. Only Anglican women were accepted; by contrast, Bedford College, founded by Elizabeth Jesser Reid, accepted pupils of all faiths, including Jews. Maurice resigned as Chairman of Queen's College after being ousted from King's because of a theological dispute. He remained however active as a history professor.

Henry Sidgwick, founder of Newnham College in Cambridge, resembled his mentor Maurice in various ways: in his unorthodox theological views as much as in his perception of women as separate beings, who needed to be protected and not burdened by onerous chores such as learning Greek and Latin.

Armed with impeccable academic credentials, Sidgwick (1838–1900) later became a great admirer of John Stuart Mill and gradually accepted Mill's views. He valiantly fought for women's access to university degrees, resigning from the Cambridge University Council when it rejected degrees for women.

Like Maurice, Sidgwick willingly dealt with the prosaic issues of raising money and finding buildings in which women attending university lectures could live. Unlike Maurice, he was an entertaining conversationalist with a proclivity for wordplay. Newnham, founded in 1871, was originally a residence, later becoming a full-fledged college.

Newnham's founder however lacked a stable character: he believed in parapsychology and had imperialist leanings. Sidgwick married Eleanor Balfour, sister of Prime Minister Arthur Balfour, and inspired her with his enthusiasm for women's education; she later became the Principal of Newnham. He infected her both with feminist and metaphysical ideas. After Sidgwick died, Eleanor believed she could communicate with him from the "other world."

A number of prominent academics contributed to the establishment of women's colleges and collaborated closely with female educators. Among the most prominent of them was the famous classical scholar Gilbert Murray. Paying tribute to him, Margaret Fry, Principal of Somerville College in Oxford, specifically highlighted the special relationships to men like Murray, who did not see himself as being a knight-errant, but as "a man who can offer help without attributing helplessness."

Enter the Educator-Entrepreneur

The contrast between the prim Christian Socialists and the brash self-made man Thomas Holloway is breathtaking. Free of any kind of religious or academic inhibitions, Holloway (1800–83) achieved more than his predecessors at one fell swoop, though he had little knowledge of education himself. The millionaire who made his money with patent medicines was urged by his wife to help women and founded an institute designed to rival Oxford and Cambridge.

Holloway excluded clerics, lawyers, doctors and indeed women from the governing board. This reflected the proclivities of the self-willed philanthropist. Pretending early in his career to being a Professor, he later had his own coat of arms. Holloway was in fact a modern Victorian: forward-looking, emphasising natural sciences while keeping both classics and modern languages on the curriculum. Royal Holloway College's founder treated the institution like a business venture; in today's terms, he was a social entrepreneur.

His mentality was highly American: after touring the Loire chateaus, he chose Chambord as the architectural model of the college. This was a typically New World approach to duplicating the Old World. Also quintessentially American is Holloway's wish to overtake his competitor: in this case, it happened to be Matthew Vassar (1792–1868), pioneer founder of the eponymous college in Poughkeepsie, New York. Holloway apparently said, "I hope I shall be able to beat Vassar into fits."

One self-made, childless millionaire measured himself against the other. Remarkably, however, one from the old country emulated a nouveau-riche of the New World. Originally from Norfolk, Vassar had made his money as a beer-brewer after a difficult childhood and without formal education. His niece prompted him to found a college that could rival Harvard and Yale. Another strong influence was Milo P. Jewett, a clergyman and founder of the Judson Female Institute in Alabama. Jewett was Vassar College's first president, forced to resign over a dispute regarding the opening date. Vassar wanted to wait until the Civil War was over; Jewett became impatient, writing a fatal letter calling the founder "fickle and childish."

Significantly, Vassar wrote to the trustees of his college in 1861 that "woman, having received from her Creator the same intellectual constitution as man, has the same right as man to intellectual culture and development." However, he still had conventional views of female "gentleness and modesty," focusing strongly on women's roles as mothers and teachers while also wanting graduates to become "skilful housekeepers." Later, his views became more progressive.

The institute was originally called Vassar Female College; later, the trustees agreed to remove the word "female" after a campaign by feminists, who considered the word degrading and even ungrammatical. This was in line with Vassar's admonition to the trustees to avoid "old beaten paths" and opt for progress. Vassar graduates were later at the forefront of feminism: Inez Milholland as a suffragette, Alice Ramsey as the first women to drive through America in her own car.

Vassar donated half his fortune to the College, putting it into a tin box and passing it to one of the trustees; he simultaneously provided land for the college buildings. Symbolically, the founder died while delivering his farewell speech to the trustees. In mid-sentence, Vassar dropped his notes; his head fell back and he passed away in the chair he was sitting in.

America's Clerical Idealists: Higher Education, but Separate Spheres

Vassar College overshadowed older initiatives for women's education that were less spectacular in both concept and endowment. In the same state of New York, ten years before Vassar, Elmira Female College was started thanks to the initiative of a local businessman called Simeon Benjamin. The real founders were a group of men calling themselves "Friends of Education" led by Reverend Isaac N. Wyckoff, who had been Principal of a girl's school in New Brunswick. The committee originally wanted to found the college in Auburn, New York, but lacked funds. With Benjamin's support, the college moved to Elmira.

There was a significant difference in funding: Benjamin provided the meagre sum of 5000 dollars, while Vassar donated more than 400,000. Lacking a proper endowment, the college struggled on for decades. However, Elmira served as a model for Jewett when he was planning Vassar. It was the first college to grant Bachelor's degrees to women. In terms of mentality, the Elmira founders were closer to Kingsley and Maurice than to Holloway. Its long-time president August Cowles was apparently a typical academic, also in the sense of being bad at fund-raising.

Oberlin College in Ohio started even earlier than Elmira. It was however more an idealistic community than an academic institution. Tuition was free and students were expected to fulfil communal tasks. Its tolerance credentials were unbeatable: Oberlin was the first college in America to admit both women and black students from the start in 1833. Three white women graduated in 1841, and in 1862, Mary Jane Patterson became the first black American women to earn a college degree. The college played a pivotal role in the abolition movement, the town forming part of the Underground Railroad with students and faculty rescuing individual black slaves.

Oberlin experienced the same financing problems as Elmira and was to a greater degree clerically influenced. Founders John Jay Shipherd and Philo P. Stewart were both Presbyterian ministers, earnest, restless characters who made great demands on their fellow men and women. Church services, held generally by Shipherd, were as important as college courses. Stewart, formerly a missionary to the Indian tribes, annoyed the boarders at Oberlin by his insistence on a "plain diet" and eventually returned to the East Coast.

Charles Grandison Finney, a prominent evangelist without any college education, who was professor and later principal at Oberlin from 1851 to 1865, succeeded the founders. The school offered a separate female curriculum called a "ladies' course," thus cementing beliefs of fundamental differences between the sexes.

The "separate sphere" ideology was strongly influenced by Emma Willard, who opened the Troy Female Seminary in New York State in 1821. Willard (1787–1870) took the progressive view that women were "primary existences," not objects of men's taste. Her school's curriculum included "manly" subjects like mathematics, science and philosophy. However, she propagated roles for educated women either at home or as schoolteachers, while rejecting suffrage.

This reactionary influence pervaded educational institutions for decades to come. By the late 1800s, almost two-thirds of all schoolteachers in the U.S. were female, with women working for lower salaries than their male colleagues. Well into the 20th century, most students and teachers at women's colleges were against suffrage; an instructor called Mabel Newcomer at Vassar was indeed reproved for participating in a suffrage rally as late as 1917.

Among America's educators, Matthew Vassar remains the great exception. The other founders of the "Seven Sisters," the women's colleges that corresponded to the male Ivy League, professed profound religiosity.

This applied to female founders as much as to their male counterparts. Mary Lyon, who started Mount Holyoke College in 1837, had a strong social conscience, reducing school fees to a minimum to attract girls from all classes. At the same time, Lyon (1797–1849) was a revivalist preacher, firmly convinced of religion's central importance. Discipline was strict, with students expected to adhere to around 70 different rules governing their behaviour and health. They were also required to participate in church services and Bible Study Groups. Fellow founder Sophia Smith was equally devout, though fees at Smith College were much higher than in Holyoke and academic standards rivalled Harvard.

Henry Fowle Durant, founder of Wellesley, was a Harvard-qualified, highly successful lawyer, who was almost fanatically religious, practising as a lay preacher for more than a decade. After the tragic death of their son, Durant and his wife decided to dedicate both the Wellesley grounds and also a large part of their fortune to "some special work for God." In a sermon delivered in 1875, Wellesley's founding year, Durant called women's education "one of the world battle cries for freedom," while equally contending: "I believe that God's hand is in it; that it is one of the great ocean currents of Christian civilization..." He both visited and preached at Mount Holyoake, which served as a model for Wellesley.

Like Mary Lyon, Durant (1822–81) had a strong social conscience, preferring the "calico" girl to the "velvet" girl and keeping the fees low. Like his fellow founders, he was a benevolent autocrat, regulating everything from the curriculum to the food eaten. Teachers were rewarded more for being devout Christians than for being talented. Unsurprisingly, former students recalled that his fanaticism drove them out of the church and led them to avoid religious issues.

The Seven Sisters were trailblazers. By the 1880s, one-third of all college students in the U.S. were female. However, an incipient conservatism kept college graduates from entering the professional mainstream. Established educationists like Edward H. Clarke of Harvard University advanced pseudo-biological arguments to prove that women were incapable of receiving a "man's education," citing alleged cases of hysteria and indeed digestive problems in coeducational schools. Prominent academics like the philosopher John Dewey however rebutted these absurd arguments. Dewey, who also endorsed suffrage, contended that both women and men profited from an educational mix, the boys learning gentleness and courtesy, the girls acquiring greater self-reliance.

Common Sense and the Sciences

Contrasting with the founders of the Seven Sisters, a group of Quaker doctors started the Women's Medical College of Pennsylvania (WMC) in 1850. Dr Bartholomew Fussell was the most important protagonist in the early phase, though he never had an official affiliation with the College. Fussell (1794–1871) had an impressive record of accomplishment as a doctor who privately instructed many former slaves and helped them escape through the Underground Railroad. Some 2,000 slaves reportedly passed through his home.

The doctor's sister Esther strongly influenced him to provide women with medical education. Firmly convinced of women's aptitude, Fussell recruited the support of other doctors, who started the college in the face of strong opposition from the medical community.

Fussell's most prominent collaborator was the obstetrician Joseph S. Longshore, who drafted the college's charter and secured its passage through the Legislature, while organising and financing the institute. In a Valedictory Address at the First Annual Commencement, Dr Longshore displayed a traditional mindset in praising the students for the "perseverance and industry characteristic of your sex" and predicting that it would take time for women to assume responsibility in a profession dominated so long by men.

The New England Female Medical College came into being in 1848, shortly before WMC. Originally a school for midwives, it later widened its scope to paediatrics. Founder Samuel Gregory was motivated partly by the perceived "gross indelicacy" of male physicians delivering babies. At the same time, Gregory (1833-72) responded bravely to attacks from the medical community in Boston, contending: "The fact of being one of the stronger sex does not render one competent."

Like Vassar, Gregory was criticised by feminists for wanting to create "female physicians," though the term "female" remained in the college name. Gregory was very much an adherent of separate spheres; however, the college played a valuable role in making it normal for women to become doctors.

Perennially short of money though it received public funds for scholarships, the College merged with the Boston University School of Medicine in 1873 and adopted a homeopathic curriculum. Dr Israel Tilsdale Talbot, who collaborated with Gregory in founding the College, was later Director of the Massachusetts Homeopathic Hospital and Dean of the School of Medicine. Thus, the College entered the medical establishment.

In Britain, women were at the forefront of the fight for medical education. Men played a supporting role as with the Edinburgh Seven, a group of female medical students who managed to attend specially organised classes at the city's university in 1869, but were denied degrees. Among their supporters were David Masson, Professor of English Literature at Edinburgh University, and Alexander Russel, editor of the *Scotsman* newspaper.

The women, notably Sophia Jex-Blake and Elizabeth Garrett Anderson, moved from the Scottish capital to London. Here, a Female Medical Society started in 1864 with the purpose of scientifically educating female midwives. The Obstetrical College set up by the Society provided surgical knowledge, enabling midwives to perform obstetrical operations. Soon, female midwives had a better education than their male colleagues did.

The major figure of the College was its Honorary Secretary, Dr James Edmunds. Edmunds firmly and eloquently believed that women were as competent as men when properly educated. He argued against the apparent preference of pregnant women for male midwives, while decrying the "careless, ignorant, drunken old creatures" serving as female midwives to the poor. However, the London School of Medicine (LSMM) founded by Jex-Blake, Garrett Anderson and other female pioneers with the support of Thomas Henry Huxley, soon overshadowed the

Society.

Huxley (1825–95) was an unusual Victorian: outspoken, combative, no respecter of titles. In professional terms, he was an evolutionary biologist known as "Darwin's bulldog" and a strong propagandist for scientific education. On the one hand, as Secretary of the Geological Society, he refused to admit women because members had to be professionals and only men qualified as such. Similarly, he barred a woman journalist from entering the Ethnological Society. On the other hand, when approached to hold separate anatomy lessons at Edinburgh University, Huxley immediately agreed; he also gave unqualified support to LSMM.

In a letter to *The Times*, Huxley declared many women superior to men both intellectually and morally. Why should careers open to the stupidest of men be closed to women? At the same time, he was a prig. Though friends with George Eliot, he never visited her together with his wife, since Eliot was "living in sin" with a man not her legal husband.

Other LSMM helpers included Ernest Hart, editor of the *British Medical Journal*, and several prominent doctors, who served as lecturers. MPs James Stansfeld and Russell Gurney provided invaluable help by getting a bill passed in 1876 enabling, though not obliging, examination bodies to accept women as medical candidates. As a leading legal authority and a Conservative MP, Gurney had the standing that the valiant William Cowper Temple, a Liberal MP who had unsuccessfully introduced various bills for women's medical education, had lacked. Stansfeld for his part helped Jex-Blake negotiate with the Royal Free Hospital so that LSMM students could get vital clinical training.

Jex-Blake (1840–1912) and her fellow campaigners had strong literary support from the novelist Charles Reade. In *A Woman Hater*, he describes in painful detail the many obstacles faced by woman doctors in both Britain and the Continent. However, female physicians enjoyed greater public support than women canvassing for suffrage did. This was understandable: they were trying to enter a profession, not determine who ruled the country.

Switzerland, Germany and the Two Ms

Unlike the Anglo-Saxon countries, education in Continental Europe was and is mostly state-run. This strongly limits the leeway for individual pioneers. Countries like France and Germany could not rely on men of action like Holloway and Vassar, though the same type of entrepreneurs existed in the economic sphere.

Ironically, the biggest laggard in suffrage was a pioneer in medical education. Switzerland's universities opened their doors to women long before universities in Germany and other Central European countries. Zurich University allowed women to attend lectures from 1840 onwards. In 1865, after long deliberations, the Senate allowed the Russian student Nadezda Suslova to register herself as a student; two years later, she qualified as a doctor. In 1870, Zurich University's Senate answered an enquiry from its counterpart at Germany's Würzburg University in positive terms, attesting that female medical students had the same rights and duties as their male colleagues and participated in all anatomic demonstrations.

Soon, women from all over the world, in particular Russia, Germany, Britain and the U.S., studied at Swiss universities. Prominent degree-takers included Rosa Luxemburg and Lou Andreas-Salomé. Liberal German professors, some of whom had immigrated to Switzerland in the aftermath of the 1848 revolution, played an important role in making Switzerland the premier country for women to study. Viktor Böhmert, a free-trade economist originally from Leipzig, was against both class and gender ideologies. He considered it imperative for women's talents to contribute to progress and pointed out that women excelled not only in the arts, but also in mathematics and natural sciences.

Russian medical students dominated for several decades in Switzerland. Prominent doctor Nikolay Pirogov, considered the father of field surgery, had supported female volunteers as nurses in the Crimean war, where, by contrast to Florence Nightingale's nurses, who remained in base camp, they served in the line of fire. Pirogov (1810–81) achieved this despite strong opposition on the part of army bureaucracy. In a letter to the czar's sister-in-law Elena Pavlovna, one of his liberal supporters, he insisted that men directed women only because the latter were treated in an "archaic and inane way." Their education needed to change. However, Pirogov envisaged limits to this education: "Not all will be doctors." By contrast, Konstantin Dmitrievich Ushinskii, pioneer of scientific pedagogy in Russia, believed both sexes had the right to the same education.

Germany was as much a mecca for mathematics students as Switzerland was for medicine. Sofia Kovalevskaya, daughter of an artillery general, showed an early proclivity for the subject; her parents hired a tutor who taught her calculus. Since women could not study at universities in Russia, Sofia attended courses at Heidelberg University, then moved to Berlin. Since this university did not even allow women to audit courses, let alone study, she took private lessons from the illustrious mathematician Karl Weierstrass, considered the father of modern analysis.

Weierstrass (1815–97) managed to have her awarded an honorary doctorate at Göttingen University in 1874 and later helped her obtain a university post in Stockholm. He corresponded with her for 20 years and proved a staunch supporter. Göttingen soon became a household name for budding mathematicians from Russia, the U.S. and Britain. Grace Chisholm Young for instance got her doctorate after finishing her studies at Girton College, Cambridge. Her "Doktorvater" was Felix Klein, a highly influential and powerful mathematician known as much for his mentoring of an entire generation of young scholars as for his work classifying geometries by their underlying symmetry groups.

Klein (1849–1925) stridently pointed out that the six women attending his courses were in every way as good as the men. He also criticised the fact that German women students practically did not exist and called for changes in the school system. Klein supported Jews as well. In the face of anti-Semitic protests, he arranged for his great friend Hermann Minkowki to become a full professor. However, he was the only professor in Göttingen to sign the ominous declaration *To the Cultural World* in 1914, in which a cross-section of the country's intellectual elite defended Germany's conquest of Belgium and its military ambitions.

By contrast, his protégé David Hilbert was an avowed pacifist. Born and brought up in Königsberg, where he studied mathematics and became an assistant professor, the mathematician had imbibed the ideas of Kant, who had spent his life in Prussia's second-largest city. Klein made him full professor in Göttingen when he was only 33 years old. Hilbert was both a friend and a rival of Albert Einstein, who appreciated his pacifist support during World War One.

Hilbert (1862–1943) was in fact against any form of authoritarianism or chauvinism. He strongly supported female students, in particular Emmy Noether, the first woman to get both a doctorate and a professorial qualification (Habilitation), this being a prerequisite for full professorship in Germany. Noether was Jewish and among her supporters was Albert Einstein. When other professors opposed Noether's Habilitation, Hilbert supposedly said, "Gentlemen, we are a scientific organisation, not a public bath." At the time, public baths in Germany separated the sexes.

Göttingen was a great exception in Prussia, which introduced university education for women as late as 1908. Other German states like Baden and Bavaria were slightly more liberal, but in general, Germany lagged behind both the Anglo-Saxon countries and Switzerland. By contrast, it was a pioneer in practical training.

In 1866, Wilhelm Adolph Lette founded an association to promote female vocational education that still exists; it offered and offers a wide spectrum of office, artisanship and trading training. The original plan was to give unmarried women from the middle classes a livelihood.

Lette (1799–1868) is a colourful figure: as a member of a student fraternity at the legendary Wartburgfest after the Napoleonic War, he was arrested. Then he became a lawyer and parliamentarian. Lette's liberality was highly functional: he categorically declared, "What we don't want, never want, even in the coming centuries, is the political emancipation and equality of women." By contrast, his successor Franz von Holtzendorff firmly supported emancipation.

Beyond that, the Lette Verein, although under the patronage of a Prussian princess, was totally under male control during Lette's lifetime. It pioneered professional training for women as telegraphists, typesetters, bookbinders and above all medical assistants.

In Austria, the Female Employment Association (FEA) resembled the Lette Verein. Founded in the same year, FEA's primary role was to help the widows of soldiers who had died during the Prussian-Austrian War. There was however one significant difference: from the beginning onwards the Austrian association was run by women, though they received legal advice from men like Dr Carl Richter. It was founded in Iduna Laube's salon and her co-founders belonged to the social elite. Perhaps for this reason, FEA was as determinedly apolitical as Lette's Association.

Richter was no exception. A large number of Austrian politicians, professors and professionals supported women's education. Beyond this, the Union of Austrian Professors offered a large variety of courses on subjects such as public-sector theory, economics and economic history. A professor of zoology called Carl Brühl was one of the few natural scientists to confirm the mental equality of women, in stark contrast to Darwin and to German scientists like Paul Julius Möbius, who published an infamous, influential pamphlet *On the Physiological Stupidity of Women*. At the Vienna World Fair in 1873, Brühl showed skeletons proving that male and female brains were of equal size.

Brühl (1820–99) created a stir by allowing women to attend free lectures. He also organised cultural evenings in his apartment primarily for women; male relatives could sometimes accompany them. Men like him inspired Rosa Mayreder, Austria's leading feminist, to remark in a letter to her fellow feminist Auguste Fickert: "It's becoming more and more impossible for me to perceive men as the enemies of women's rights."

C. Entrepreneurs: The Masculinity of Money

Men have traditionally dominated the economic world. Female entrepreneurs and managers still form a minority; wage disparities between male and female employees remain persistently high. The masculinity of money is a fact proven by behavioural research: Implicit Association Tests demonstrate the connection made between men and wealth.

The link between masculinity and money is particularly strong in countries with highly developed financial markets like the U.S. and Britain. Stock exchanges and trading have promoted a macho culture well symbolised by the "Big Swinging Dicks," a designation for particularly successful stockbrokers and exchange traders. The link between the male genital and money-making is as apparent as visions of supremacy. In a Master of the Universe culture, men are subjects while women are objects.

Artisanship is different. In Continental Europe, particularly in the German-speaking countries, access to the professions was historically free and only later restricted to men. In 15th-century Cologne, girls went through the same four-year apprenticeships as boys. Of the 15 companies that rented wheels from the city council to twine yarn, women ran five.

Similar developments are reported from the cities of the Hanseatic League that dominated trade in Northern Europe. In Lübeck, the North German city prominent for its trading role, the economy depended largely on Gertrude Morneweg, a widow who financed major trading families. The law allowed her to carry out all trading transactions in her own name.

Protestantism and the cult of domesticity later led to legal restrictions based on the belief that a woman's place was in the home. In 17th-century New York, Margarete Hardenbroeck, daughter of a German emigrant, served as an agent to her cousin, trading in a variety of commodities including cooking oil and vinegar. After her second marriage to a Dutchman called Frederick Philipse, Hardenbroeck (1637–90) continued doing business under the Dutch law then valid in New Amsterdam. In 1664, however, the British gained control of what would then become New York and put an end to her legal independence. British common law applied; thus, the profits from her business automatically belonged to her husband.

European laws later excluded women from professions. Despite this, women were able, generally with the help of relatives and friends, to exploit their own artisanship skills. This is particularly true of two doll-makers in Germany.

Margarete Steiff managed to become one of the world's most successful manufacturers of dolls despite the fact that she was born in a small village in Swabia and suffered from polio. Steiff (1847–1909) learned to sew as a child, and at the age of 16, she had saved enough to buy herself a sewing machine. Her cousin's husband Adolph Glantz, a factory-owner, recognized her talent and strongly supported her, both financially and morally. She also had a close relationship with her brother Fritz; he and his sons helped coordinate production and marketing.

Fritz's son Richard created the Teddy Bear that was spectacularly successful in the U.S. Another nephew of hers, Franz, invented the famous Button-in-ear that has since become a registered trademark and characterises the Steiff animal-dolls.

A generation later, Käthe Kruse had less ostensive male support. Starting life as an illegitimate child in poor conditions, she initially had a successful career as an actress in Germany and abroad, then fell in love with a sculptor called Max Kruse, who designed stage sets for Max Reinhardt in Berlin. Käthe (1883–1968) had a daughter born out of wedlock in Switzerland and asked Max to send her a puppet. He abruptly refused, telling her that he found puppets disgusting and that she should make one herself. Kruse did so and soon discovered that her life-like dolls were in great demand, displaying them in one of Berlin's leading departmental stores. Soon, orders came from the whole world and the dolls were manufactured in large sets.

Doll-making can be considered feminine artisanship; locomotive manufacturing hardly so. This makes the career of Sophie Henschel all the more extraordinary. By contrast to Steiff and Kruse, she grew up in privileged surroundings and then married the heir to a dynasty of train builders. Initially regarded by the bridegroom's family with a certain reserve because she was rumoured to be a bluestocking, Sophie married Oskar Henschel with her brother's blessing. He thought it excellent that she was marrying a "man of progress" rather than a "soldier marionette"; at the time, army officers were considered the perfect husbands for upper-class women.

From her father, who was a successful landowner with a strong social conscience, Sophie learned both the basics of business and the need to treat those dependent on her well. Beyond that, her father insisted that only she had access to her fortune. Appropriately, separation of property was part of the marriage contract.

Oskar Henschel was both enlightened and open-minded. He asked Sophie what she would like as a wedding present: a gift or a party for the workers. Unsurprisingly, she chose the latter, and this set the tone for a remarkably egalitarian partnership. Instead of a honeymoon, they visited business friends of Oskar.

With full support from her husband, Sophie (1841–1915) became a locomotive expert with intimate knowledge of everything that happened in the factory. When Oskar died in 1894, Sophie ran the factory until her son Karl came of age in 1900. Characteristically, two days before she gave up her managerial position, she asked Karl in no uncertain terms to give her in writing a pledge that he would consult and inform her on all matters.

Quakers and Traders

In Britain, common law grossly discriminated against women engaging in any form of entrepreneurial activity. Salaried women were equally disadvantaged and, over a large period of time, the trade unions were disinclined to advocate women's rights. Union leaders were stridently masculine, masquerading as women's protectors when it came to justifying unequal pay and working conditions. In 1875, the Secretary of the Trade Unions Congress (TUC) Henry Broadhurst thought it the unions' mission to work towards a situation "where wives and daughters would be in their proper sphere at home, instead of being dragged into competition for livelihood against the great and strong men of the world." Men invited public disgrace if they allowed their wives to work.

As in other fields, the Quakers proved to be the exception to the general rule. Approving as they did the education of girls and their right to speak at religious meetings, members of the Society of Friends belonged to the most enlightened entrepreneurs on both sides of the Atlantic. Among their ranks in Britain were industrial dynasties like the Cadburys, the Frys and the Rowntrees. George Cadbury provided employees with a wide range of facilities like canteens, sports grounds and educational facilities. Persons of both sexes operated Works Committees. Cadbury's (1839–1922) vision of practical Christianity certainly included women. His wife Elizabeth was equally committed to social causes. Fellow industrialist Joseph Rowntree was a friend of social reformer Charles Booth and a committed philanthropist.

In the United States, Rebecca Lukens' father supported her. He had founded a steel mill that made wheel rims and barrel hoops. He introduced her to steel-manufacturing and her later husband, Charles Lukens, though educated as a doctor, joined the business. Rather like Sophie and Oskar Henschel, the Lukens formed an egalitarian partnership. When Charles died, Rebecca (1794–1854) carried on the business and developed a great commercial aptitude, taking care of pricing and of negotiations with the banks.

A range of non-Quaker industrialists similarly provided facilities that eased working women's lives. In the case of William Lever, later Lord Leverhulme, this meant building schools where girls had special classes in subjects like cooking and shorthand. Women also profited from the garden villages built by Lever Brothers, where the company provided accommodation in cottages and facilities that included a theatre, a library and an open-air swimming pool.

William Rathbone VI, scion of a family prominent in general merchandise in Liverpool, perceived business activity as a way of achieving social goals. Rathbone (1819–1902) strongly promoted nursing, after experiencing the good work done by a nurse when his wife was dying in 1859; his friendship with Florence Nightingale also motivated his support. He later established a Training School and contributed to the founding of Queen Victoria's Jubilee Institute for Nurses. His wife Emily closely cooperated with him and later served as Lady Superintendent of district nurses. One of his six children was the politician Eleanor Rathbone. Like her father, she worked from an early age among the poor in Liverpool.

In 1838, Charles Jenner founded a store for high-quality linen and silk in Edinburgh, which later became the city's leading department store. He and his colleague lost their jobs as employees at a draper's store because they had gone off to the races instead of reporting for work. However, they had betted on the right horse and used the proceeds to set up their own enterprise.

Jenner (1811–91) firmly believed that women were vital for his business, both as customers and employees. Known as the Harrods of the north, Jenner paid its shopgirls above-average wages, which apparently did not keep some of them from allowing customers to take them out for dinner and to bed. Jenner was a public benefactor, becoming the first Director of the Royal Hospital for Sick Children; his actions reflected to a greater degree shrewd business psychology rather than charity.

In the 20th century, Quaker businessman Ernest Bader was a pioneer in making employees into business partners and owners. The chemical company founded on Quaker principles in Northamptonshire became the Scott Bader Commonwealth in 1951. It has always sought to provide equal opportunities to all employees, whether male or female. The company received the Gandhi Foundation International Peace Award in 2014 in recognition of its business model.

Similarly, John Lewis Partnership is a beacon of profitable, enlightened enterprise in Britain today. John Spedan Lewis, son of the company's founder, was shocked by the disparity between the wealth owned by his family and the salaries paid to staff in the company's department stores. Spedan (1885–1963) was a canny philanthropist who took over his father's second shop, Peter Jones, and turned it into a profit-making enterprise. In 1928, he founded the John Lewis Partnership and by 1950, ownership of the company devolved to the employees.

In the meantime, Spedan provided an unusual range of

opportunities for female employees. While recruiting women as normal staff, he also selected a group of highly educated women for managerial positions. In the years after World War One, with women often excluded from the workforce in favour of men returning from the war, the Partnership was one of the few companies that offered high-level employment.

Strong women certainly inspired Spedan: his mother Eliza Lewis was one of Cambridge University's first female graduates and his wife, Sarah Hunter, who had a graduate degree from Oxford, reinforced his belief in women's managerial capabilities. She had a visible influence on staff training and management development within the Partnership.

Spedan was as much a workaholic as a benefactor. His former secretary and housekeeper recalls him working seven days a week and others remember him as being both vain and cantankerous. However, he displayed great courage and vision in rejecting his father's Victorian brand of cutthroat capitalism and opting for an enlightened, cooperative model. Fittingly, in a BBC online poll in 2002, John Spedan Lewis was voted Britain's greatest business leader.

A remarkable range of male personalities has supported women in the working world. Lord Reith was perhaps the most surprising of them all. The self-important, authoritarian founder of the BBC seems an unlikely candidate for the role of mentor. Yet, John Reith (1889–1971) appointed a large cross-section of women and gave them a great degree of autonomy. He supported executives like Hilda Matheson, Director of Talks, though he later forced her out of the BBC. Another example was Mary Somerville, who visited him while studying at Oxford and who later started as an educational assistant, ultimately becoming Director of School Broadcasting. A third example was Isa Benzie, who started as a secretary and rose to become Foreign Director.

Often however, Reith felt uneasy about intelligent women

and on several occasions called them "weird." He was happier in the company of devoted secretaries and assistants whom he treated with great consideration.

Beyond this, Reith's largesse had its limits; no woman became a member of his Control Board and his style of leadership was certainly paternalistic. In one memo, he expressed his private opinion that there was no reason why a woman should not become a Station Director, though he quickly added the proviso that it would be extremely difficult to find one. Privately, Reith was both an autocrat and a womaniser. He forced his wife Muriel to stop working when she married him and later had squalid affairs with several women.

Another mighty man who valued female assistance was the legendary American newspaper tycoon William Randolph Hearst, who inspired Orson Welles' film *Citizen Kane*. After recruiting Alice Head as assistant editor of one of his magazines, Hearst (1863–1951) developed such respect for her that she rapidly rose in the hierarchy, then becoming editor and managing director of the English edition of *Good Housekeeping* from 1924 to 1939. Head (1886–1981) was the highest-paid woman in Britain at the time. Hearst trusted her with a variety of missions in Europe, including eccentric jobs like procuring giraffes for his private zoo.

Equality in Difference: The French Recipe

In France, Julie-Victoire Daubié was the country's first woman to do her school-leaving exams (baccalauréat) in 1861 and equally the first to obtain a university degree (licence) in 1872. Daubié (1824–74) later became a journalist, greatly supported by the Saint-Simonean industrialist François Barthelemy Arlès-Dufour.

Arlès-Dufour (1797–1872) was a self-made man in the silk industry, who married his boss Dufour's daughter and, as a feminist signal, gave himself a double-barrelled name. He accompanied Daubié to Paris, where she received the baccalauréat. As a railway pioneer, the silk industrialist was also one of the Suez Canal initiators. Dufour was a great reformer who fought for relief of the poor and for peace; he was also an amateur homeopath. He visited England to investigate factories in the 1820s; his radical liberal ideas show the influence of Richard Cobden and John Bright.

Equally assiduous in the field of law was the Belgian advocate Louis Frank. Born in a liberal Jewish family, he entered the fray in 1888 at the age of 24, fighting for Marie Popelin, a Belgian fellow student, who attempted without success to take the oath as a lawyer.

Frank (1864–1917) was more successful supporting Jeanne Chauvin, a French lawyer. Her application to join the Bar in Paris, though rejected by a court verdict, gained success through legislation passed by the French National Assembly. Frank publicised her cause widely, emphasising the injustice of the Napoleonic civil code.

Later, Frank cofounded the Belgian League for Women's Rights and was its first secretary-general until forced out by both male and female board members because of his autocratic leadership style. Ironically, Marie Popelin replaced him. Furious at this, he publicly said that till then, the best champions of women's rights had always been men and that women, left to themselves, would not be able to "generate a Stuart Mill." Despite this, feminists held him in high regard. His *Grand catéchisme de la femme,* a feminist manual, was translated into six languages.

Other combatants for women's education rights included the playwright Ernest Legouvé. His lectures on the moral history of women at the prestigious Collège de France included the accusation that the French Revolution had failed, because it ignored women's rights.

Intriguingly, Legouvé (1807–1903) considered fraternity to be a feminine virtue that derived from women's love. His advocacy of better education led to his becoming the inspector-general of female education at secondary schools. His ideas were greatly admired by feminists across Europe, ranging from John Stuart Mill to the German feminists Hedwig Dohm and Lily Braun.

Legouvé propagated equality in difference, emphasising the fundamental divide between the sexes and insisting on women's moral superiority. While supporting their demand for a professional vocation, he denied their need to vote.

Other reformers were decidedly more enlightened. Ferdinand Buisson was a man of many roles. As director of primary education in France, he firmly supported compulsory, secular education. As a deputy in parliament, Buisson (1841–1932) was a prominent member of the Commission for Universal Suffrage and an unconditional supporter of the cause. As a pacifist, he won the Nobel Peace Prize because of his work towards French-German reconciliation. As a member of the country's Protestant minority, Buisson was in many ways an outsider. His espousal of the Dreyfus cause and his criticism of the Versailles treaty after the First World War made him a target for clerics and conservatives alike; at the age of 87, he was physically assaulted by students when speaking at a peace rally.

Buisson also supported coeducation both as editor of the *Pedagogic Dictionary* and as a promoter of Paul Robin (1837-1912), who became the Principal of the Prévost Orphanage, which he transformed into one of the country's leading reformed schools. Robin's credo was éducation intégrale, an all-round approach that included intellectual, manual and physical education for boys and girls alike. Unsurprisingly, this enraged conservative circles, and in 1894 Robin lost his position, later committing suicide.

One of Robin's few supporters was the speaker and writer Léopold Lacour. Lacour (1854–1939) qualified with distinction from the prestigious École Normale Supérieure, one of the country's leading grandes écoles, and was briefly active as a schoolteacher, before becoming a free-lance writer and speaker. He was one of the Third Republic's most prominent feminists and, like Buisson, a radical humanist. Lacour's major work *Humanisme intégral,* published in 1896, calls for the complete emancipation of women.

Beyond supporting co-education, Lacour documented the feminist cause, writing a book on pioneer feminists like Olympe de Gouges. This led to his being insulted by misogynist writers like Dumas and Zola, who called him a "vaginard." Advocating sexual freedom, Lacour lived accordingly, dividing his erotic attentions between his wife and his long-term mistress.

Buisson had seen to it that Robin was appointed in 1880 and had also staunchly supported him, but was vilified himself by clerics, conservative scholars and journalists alike. In the struggle between Catholic conservatism and modern, enlightened attitudes, the former mostly triumphed.

Women's Minds: Progress through Protestantism?

In the second edition of Buisson's *Pedagogic Dictionary,* the description of the term "coeducation" includes a critical view of the moral objections that held up progress in France. By contrast, "In countries with Germanic races [sic] and Protestant education, where women enjoyed greater independence and where the sexes mixed more freely, there were many mixed schools."

Published in 1911, the Dictionary made no secret of the fact that the situation in Britain, Germany, Switzerland, Holland and the Scandinavian countries was more advanced. Pride of place was however given to the United States, which as a country invalidated the moralistic arguments against coeducation in France. The Americans believed that in getting to know one another at an early age, the boys would be less boisterous and the girls more serious.

Protestant countries were certainly more prone to promoting mental individualism. Religious dissenters, in particular the

Quakers, were already running coeducational schools in both England and New England during the 18th century. Coeducation flourished particularly in the northern and western regions of the U.S.; mixed schools mirrored the mingling of the sexes in church and reflected the norms of a frontier society, where separate spheres for women and men were hardly feasible. By the 1890s, the majority of schools were coeducational.

However, a large protest movement developed, both in the U.S. and in Europe. Moralistic arguments about the impropriety of boys and girls mixing freely were augmented by the pseudo-professional findings of doctors, who proclaimed that coeducation would stress the delicate dispositions of the girls undergoing it. Single-sex schooling was a rallying-call for conservatives of all faiths with Catholics in the forefront. The *Catholic Encyclopedia* argues that the practice whereby men teach boys and women girls is sanctioned by tradition and facilitated by the male and female religious orders that run schools. With regard to coeducational schools, it points out, "While the boys probably part with some of their roughness it is by no means certain that the delicacy of feeling and the refinement of manner that are expected in girls gain much by the association."

Clichés of this kind have been at the forefront of attempts to protect girls and women from the stress involved in interacting with males and in developing their individuality. Progress has been stronger in countries with different Protestant denominations, in particular the U.S. and to a certain extent Great Britain, where however Anglicans prevail over other forms of Protestantism to a great degree. Countries with unified Protestantism such as Germany, where the Lutheran faith predominates, lag behind pluralist societies.

Another reason why progress in opening higher education to women has been stronger in the Anglo-Saxon countries has to do with the fact that they are to a greater degree free-market societies. Entrepreneurs like Vassar and Holloway pushed ahead and established pioneer colleges. By contrast, in countries with state-run education, progress was slow because reformers had to undertake the "long march through the institutions of power" that the German activist Rudi Dutschke was advocating in a more global context in the 1960s.

4

Women's Bodies: Abolitionists, Abortionists, Birth-Controllers

> *Constant companion, (& friend in old age) who will feel interested in one. —object to be beloved and played with. —better than a dog anyhow.*
>
> Charles Darwin

Traditional male prejudice, dating back to the Greek and Christian philosophers, postulates that women are not only less intelligent than men, but are also morally weaker and sexually susceptible. Eve succumbs to the Devil's persuasion and then corrupts Adam. Women are basically animalistic temptresses; this is also an implicit justification of rape, with men succumbing to women's malign influence. In more modern times, a racial component augments this prejudice: black women, like black men, supposedly have huge sexual appetites.

Charles Darwin (1809-82) gave prejudice a scientific foundation. His famous theory of evolution postulated that males were more advanced, while adult females resembled the youth of both sexes, immature, though capable of "greater tenderness and less selfishness." Women were thus, to revert to the famous quote at the beginning of this chapter, ideal companions, "objects" to be played with, certainly better than dogs. Those were the notes he scribbled on the back of a letter regarding the pros and cons of marriage.

Darwin's analogies derived strongly from the animal world: "No one disputes that the bull differs in disposition from the cow, the wild-boar from the sow, the stallion from the mare..." Women, important for breeding purposes, needed to be looked after and guided. Any kind of militancy would threaten "the orderly process of evolution."

As early as 1800 BC, the Code of Hammurabi viewed women's bodies as men's property. Rape was thus a property crime, not a crime against humanity. English common law, as codified by Sir William Blackstone in 1769 and soon adopted in the U.S., gave husbands unrestricted rights over the property and bodies of wives. They could beat or rape their wives with virtual impunity, as the case of Caroline Norton indicates. Similar rules applied in Continental law, particularly in the Code Napoléon.

Women's supposed bodily weakness served as an argument to bar them from higher education and the vote. Arguments were often openly biologistic: for instance that too much education could result in frigidity, or that women were too emotional to be able to vote. This concentration on the female body reduced women to social roles as wives and mothers.

The dichotomy between mind and body corresponds with the distinction made between mentally talented men and "body-limited" women. Early feminists addressed this prejudice, protesting that the "mind had no sex" (Poullain de la Barre) and that rationality was universal (Mill, Wollstonecraft). Both male and female feminists concentrated on broadening women's minds through education, while demanding their right as intelligent beings to vote. Parallel to this, others fought for the dignity and independence of the female body. The three theatres where women and like-minded men played major roles were the abolition of prostitution, abortion and birth control.

A. Protecting Prostitutes

A major movement for radical change focused on women who sold their bodies. The campaign against the forcible inspection of prostitutes for venereal diseases in England led by Josephine Butler marks the propagation of an often-restated fact: A woman's body belongs to her and is inviolable.

Here, we encounter a significant difference to the campaigns addressing women's minds. Leading protagonists of abolitionism were predominantly female. Butler (1828–1906) was for women's bodies what Mill was for suffrage. However, men played vital roles as doctors, politicians, civil servants, clerics and publicists.

The Contagious Diseases Acts (CD) passed between 1864 and 1869 ignited protest for several reasons. Venereal disease was rampant in the armed forces; alone in the navy, over 100,000 total sick days per year were registered. Cases of syphilis had been rising since the early 19th century; during the Crimean War, the high number of deaths not caused by warfare incited health investigation. Addressing this issue, the CD Acts made prostitutes solely responsible for syphilis, gonorrhea etc. This empowered the police to both arrest them and subject them to gynaecological tests. Soldiers on the other hand were not prosecuted, the visits to prostitutes being considered unavoidable. This was a blatant case of double standards.

Beyond their manifest unfairness, the Acts passed Parliament surreptitiously, parallel to similar bills applying to cattle. Implicitly, the law treated "fallen" women like cattle. Several parliamentarians criticised CD as a conspiracy against womanhood.

Among the first in the medical profession to protest were two doctors from Nottingham. Charles Bell Taylor, a renowned ophthalmic surgeon, was a man of strong convictions and ascetic behaviour. Known never to have had more than two meals a day, Taylor (1829–1909) abstained not only from alcohol and tobacco, but also from tea and coffee. He was a strong exponent of individual rights, also opposing compulsory vaccination and vivisection.

The surgeon immediately attacked CD in a pamphlet with the eloquent subtitle *Showing how the New Law Debases Women, Debauches Men, Destroys the Liberty of the Subject and Tends to Increase Disease*. His colleague Charles Worth, also a surgeon, sent a telegram to Butler urging her to head the repeal campaign with the argument that women needed to have representatives of their own sex lead the charge.

Among those who rallied to the cause in the first phase of protest was the clergyman Robert Eli Hooppell, who cooperated with Bell Taylor in organising meetings and later started a weekly called *The Shield* dedicated to CD repeal. Hooppell (1833–1895), who also fought for temperance, had a provocative approach, displaying a speculum at public meetings. This led Butler to dismiss him from the position of secretary of the Northern Counties League for Repeal.

Parliamentarians and Priests United

Butler got strong support from parliamentarians as well. Most prominent among them was the Liberal Sir James Stansfeld, who served as President of the National Association for the Repeal of the Contagious Disease Acts, this being the male equivalent of the Ladies' Association headed by Butler, of which he was vice-president. Stansfeld (1820–1898) was a prominent radical, supporting both the Italian and Polish freedom movements. He was Lord of the Treasury in the first Gladstone ministry and occupied other prominent positions. As President of the Local Government Board, Stansfeld appointed a woman as Inspector of Workhouses in the face of strong opposition.

The radical's open support for CD repeal deprived him of a government post in Gladstone's 1880 administration. Stansfeld fought in parliament over a period of ten years for the repeal of the CD Act. He called government statistics "faulty and deficient" and skilfully cross-examined medical witnesses as a member of the Committee of Enquiry. Parliament adopted the report written by him, though only a minority of committee members signed it. Butler organised prayer meetings throughout the entire night of final debate.

Stansfeld could count on support from his wife Caroline

(1816–1889), who also came from a radical dissenting family. Her father had very progressive views on women's rights, allowing his daughters to mingle with prominent reformers and even to smoke cigars. When a radical Unitarian minister married the couple, they exchanged rings as a token of equality. Both supported woman's suffrage; Stansfeld also campaigned for medical education.

Another staunch supporter was Stansfeld's Liberal colleague Henry Joseph Wilson. Also from a family of non-conformist radicals. Wilson (1833–1914) ran the anti-CD campaign in the Northern Counties, sending out petitions, distributing circulars and organising conferences. Like Stansfeld, Wilson was a true liberal, coming out for Home Rule in Ireland and opposing the Boer War.

Other politicians of the Liberal Party played important roles in the years before Stansfeld started his agitation. William Fowler introduced a Repeal Bill as early as 1870 and withdrew it when the government appointed a Royal Commission. Later, Harcourt Johnstone introduced Repeal Bills unsuccessfully every year.

Stansfeld, Wilson and their supporters finally prevailed in the House of Commons; in 1885, the CD Act was repealed. This however applied to Britain, not to the colonies. Butler then founded the British Committee of the International Abolitionist Federation (IAF), pressing for the extension of repeal. Wilson's friend George William Johnson, who held a high position in the Colonial Office, supported her. After he resigned his post in 1917, Johnson served as Vice-Chairman of the British Committee.

Johnson (1857–1926) was a remarkably enlightened civil servant with a strong sense of justice that extended both to the colonial people under British rule and to his own family. He for instance rejected the idea of being the "master of the house." As the son of liberal nonconformists, Johnson was exposed to religious discrimination at an early age. He fought for the complete legal equality of the sexes, as also for suffrage and for abolition in the colonies. His views were expressed in *The Evolution of Woman, from Subjection to Comradeship*, a magisterial analysis of women's rights from antiquity to the early 20th century.

Another prominent parliamentarian playing an important role in tackling the "licensing of immorality" in India was Cambridge professor James Stuart. An early supporter of Butler, Stuart (1843–1913) was one of the first male activists for women's education and an unconditional supporter of suffrage for all women, whether married or unmarried. Like Stansfeld, Stuart suffered for his radical views, never achieving a government position despite his enormous talents. A remarkably versatile man, Cambridge's first Professor of Mechanism was a great advocate of practical training. Later, when his father-in-law Jeremiah Colman died, Stuart ran the eponymous mustard-manufacturing company.

Stuart persistently confronted the Undersecretary of State for India with unpleasant truths: in 1888, he highlighted the cynicism underlying the Act, quoting the medical officer of a cantonment who had complained that the matron did "not take trouble to attract good-looking women" and should therefore be replaced. Beyond that, a Surgeon-Major in the North-Western Provinces had reported that the rate of venereal diseases had risen. That year, the Act was suspended in India.

Prominent clergymen had supported the parliamentary battle for repeal. During the night of the debate, Cardinal Henry Edward Manning, the prominent Catholic leader, argued with Irish parliamentarians in the lobby to gain their support for repeal. Ten years before this, Manning (1808–92) had condemned the Acts "on every ground of Christian and natural morality," regarding them "with the strongest repugnance."

Alfred Dyer, a Quaker activist, similarly moved from agitation in Europe to India, where his reports included an embarrassing memorandum from the Quartermaster General in

India related to providing "attractive women" in "proper houses." Before this, he had created a great stir with the story of a housemaid, kidnapped and held in a brothel in Brussels. Dyer closely cooperated with Butler and members of the local Federation in Belgium, one of whom helped the 19-year-old girl escape to England from a hospital, where she received treatment for VD. He later published a bestseller, *The European Slave Traffic in English Girls*.

From Social Purity to Repression

Originally called the Christian Revival Association, the Salvation Army (SA) came into being in 1865. From the beginning onwards, its founders William and Catherine Booth strongly opposed sexual trafficking. Authoritarian leadership and the innovative use of resonant symbols such as uniforms, popular music and military language characterise the SA on the one hand. On the other hand, the Army granted women more authority and freedom of action than in most other Protestant institutions.

The Booths were already cooperating with Josephine Butler when a 17-year-old girl, lured into a brothel after being offered a housemaid's job, escaped to the SA. After this happened, Butler, Booth and others contacted William Thomas Stead, editor of the *Pall Mall Gazette*. Stead (1849–1912) was a strong supporter of both the Army and the Liberal Party, thus a kindred spirit and a great propagandist with Puritan inclinations. He had already campaigned against the CD Acts and published reports on child prostitution. Beyond this, Stead practiced gender fairness as the first editor in Britain to pay female journalists the same wages as their male colleagues. A campaigner for many causes, he died on the Titanic in 1912 while on his way to America to hold a lecture on world peace at New York's Carnegie Hall.

Stead is best described as an early master of investigative journalism. He pro forma kidnapped a 13-year-old girl to show how easy it was to do, and was then convicted to a three-month prison sentence. The real sensation was his article series, *The Maiden Tribute of Modern Babylon,* which described child molestation and rape in lurid language, accusing rich men of dishonouring poor girls.

Stead concentrated on girls older than 13, the scandalously low age of consent at the time. In one article, he wrote, "The law, indeed, seems specially framed in order to enable dissolute men to outrage these legal women of thirteen with impunity." He also bemoaned the physical ignorance of the mostly Protestant girls involved, pointing out that Catholic children were more aware of the facts of life. The crusading journalist played a major role in getting the Criminal Law Amendment Act passed in 1885, which increased the age of consent to 16. However, this Act also made "indecent acts" between consenting males a crime, thus exposing homosexuals to legal repression.

Stead's emphasis on social purity was well-meaning, but opened the door to social repression. "White slavery" created a moral panic, diverting attention from the social factors leading to prostitution. It also created images of women as helpless objects in need of assistance. This became particularly apparent during the manhunt against Jack the Ripper from 1888 onwards; vigilance committees put pressure on lower-class women, while respectable women were essentially under house arrest at night.

A further side effect of the social purity campaign was ethnocentrism and intolerance. Stead had imperialist tendencies as a strong supporter of Cecil Rhodes, though he was an opponent of the Boer War. Dyer avidly described "wealthy Continental debauches" violating innocent English girls. Benjamin Scott, one of Stead's collaborators and chamberlain of the City of London, called prostitution "the filthy product of pagan depravity," singling out France as a particularly vile country.

This ethnocentric bias was no male monopoly; Millicent Fawcett considered "British womanhood" superior to that of the Continent. Butler was also susceptible to feelings of superiority;

she saw Indian women as "helpless, voiceless, hopeless," rather like homeless children.

William Alexander Coote is the typical example of a dangerous zealot. He was a religiously inspired moral reformer, who started as a trade unionist and moved on to become secretary of the National Vigilance Association founded by Stead. Coote (1842–1919) led an international campaign against the "white slave" trade. He considered legislation important as a way of "whipping most of the citizens into a condition of obedience." Butler later distanced herself from him. As with Dyer, the social purity movement attracted unbalanced characters with a penchant for extremist behaviour. George Bernard Shaw described Coote as being "intensely stupid" as far as art was concerned and "something of a monomaniac" in sexual matters.

The late Victorian Age was full of troubled Puritans at all levels of society. Four-time Prime Minister William Gladstone is an excellent example. He played a role in rescuing and rehabilitating prostitutes while also enjoying the company of well-known courtesans. In his diary, he once confessed to "adultery of the heart." His famous opponent of the Conservatives, Benjamin Disraeli, by contrast was a man of the world, as illustrated by the apocryphal story that when accosted by prostitutes in Green Park, he responded: "Not tonight, my dears, not tonight."

Continental Europe: Separate Efforts for Common Goals

There was a significant difference between Britain and the Continent: laws regulating prostitution in countries like France dated back to the Napoleonic period. From 1804 onwards, France established official brothels with registered prostitutes subject to regular medical checks. This precluded the drama of the CD Acts. The main emphasis was on combatting venereal disease (VD).

Ghénia Avril de Sainte-Croix, the French Josephine Butler,

lacked French male allies. She was Head of the IAF French section and active in the International Council on Women. Fittingly, her principal male supporters came from abroad and included Henry Wilson Harris, an English MP and long-term editor of *The Spectator*, as well as the American social-purity activist Bascom Johnson.

In France, Sainte-Croix (1855–1939) and other female abolitionists like Sarah Monod mostly belonged to the country's tiny Protestant minority and gained the support of sympathetic relatives. Sarah's cousin Henri, Head of the Public Health Department in Paris, supported the campaign against regulated prostitution, though he did point out: "It is not my task to examine whether or not a society should tolerate brothels." As late as 1898, Sainte-Croix expressed her indignation about this attitude in her often-quoted article *La serve* (*The Female Serf*). Similarly, the influential industrialist and statesman Jules Siegfried supported his wife and other members of the French National Women's Association.

Perhaps the most striking male campaigner against regulated prostitution was the radical journalist and parliamentarian Yves Guyot. In works like *La Prostitution*, published in 1882, Guyot attacked what he called the barbarous brutality of men, who under the guise of gallantry misused women, enjoying prostitutes' bodies while condemning the trade. This made Guyot (1843–1928) a close collaborator of Josephine Butler, to whom he dedicated his book on prostitution. Later, they had fundamental disagreements. Guyot was particularly against the regimentation of prostitution; his attacks on the Prostitution Section of the Criminal Investigation Department apparently led to its dissolution in 1881. Butler and he were fighting for the same cause, but in completely different environments.

The situation in Germany was largely similar. Anna Pappritz, the country's major campaigner, met Butler in 1895 and, inspired by her, founded the German branch of IAF in 1899. Apart from this, she edited the magazine *Der Abolitionist*. Pappritz (1861–1939) had a strong sense of morality and saw female sexuality exclusively in the context of married life. This led her to oppose those who, like Helene Stöcker, advocated a new autonomous sexuality for women. Both however were committed to abolishing prostitution; Pappritz believed that stable marriages were the solution, while Stöcker had a more modern view of sexual relationships.

Gertrud Guillaume-Schack was even more progressive, founding the German Cultural Association as early as 1880 as a branch of IAF. Schack (1845–1903) had the courage to speak openly in public about sexuality, often to female workers, and joined the Social Democrat Party (SPD), whose Chairman August Bebel was a great supporter of suffrage for women. Later, in the context of Bismarck's anti-socialist laws, she immigrated to England and was in close contact with Friedrich Engels, who rather patronisingly called her "Mother Schack." Both Pappritz and Schack lacked male support.

Parallel to their agitation, male morality campaigners from both the Protestant and Catholic churches attacked prostitution. Samuel Keller, a German preacher born in St. Petersburg and forced to flee Russia for political reasons, became general secretary of the Ethical Foundation (Sittlichkeitsbund). Other churchmen were followers of Adolf Stoecker, the controversial leader of the anti-Semitic Christian Socialists during the Kaiserreich. Stoecker (1835-1909) attacked both capitalism and leftist movements as being under Jewish control. For some time, he had a strong influence on Kaiser Wilhelm II.

Ludwig Weber, who played an important role in Protestant social welfare, founded an Ethical Association to preempt the formation of a feminist organisation. To the dismay of all present, he dominated the proceedings at the founding meeting of the Evangelical Women's Association. Weber (1846–1922) was Head of the Protestant Workers Association and remained close to

Stoecker until the end of his life. A similar combination of social reform and conservative political views can be perceived in Wilhelm Philipps, the preacher and publicist who co-founded the reactionary Deutschnationale Volkspartei (DNVP) during the Weimar Republic.

In 1906, *Der Abolitionist* published the text of a speech that the Swiss priest Emile Hoffet had held on the subject. Hoffet (1873–1946) called the state regulation of prostitution unjust and traced the causes of prostitution to poverty, while also criticising the "dissoluteness of human nature" and the disgusting proclivity of men to indulge their base instincts.

Thus, the rhetoric of Keller, Weber, Hoffet and others did include strong criticism of male behaviour in reducing women to "white slaves." All of them considered the treatment of prostitutes like commodities to be an enormous sacrilege. Keller (1856–1924) called the medical checks on prostitutes "modern witch-trials." By contrast, the liberal press criticised the churchmen for being philistine and acting as "intolerant apostles of morality." Journalists even implied that their prudery was a cover-up for prurience.

This mixture of strong morality and an ethnocentric mentality was no prerogative of male campaigners. Katharina Scheven, a close collaborator of Pappritz, found it important to save German women, because they were more innocent than their Jewish or foreign counterparts. Käthe Schirrmacher was explicitly anti-Semitic both in her articles for *Der Abolitionist* and in her activities as a DNVP parliamentarian. Ethnocentric bias in Germany was at least as strong as in Britain.

From Antebellum Reform to Puritanical Restrictions

The situation in the U.S. was closer in many ways to the Continent than to Britain. There was no coherent abolitionist movement revolving around an individual personality like Butler. America also lacked the drama of the CD Acts.

Prostitution, while tacitly tolerated, was not regulated as in France and Germany.

The Magdalen Society founded in 1830 with the support of wealthy women took early action against "licentiousness." The most prominent member of the New York-based Society, Reverend J. R. McDowell, attacked girls who were "ignorant, vain and idle" and were trying to emulate their wealthy neighbours, thus laying the base for their ruin as "easy prey to the profligate libertine." This was in his Annual Report to the Society, which later closed. McDowell (1780–1868) continued to preach against moral iniquity, later supported by the New York Female Moral Reform Society (FMRS), run by Lidia Andrews Finney, wife of a revivalist preacher.

FMRS tried various strategies, entering brothels and praying with prostitutes, agitating for state intervention and threatening to publish the names of brothel patrons. This is a good example of pre-civil-war reform with men and women working together. However, it did not lead to state action or legislation.

During most of the 19th century, prostitution was considered a "necessary evil." Since its regulation was a state domain according to the Tenth Amendment of the U.S. Constitution, conditions in individual states greatly varied. Though considered illegal under vagrancy laws, brothels and streetwalkers were mostly tolerated.

In the context of the Industrial Revolution that expanded across the country in the 1830s and 1840s, poverty and unemployment drove many working-class women in the cities into selling their bodies. The material temptation was strong: the women could make four times as much as what servants or workers earned. Beyond this, prostitutes were far freer than "normal" women: they married later, were divorced more often, owned their own property and used contraceptives.

Brothel madams considered themselves businesswomen and often supported charitable causes. This was equally true of black madams like "Mammy" Pleasant and "Babe" Connors, who also fought for desegregation in San Franciso's streetcars. Pleasant has in fact been called the "mother of the civil rights movement."

After the Civil War and in the face of increased immigration, medical experts like William Sanger, author of *The History of Prostitution,* recommended European-style regulation. Sanger pinpointed the phenomenon's major cause as being poverty, not female depravity. France and Prussia were considered regulatory models and when the European Medical Congress of 1873 advocated medical checks of women, American experts concurred.

The public mood then changed in the 1880s. A curious temporary alliance between social-purity crusaders and early feminists came into being, comparable to the connection between the temperance movement and suffragists. Prostitution became an absolute, not a necessary evil, a scourge on national purity. While free-love feminists stressed a woman's right to refuse sex, even in marriage, the purity activists were far closer to middle-class morality. Their criticism of the sex drive as deviating from a focus on work and material success was potently Puritanical.

Women's and Men's Groups coexisted, remaining strangely separate. Vice commissions were generally dominated by men, while women organised themselves mostly in religious groups like the Women's Christian Temperance Union. Inspired by events in Britain, they campaigned to raise the age of consent and called for the abolition of brothels.

Men concentrated more on eradicating organised vice and on health issues. Many were doctors like Prince Albert Morrow, marking a transition from social purity to hygiene. Morrow however saw VD not merely as a medical issue, blaming it on male promiscuity and double standards. Others concentrated on the economic issues involved. The Illinois Senate Vice Committee was particularly clear-minded, pinpointing poverty as the main cause of prostitution.

Members of the Commonwealth Club Committee in California were mostly doctors, insisting on scientific evidence and in the process ignoring women reformers. However, after women gained suffrage in the state in 1911, they successfully pressured the state legislature to abolish prostitution and put an end to the Municipal Clinic of the Health Board, which had hitherto played a regulatory role.

Ethnocentrism and "White Slavery"

Ethnocentrism in the U.S. was even stronger than in Britain and the Continent. Social-purity activism focused on pure Anglo-American girls coerced and misled into "white slavery." They became the easy prey of degenerate immigrants. Abolitionist rhetoric lost all sense of proportion.

The White Slavery slogan gave Puritans traction and led to restrictive legislation. Innocent young girls lacked "agency"; they were not interacting with society as professional prostitutes did, but were its victims. They belonged to society and were not its outcasts; hence, they needed to be rescued. Lurid White Slavery stories, well comparable to W.T. Stead's *Modern Babylon* series in England, came out in the early 1900s.

Republican Congressman James Robert Mann, who made history as originator of the Mann Act of 1910, rendering the interstate transportation of prostitutes illegal, went as far as declaring: "All of the horrors which have ever been urged, either truthfully or fancifully, against the black-slave trade pale into insignificance as compared to the horrors of the so-called 'white slave trade'." Mann (1856–1922) was a skilled parliamentarian and a "master legislator" responsible for food and drug laws. He also served as House Minority Leader. By contrast, California's State Senator Edwin Grant failed to gain reelection because he acted against the vested interests of his San Francisco constituents in opposing prostitution.

Grant had supported the Red Light Abatement Act together

with other purity stalwarts. The Act held property owners responsible for the use of their premises. Individual citizens could file petitions against both brothel owners and their licensers and get injunctions. San Francisco's red-light district Barbary Coast overshadowed similar areas in other cities. Thus, the Abatement Act threatened the livelihoods not only of prostitutes but also of the men behind the trade. By the 1920s, red-light areas had virtually disappeared in America's cities.

Another campaigner in San Francisco was Bascom Johnson, a Yale-educated lawyer who acted through the American Social Hygiene Association. Johnson was proud of the fact that he had filed numerous court suits against brothels in Barbary. During World War One, Johnson (1878–1954) travelled to France to curb prostitution affecting U.S. soldiers. Several other activists played equally important roles in what was really a campaign for social purity.

The disparity between Britain and the U.S., in particular the lack of solidarity in America between those fighting for the same cause, illustrates the importance of centralised power mechanisms and personal ties. Butler's social contacts and her impeccable higher middle-class respectability were of vital advantage.

B. Birth Control: Respectable Women's Bodies

Abolitionism focused on a fringe group of social outcasts, attempting to protect them and give them self-respect. Birth control was a universal issue, affecting a large percentage of adult women. Prostitutes provided sexual pleasure for money, implicitly accepting the consequences; could and should respectable women enjoy sexuality without facing its consequences? This was both a moral and a political question.

Thomas Malthus was the first to urge birth control for existential reasons; his law postulated population growth outpacing agriculture, thus creating famine. Malthus's recipes to regulate births were highly traditional: celibacy or late marriage.

Utilitarian Jeremy Bentham is often considered the first to advocate contraceptives. However, an opaque reference to "spunges" in the context of a tract on the *Situation and Relief of the Poor* serves as evidence.

The working-class radical Francis Place was a real pioneer. Despite great poverty, Place (1771–1854) was well read, strongly influenced by radical thinkers like Paine and Godwin, but also by Bentham and James Mill. While hating the landed classes, he also abhorred violence, resigning from the London Corresponding Society because some members espoused rough methods. Place was against trade unions because they, according to him, damaged the fabric of society.

The radical had good personal reasons to promote birth control: he fathered 15 children. Well aware of Malthus's gloomy predictions, Place criticised him for being ignorant of the conditions in which the poor lived. He equally attacked Malthus for having the illusion that the poor would refrain from sex until economically capable of supporting a family.

Place's *Illustrations and Proofs of the Principle of Population* is the first book to advocate contraception openly. Beyond this, he published several handbills, mostly counselling readers to use a vaginal sponge, while also advocating coitus interruptus.

Place's most important disciple was equally versatile. Richard Carlile, who also propagated universal suffrage and freedom of the press, had a strong satirical streak, landing in prison for his parody of the Book of Common Prayer. Carlile (1790–1843) was a remarkable humanist, truly believing in equality between the sexes and in the fact that men and women had the same sexual appetites. For him, birth control and sexual emancipation were closely linked.

In *What is Love?* Carlile pleads for free love as opposed to purely matrimonial sex. He specifically advocates contraception, in particular the sponge, though also mentioning condoms, coitus interruptus and interfemora (ejaculation between the thighs of a woman).

Carlile goes as far as calling for a "new attitude to physical love – secular, open, celebratory and hedonistic, rather than Christian, clandestine, condemnatory and prim," as M.L. Bush, editor of the new edition of the book, puts it. Men and women are equal because they have the same sexual appetites. Carlile strikingly points out: "I am not for treating women as the mere breeding machines for the human race and men as the directing lords of the aggregate machinery." However, he draws the line at homosexual sex.

What is Love? was published in 1825. Thirty years later, a similar work again evoked the pleasure of sex. George Drysdale's *Elements of Social Science*, written at the age of 27 and soon translated into all major European languages, includes the hypothesis that the fear of having more children led men to visit prostitutes while inhibiting female sexuality. Like Carlile, Drysdale (1825–1904) fervently endorsed heterosexuality, while strongly condemning masturbation. Similarly, he describes various contraceptive techniques, including vaginal sponges and douches (flushing out sperm from the vagina with tepid water).

From Radical Fringe to Establishment

In 1825, the same year as *What is Love?*, a pamphlet published by a rich liberal attacked the sexual subjugation of women. William Thompson, an Anglo-Irish property owner with profoundly enlightened views, had significantly improved the welfare of his tenants through both agricultural innovations and children's education. As an egalitarian, Thompson (1775–1833) supported both the French Revolution and Catholic Emancipation. There are many parallels to John Stuart Mill, including Thompson's background in Utilitarian philosophy and his deep friendship with Anna Wheeler. She had separated from her alcoholic husband and propagated feminist views, influenced both by French philosophers and by Mary Wollstonecraft.

Specifically in Ireland, Thompson saw the danger of uncontrolled population growth increasing poverty. Beyond this, he had a remarkable sense of empathy for the underprivileged, whether men or women. This led him to write the pamphlet *Appeal of One Half of the Human Race*, in which he gave co-authorship to Anna Wheeler in the same spirit of generosity that infused Mill.

This remarkably eloquent text addresses the "Women of England" and openly confronts them with their pretence of enjoying the "banquet of bought or commanded sensuality." Simultaneously, the pamphlet pilloried men for their "domineering hypocrisy" in denying women the same sexual enjoyment that they indulged in. Thus, contraception became part of a far larger emancipation concept.

The same harmony of interest existed between a prominent pillar of society and his wife. Viscount Amberley, eldest son of the former Prime Minister Lord John Russell, had John Stuart Mill as godfather. Amberley (1842–76) appalled Victorian Britain with his radical views as a religious agnostic and a propagator of women's rights. His support for birth control cost him a parliamentary seat at the election in 1868.

His wife Lady Amberley (1842–74) equally supported contraception as an inherent part of feminine equality. She had an open relationship with the tutor of her children with the approval of her husband. Lady Amberley's views enraged Queen Victoria and incited the quotation that feminists ought to be whipped, cited at the beginning of this book's Prologue. Sadly, both Lord and Lady Amberley, the parents of the famous philosopher and feminist Bertrand Russell, died in their early thirties.

From Theory to Practice

The early propagators of birth control (BC) came from many professions, not however from the medical. Yet, one of the 20th century's most remarkable doctors almost single-handedly made

BC both respectable and legal. Bertrand Dawson (1864–1945) combined impeccable academic qualifications with an intense dislike of religious dogma. He soon became a Neo-Malthusian, which led him to explore different methods of contraception. In early years, Dawson wrote a pamphlet called *Few in the Family, Happiness at Home*, advocating family planning.

The doctor was remarkably versatile: he ran a successful practice on Harley Street, was a consultant at the London Hospital and soon attended high-level house parties, where hosts considered it advisable to have a doctor in attendance. His social skills soon matched his medical abilities and Dawson became one of the King's doctors in 1907. Now an establishment figure, he distinguished himself in World War One, acting as a consulting physician in France and researching trench fever.

Dawson became a baronet in 1920 in addition to the CB and KCMG titles he had accumulated in earlier years. He then went on to be a pioneer of medical planning by heading a committee that called for state-organised health protection, later put into practice when the National Health Service came into being after World War Two.

Dawson soon joined the battle for contraception. Both the Catholic and Anglican churches were firmly against BC, considering it both immoral and artificial. The Church of England then made the great mistake of inviting Dawson to address its congress on sexual relationships in 1921.

Dawson used the occasion to marshal both humanistic and pragmatic arguments for contraception, accusing the church of being out of touch with the modern world. A huge controversy ensued; calls for his dismissal as Royal Physician were counterbalanced by support from within the establishment; even *The Times* endorsed his viewpoint. Writing in Margaret Sanger's *Birth Control Review* in 1928, Dawson's willingness to call a spade a spade is apparent in sentences like "To ask that this generation should go back to the helter-skelter method of having families is like crying for the moon." Similarly, he contended that "the proper time for intercourse is when the desire is mutual." For this reason, Dawson rejected any kind of abstention or restriction of sex to "safe periods," since these were periods "when a woman's desire is at its lowest."

By 1930, opinion within the Anglican Church was split, though contraception was only officially accepted as late as 1968. Dawson remained an establishment figure as the King's physician, putting an end to George V's life in 1936 by giving him a lethal injection.

The doctor was also a major force in the parliamentary movement to legalise contraception. Various Ministers of Health shilly-shallied on the issue, while individual members of the Labour Party and personalities like H.G. Wells and Dora Russell canvassed for BC. The official Labour Party viewpoint was, however, that BC was not a political issue. Prominent Liberals like Viscount Buckmaster also supported BC, mainly for eugenic reasons, to stop the "underfed reproducing at a rate which is nearly double of anybody else."

By 1931, the Ministry of Health allowed BC counselling for health reasons. Progress depended on the initiative of individual medical officers. In 1934, a bill proposed by Dawson liberalised both BC counselling and the sale of contraceptives. It passed the House of Lords by 45 votes against six, a signal triumph for Dawson and his allies. Here again, the doctor carried the House with his strident rhetoric, calling BC "a part of our social fabric. To oppose it is just to beat the air."

Parallel to this, a number of BC clinics were founded in the wake of Marie Stopes' pioneer enterprise in 1921. A vibrant network of Groups, Centres and Committees coordinated activities. Their protagonists included two Nobel Prize-winners, several Presidents of Royal Societies and Colleges, not to speak of a number of Oxbridge professors. As was the case with suffrage, the BC cause attracted high-level supporters.

Fellow Travellers of Stopes and Sanger

The great female protagonists of BC used men rather than really collaborating with them. Marie Stopes (1880–1958) had the right parents: her father was a celebrated scientist, her mother a feminist and suffragette. She also had the right education and great natural gifts. Winning a science scholarship to University College London and passing a dual honours degree, she did her doctorate at Munich University.

After carrying out botanical research in Japan and Canada, she married the Canadian scientist Reginald Ruggles Gates, only to discover after researching the subject in the British Museum that he was frigid. Thus still a virgin, Stopes went to court and had her marriage annulled. Gates believed she had been unfaithful; evidently, they were emotionally mismatched and held different social views.

Stopes then married Humphrey Roe, a wealthy manufacturer, who supported her BC research and funded England's first clinic. Later, Stopes expanded her scope in terms of both clinics and contraception instruments, designing a vaginal cap. She dominated the marriage, actually getting a contractual right to have affairs with other men while remaining married.

Like Gates, Stopes was a fervent believer in eugenics, advocating sterilisation not only of the insane and feeble-minded, but also of "revolutionaries" and "half-castes." BC clearly aimed at reducing the reproduction rate of the lower classes and of undesirable human beings. Unsurprisingly, Stopes admired Hitler, sending him a book of her poems with an unctuous letter as late as August 1939; she was both strongly anti-Semitic and homophobic. Britain's BC pioneer certainly was consistent in her eugenic convictions: when her son Harry Stopes-Roe married a myopic woman, she disinherited him.

This contrasts with great courage and initiative in fighting for a woman's right to decide when to give birth and when not. Stopes also had great persuasive skills, managing to enlist the support of many influential men, particularly in the medical profession. This became apparent when she filed and won a court case for libel against Dr Halliday Sutherland in 1923, who had written a book in which he called her activities a "monstrous campaign." Testifying for her were a vice-president of the British Medical Association, a professor of University College London and several distinguished obstetric surgeons and gynaecologists. The protocol of the proceedings shows that, conversely, several female doctors testified for the defence. This demonstrates how the issue transcended gender boundaries.

Stopes' great inspiration was American pioneer Margaret Sanger. There are strong parallels in their lifestyles and political views. Both seemed to be doing the right thing in alleviating misery and increasing personal freedom for the wrong, racist-elitist reasons. In particular, they were helping the poor in order to eliminate their procreation; their motivation was at least as eugenic as it was humanistic.

Sanger (1879–1966) however had a more moderate viewpoint; she openly criticised Hitler and Mussolini as rulers of totalitarian countries where mothers were forced to produce babies as cannon fodder and was shocked by fascist ideology. Beyond that, she had friendly contacts with prominent black leaders like W.E.B. du Bois, opening a clinic in Harlem with black medical staff after receiving a request from a social worker. She also cooperated in the Negro Project designed to offer BC to poor black Americans. While convinced of the superiority of the white race, she was personally against race discrimination.

Sanger had the good fortune of being born to a Catholic father who later became both an atheist and an activist for women's suffrage. By contrast, her mother demonstrated the dangers involved in "normal" familial sexuality: 18 pregnancies in 22 years, death at the age of 50 from tuberculosis and cervical cancer. Margaret's first husband, architect William Sanger, firmly supported her BC activities and even went to jail for distributing one of her pamphlets. Margaret herself had fled to England in 1914 to avoid prosecution for both obscenity and assassination under the Comstock Law of 1873, which prohibited the distribution of BC literature. There, she had relationships with prominent sexologist Havelock Ellis and with the writer H.G. Wells.

Later, she married a rich South African oil magnate called J. Noah Slee, who funded her BC activities, just as Humphrey Roe had supported Stopes. The relationship seems to have been less one-sided than Stopes-Roe, though they maintained separate apartments in their house in Tucson, Arizona, and apparently quarrelled on many issues.

Sanger invented the term birth control and defined it as a "scientific means" of helping parents to fulfil their responsibility "with due regard for the health of the mother, the economic circumstances of the family and the right of a child to be wanted and to be cared for properly." More than anyone else, she made BC standard practice, it being progressively legalised in the U.S. by court decisions in 1918 and 1936. None of the male activists even came close to her knowledge of the subject, not to speak of her influence across the world.

Sanger has been criticised for her views on racial hygiene and for her support of the 1924 Immigration Restriction Act, in particular her famous comment about not admitting "certain aliens whose condition is known to be detrimental to the stamina of the race, such as feebleminded, idiots, morons, insane, syphilitic, epileptic, criminal, professional prostitutes and others..."

The eugenics movement in fact united men and women of high social stature with varied objectives: pure racists such as Lothrop Stoddard, a historian with a doctorate from Harvard, and BC activists, who used eugenics as a mental framework. The same applied to Britain; the first international eugenic congress held in 1912 united luminaries like Major Leonard Darwin, son of the famous biologist and Head of the country's Eugenic Society, Sir Thomas Barlow, President of the Royal College of Surgeons, as well as Chief Justice Lord Alverstone and the Bishop of Oxford.

American Pioneers and their British Allies

One of the pioneers whom Sanger admired was Charles Knowlton, a doctor who published the country's first contraception tract as far back as 1832. *The Fruits of Philosophy* proposed contraception from a medical standpoint, enumerating methods such as the rinsing of the vagina (douche) or insertion of a sponge dipped in chloride. Prosecuted several times, Knowlton (1800–50) went to prison for writing the book, but later established himself as a doctor in Western Massachusetts.

The *Fruits* became a cause célèbre in Britain when Charles Bradlaugh, a prominent atheist and republican, and his collaborator Annie Besant decided to publish the book in 1877. They were promptly prosecuted and convicted; fortunately for them, the Court of Appeal acquitted them on technical grounds. Bradlaugh (1833–91) was at the cutting edge of radical issues like trade unionism and women's suffrage, rather like Richard Pankhurst. A brilliant amateur lawyer, he finally gained a seat in the House of Commons after repeatedly being refused membership because of his atheist creed and his refusal to swear allegiance on the Bible.

Bradlaugh's comrade-in-arms Annie Besant was an extremely independent woman, who arranged a legal separation from her clergyman husband and gravitated to radical causes. These included BC, trade unionism and school reform. She published her ideas on BC in a book called *The Laws of Population* and contributed to the *Fabian Essays*. Besant (1847–1933) later drifted into theosophy and transferred to India, where she joined the Home Rule movement.

Other pioneers came out of the Utopian movements in the 19th

century. Their BC prescriptions were understandably less practicable than those of Knowlton. Robert Dale Owen was the son of the famous social reformer Robert Owen, who had founded the Utopian settlement New Lanark. One year before Knowlton, Owen (1801–77) published *Moral Physiology*, addressing it to "Young men and women! You who, if ignorant, are uncorrupted also" and sternly informing "libertines and debauchees" that the book was certainly not meant for them. Owen recommends coitus interruptus as the best method, calling it a "trifling diminution of physical enjoyment." The book continues in this well-meaning, sententious vein, rejecting both vaginal sponges and skin condoms as being too expensive.

Equally illusionary were the ideas of John Humphrey Noyes, founder of the Oneida community, which attempted to abolish monogamous marriage and replace it by a system of communal living. The method of BC propagated by Noyes including coitus reservatus, the male stimulating the female without ejaculating, favoured women, who were allowed to achieve orgasms without having to fear the consequences. Sexual equality was as much an imperative of the Oneida community as intellectual parity. Oneida, an odd mixture of work ethic and free-love ethos, ultimately failed and Noyes (1811–86) fled to Canada in the face of legal action against him for immorality.

Sex radicals coexisted with the Utopians and endorsed their ideas. The journalist Moses Harman not only demanded that women determine their own procreation; he also propagated free love and advocated abolishing marriage, which in his opinion enslaved women. Needless to say, Harman (1830–1910) was prosecuted and imprisoned. Fellow journalist Ezra Heywood suffered the same fate under the Comstock laws and landed in court for mailing "obscene material." Heywood (1829–93), who also advocated the woman's vote, was arrested five times in the course of his life. Both were in their own ways martyrs for women's rights; Wendy McElroy has called Harman "the paradigm of a male feminist."

In speeches and books, Sanger paid tribute to Noyes, Owen and in particular Knowlton. Her own importance as the catalyst of BC is demonstrated by a wide spectrum of supporters: they ranged from the Rockefellers to the British anarchist Guy Aldred, who together with his partner Rose Witcop published Sanger's *Family Limitation*. They were immediately arrested and prosecuted, receiving prominent support from Bertrand and Dora Russell, and also from John Maynard Keynes.

While Sanger is a household name, her mentor Emma Goldman is often forgotten, though her approach to BC was more humanistic. Goldman (1869–1940), an avowed anarchist and feminist, discovered the misery of poor women constantly pregnant while working as a nurse in New York's Lower East Side, where Sanger was also active. She saw BC as a means of achieving revolutionary change and suffered arrest several times for writing and lecturing on the subject. Though they were initially close, Sanger later disassociated herself from Goldman, profiling herself successfully as BC's single pioneer. Oddly enough, Goldman exalted free love while rejecting female suffrage, perhaps because it did not rhyme with her anarchist convictions.

Goldman's great ally was her lover Ben Reitman, a colourful figure who called himself "a rascal by nature, a celebrity by accident." Reitman (1879–1942) qualified as a doctor, but lived for a time as a hobo. He performed illegal abortions and managed Goldman's lecture activities, often speaking himself at public meetings. Her intellectual friends found him vulgar, but the doctor was a true soldier of the cause, once serving a six-month sentence for selling BC pamphlets and also getting beaten up.

Though both believed in free love, Goldman suffered under Reitman's perpetual infidelity and separated from him after he was released from prison. Also imprisoned was a young activist from a rich New York family. Van Kleeck Allison had distributed

Why and How the Poor Should Not Have Many Children, a book written by Goldman and Reitman.

Doctors: From Quacks to Innovators

The attitudes and interests of the medical profession enormously influenced the social acceptance of BC. In 19th-century America, most doctors publicly denounced BC, though they were known to privately give advice on contraception or even perform abortions.

Edward Bliss Foote was the great exception. Despite his strict Presbyterian upbringing, he was a freethinker with the courage of his convictions. These included the need for free access to contraception, women's suffrage and, curiously, polygamy. Foote believed that monogamy made women sexually apathetic and men impotent.

Before qualifying as a doctor, Foote (1829–1906) published *Medical Common Sense*, dealing here with "the best ways to control reproduction." In a later edition, he described methods that he had apparently invented, like a membrane envelope type of condom made of fish bladder, a rubber penis cap, a "womb veil," a rubber diaphragm, and even an electro-magnetic preventive machine.

This was obviously quackery, but Foote's intentions were serious. Criticising the elitism of his medical colleagues, he genuinely tried to reach common people with his recipes. A great opponent of the Comstock Law, he was inevitably indicted and fined for selling supposedly obscene pamphlets. To overcome these restrictions, he opened a "Sanitary Bureau" that sold both his books and a variety of contraceptives. Foote's wife and sons assisted him in his endeavours.

While Foote was clearly a maverick, Abraham Jacobi and William Josephus Robinson were pillars of their profession. Jacobi (1830–1919), a Jewish doctor born, educated and imprisoned in Germany for revolutionary activities, came to the

U.S. in his mid-20s, rapidly becoming a distinguished physician. Later, he was professor at Columbia University, a pioneer of paediatrics and President of the American Medical Association (AMA). Jacobi called on doctors to provide BC advice. His arguments for contraception had a distinctly eugenic tinge: "unfit children" were "useless" and should not exist.

Robinson apparently induced Jacobi to mention contraception in his 1912 Presidential Address to the AMA. Like Foote, Robinson (1867–1936) was a strong Comstock opponent and demanded that doctors be educated in methods of contraception. His book *Birth Control or the Limitation of Offspring* reached 48 editions. After Margaret Sanger's indictment, he organised public meetings to support BC at the New York Academy of Medicine. Robinson's arguments had an even stronger eugenic tendency: he called for sterilisation of persons he considered insane, moronic or perverted.

Robinson advocated the medicalisation of BC; however most doctors disagreed, considering it out of their domain. One ally was Robert Latou Dickinson, a distinguished gynaecologist and President of both the American Gynecological Society and the American College of Surgeons.

Dickinson (1861–1950) had a deep interest in sexual pathology and assembled more than 5,000 sexual case histories in the course of his career, strongly influencing Alfred Kinsey. While agreeing with Sanger's principles, he firmly believed that only doctors had the authority to deal with BC. Both had strong personalities and clashed; they founded rival clinics, but Dickinson's was far less successful in attracting patients. Ultimately, Sanger prevailed, helped by a court ruling, *U.S. v. One Package* (1936), and a new readiness by AMA to actively investigate contraception.

Sanger and Dickinson both influenced Clarence Gamble, who united a Harvard medical degree with an enormous fortune as one of the Procter & Gamble heirs. Gamble (1894–1966) endorsed population control for both eugenic and racist reasons. He apparently drafted the proposal for the "Negro Project" launched by Sanger's Birth Control Federation in 1939, which proclaimed, "The mass of negroes, particularly in the South, still breed carelessly and disastrously..." Sanger herself seems to have realised the dangers of their mutual enterprise. In a letter to Gamble in 1939, she calls for black participation in the project, pointing out: "We do not want word to go out that we want to exterminate the Negro population..."

Gamble generously funded public-sector contraception in North Carolina from 1933 onwards. At the time, the state had three clinics; by 1939, it had 62, second in number only to New York. Gamble brought a great degree of private-sector individualism to BC; his field workers were paid by and answerable to him alone. His disregard for hierarchy and bureaucracy led to conflicts with Family Planning organisations like Sanger's International Planned Parenthood Federation. After World War Two, he funded BC across the world.

The Pill's Mother and Father

During the war and the post-war period, the U.S. profited from large numbers of talented immigrants fleeing Europe mostly for racial reasons. This was particularly true of the self-styled "mother" of the pill, Carl Djerassi. Of Austrian-Jewish decent, he developed an oral contraceptive that transformed female sexuality, providing a safe and easy form of birth control.

Djerassi (1923–2014) had far-reaching literary and cultural interests as the author of several novels and as a skilled art collector. He also saw the pill as a vital social factor contributing to the feminisation of men; in fact, he called himself a male feminist. On the other hand, Djerassi publicly bemoaned the fact that because of the pill, there was "no connection at all between sexuality and reproduction," while calling on the pharmaceutical industry to provide a pill for men.

Gregory Pincus had better credentials than Djerassi. At a

dinner party in New York in 1951, Sanger persuaded him to research an oral contraceptive. Pincus (1903–67), of Russian-Jewish descent, had achieved the in vitro fertilisation of rabbit eggs as early as 1934. His invention was publicly denounced; this affected his academic career. Together with the gynaecologist John Rock, who was already testing chemical contraception on women, he conducted first trials. Rock (1890–1984) was far more an establishment figure, born in Massachusetts and with a Harvard medical degree. As early as 1931, he had signed a petition to legalise birth control, well aware of the pain suffered from unwanted pregnancies. Thus, he was well qualified to conduct the clinical appraisal of the new contraceptive.

One of his key assistants was Stephen Fleck, who fled from Nazi Germany, took his degree from Harvard Medical School and had a major role in basic research for the pill. Fleck (1912–2002) and his wife were also politically active and contributed to the success of *Griswold v. Connecticut*. As early as 1965, the case made BC legal within the state of Connecticut.

Both Pincus and Rock were less overt in their support of the pill as a tool of women's emancipation; Rock was a devout Catholic who tried in vain to convince the Catholic Church to approve oral contraception. There is also no evidence that Pincus, despite his fateful meeting with Sanger and financial support from Katherine McCormack, had feminist inclinations. Both were straightforward scientists without greater aspirations.

Bill Baird was the exact opposite. His scientific qualifications were flimsy, comprising one year in medical college, but some observers call him the father of abortion rights. Forced to give up his studies for financial reasons, Baird (1932–) worked for a contraceptive manufacturer until experiencing his epiphany in 1963, when a black woman died in Harlem Hospital after trying to abort herself with a coat hanger. After experiencing this first-hand, he started teaching and distributing literature on contraception with a mobile van and was duly prosecuted. Ultimately, the New York State Legislature changed the existing laws against propagating contraception. The State Senate even appointed Baird to a committee charged with drafting new legislation.

Then, students at Boston University invited him to lecture in 1967 on the subject, flouting a state law prohibiting the provision of devices and information on BC to the unmarried. Baird was promptly arrested after the lecture and prosecuted. Acquitted for presenting information, he was condemned to a jail sentence for distributing devices. Ultimately, the U.S. Supreme Court overturned the activist's conviction in *Baird v. Eisenstadt*, underlining the right to privacy and freedom from "unwarranted government intrusion" into the decision of whether to bear or beget a child. Famously, Chief Justice William O. Douglas pointed out while passing judgment in 1972: "The teaching of Baird and those of Galileo might be of a different order, but the suppression of either is equally repugnant." This logic also led to legalisation of abortion in the *Roe v. Wade* judgement a year later, in which the Baird case played an important role.

Despite these successes, Baird remains a highly controversial figure, hailed by some, while condemned by conservatives, prominent feminists like Betty Friedan and even organisations like Planned Parenthood. This seems partly because of his self-dramatisation and his lack of respectability. Planned Parenthood called his efforts an "embarrassment," Betty Friedan implied that he was a CIA agent, her fellow feminist Robin Morgan called him a male supremacist, while the National Organization for Women declined support, openly admitting to sexism by stating that if his name had been "Wilhelmina Baird," they would have supported him. Ironically, the Playboy Foundation supported Baird's legal defence. His second wife Joni openly accused feminists of a "deliberate effort to revise, suppress, or invalidate the contributions made to the reproductive movement by men." Whether or not such claims are justified is a question of standpoint. However, Baird's achievements are manifest.

C. Abortionists: Quacks and Professionals

BC and abortion are parallel causes that attracted male supporters of different types. Harvey Karman for instance was a talented impostor. He came from a poor family and was a high-school dropout before becoming a GI in World War Two. After the war, the soldier-integration programme financed his university education in theatre science and psychology. Discovering an interest in medical studies, Karman (1924–2008) bestowed a PhD on himself and was soon involved in organising abortions. The so-called doctor started by counselling women and helping them travel to Mexico; later he conducted abortions himself and invented the Karman Cannula, a thin flexible plastic tube that could be inserted into the womb.

Though repeatedly jailed, "Dr Karman" continued to publicise his Cannula; by the 1970s, women across the U.S. used it. This success contrasts with his pseudo-medical activities. In 1956, Karman was convicted of killing a woman by attempting to abort her using a speculum and a nutcracker. The "super coil" he developed first experienced a field test in Bangladesh on women who had been raped by soldiers during the war of independence from Pakistan in 1972; numerous complications suffered by the women led to a local investigation. A further attempt on inserting the supercoil the same year in Philadelphia failed.

Opinions on Karman differ dramatically. Malcom Potts, Professor of Family Planning at Berkeley, said he achieved more for safe abortion than "practically any other person in the world," while Carol Downer, founder of women's clinics in California, denounced his "irresponsible experimentation."

By contrast, opinions on Kermit Gosnell are universally negative. Gosnell (1941–) had a medical degree, but was not a licensed gynaecologist or surgeon. Himself an African-American, he started in Philadelphia providing abortions to mostly black American and minority women. Often praised for providing medical services to the poor, it was later revealed that he was taking up to 3,000 dollars for performing abortions at a late stage. In 1972, Gosnell performed 15 abortions using Karman's supercoil, causing haemorrhages on 11 of the women treated.

Despite repeated complaints, both from practitioners and the relatives of fatally injured patients over a period of several decades, Gosnell was only arrested in 2011, after a raid the year before by investigators of the FBI and state police found horrific evidence at the "Women's Medical Society" he ran. Sanitary conditions were disgusting, the women were treated by untrained staff and abortions were often performed after the 24-week gestation period prescribed by law. Further evidence included the use of infected instruments and frequent deaths caused by incompetence. Gosnell's crowning crime was murdering infants by severing their spinal cords with scissors. In 2013, Gosnell received a life sentence without access to parole; the doctor waived his right to appeal and thus avoided the death sentence. Clearly, he had been masquerading as a social worker while making money at the expense of socially deprived women.

The deeds and misdeeds of other practitioners pale by contrast. Nathan Rappaport was imprisoned a number of times for carrying out apparently more than 25,000 abortions. Rappaport openly admitted that he started doing abortions during the Depression in 1933 after his medical practice declined. The doctor was a prominent member of the underground abortion circuit, feted by many feminists. However, his major motive was apparently moneymaking; he reportedly charged as much as 500 dollars per patient.

This makes Rappaport less idealistic than Robert Spencer, who practised abortions from 1919 until his death 50 years later. Spencer (1889–1969) was the "angel" of Ashford, the small Pennsylvania town in which he lived and operated. Local citizens supported him, in part because his practice brought business to hoteliers, dressmakers and other tradespeople. Spencer's charges were distinctly moderate at around 50 dollars a client; he was finally charging 200 dollars towards the end of his life. Arrested and acquitted twice, he died before the third case came to trial. By contrast to Gosnell, his clinic had excellent operating conditions and he took great care of his patients.

The same applies to another Pennsylvania doctor: William Jennings Bryan Henrie in Grove. Henrie (1896–1972) performed abortions for around 25 years before going to prison in 1962 for first-degree manslaughter, when a woman died after he aborted her child. His practice was known as the "abortion mill of the nation" and he claimed to have carried out 5,000 operations. Henrie was one of Grove's most respected citizens. The day before he went to prison, 500 guests joined a farewell picnic. A photo taken on the occasion shows the doctor posing with a large number of children and their mothers. Like Spencer, he had moderate charges and exempted the poor from payment, though he later contended that he had made two million dollars from his work, revising this figure to eight million dollars for 20,000 abortions at a later stage. A local newspaper reported that business in the town profited from his activities, which would also explain his popularity.

Henrie, like most of the other doctors, was not conscious of his role as a defender of women's rights over their own bodies. He began reflecting on this while in jail and, when released, became an activist for legalising abortion.

Henrie and Co. helped in individual cases. The impact of Seymour L. Romney was far larger, because he and his colleagues pressurised the New York State Legislature to regulate the issue. After this was achieved and after the *Roe v. Wade* case at the Supreme Court legalised abortion across the country in 1973, Romney (1917–2010) realised that in practical terms, most regions in the U.S. lacked abortion services. In the early 1990s, he founded Physicians for Reproductive Choice and Health, an association that campaigns for universal access to abortion facilities.

Romney was sensitised to the need for legalisation after having performed a hysterectomy in the early 1940s on a 16-year-old girl. An abortionist, who had inserted a darning needle into her uterus, had perforated it. Later, Romney became a professor at Albert Einstein College in New York, thus able to propagate responsible abortions in an urban milieu.

Founding Fathers of the Abortion Movement

Doctors like Romney formed loose coalitions with journalists, politicians and even members of the clergy, all advocating a liberal approach to reproductive rights. Perhaps the most influential of all was Lawrence Lader, who did more than anyone else to publicise the need for abortion. Lader (1919–2006) became aware of the subject when writing a biography on BC pioneer Margaret Sanger, who was ironically a great opponent of abortion. The writer was convinced that new technologies were facilitating safe abortions and campaigned tirelessly for liberalisation. His book *Abortion* changed public attitudes and was amply quoted in the landmark *Roe v. Wade* Supreme Court case.

Lader cofounded and headed the National Association for the Repeal of Abortion Laws (NARAL), leaving it to found a more radical group. In the course of his career, he advised more than 2,000 women on where to get abortions, even opening a laboratory to manufacture the French abortifacient RU-486. Prominent feminist Betty Friedan, one of NARAL's cofounders, fittingly called him the "founding father of the abortion movement."

Among the politicians, Percy E. Sutton was one of the pioneers. Sutton (1920–2009), a black lawyer born in Texas and persecuted at an early age by the police, later served as defence attorney for Malcolm X and the Black Panthers. He also became Borough President of Manhattan, thus both challenging and becoming a part of the Establishment. Sutton was a key speaker at NARAL's founding ceremony and introduced pro-choice legislation in the New York State Assembly as far back as 1965, working closely with City Council Member Carol Greitzer and other NARAL activists.

Where Sutton failed, Franz S. Leichter and others succeeded. Leichter (1930–), of Jewish origin like Lader, came to the U.S. in the 1930s as a refugee child. His mother, the famous Austrian feminist Käthe Leichter, perished in a concentration camp. After achieving a doctorate in law from the Harvard Law School, Leichter became a prominent Democratic member of the New York State Assembly and Senate for 30 years, gaining a reputation as an anti-establishment gadfly. Just as Sutton collaborated with Greitzer, Leichter introduced an abortion bill to the New York Senate in 1970 together with Constance Cook.

After long and heated discussion, the bill finally passed the Senate in 1970 and entered the State Assembly in a slightly modified form. Here, discussion was even more acrimonious and the vote only passed because at the last minute, a Democrat from a Catholic constituency decided that his conscience was more important than his career.

George M. Michaels was a personal pro-choice supporter; however, his constituents in Cayuga County were strongly pro-life and Michaels (1910–92) originally voted against the bill, resulting in a stalemate. Before the Speaker was forced to cast his vote, the Congressman made an emotional intervention, saying that he realised he was ruining his chances of reelection, but that he could not with a good conscience contribute to defeating the abortion cause. He then reversed his vote and the bill passed parliament, with the Speaker also voting pro-choice. Intriguingly, the attitudes of his sons, both of whom strongly urged him not to defeat the bill, had influenced his decision. Michaels' prescience was justified; his constituents refused his nomination and the law firm he later founded also failed. Effectively, he ruined his life for a good cause.

Abortion was a supremely feminine issue decided by men; at

the time, of the 207 members of the New York State Legislature, only four were women. Republicans controlled both Houses, which highlights the fact that pro-choice had bipartisan support. In the Senate, 18 Democrats but also 13 Republicans supported the bill, 20 Republicans and six Democrats voted against it. Earl Brydges, the highly Catholic majority leader of the Senate, could have intervened against the bill, but nobly chose not to, abiding by the majority decision. The New York vote was of crucial importance, being the most important milestone before the Supreme Court decision legalising abortion on a national basis.

Parallel to the politicians, a sizeable group of Protestant clergymen and Jewish rabbis united under the banner of the Clergy Consultancy Service to provide abolition advice. Howard Moody was at the forefront. Moody (1921–2012) was a highly unusual priest: a former marine sergeant, he ministered at Judson Memorial, a small Greenwich Village church with a tremendous influence on public opinion.

Moody endorsed a variety of causes, from help for drug addicts and prostitutes to aid for AIDS victims. As early as 1957, he started helping women to get abortions, firmly believing in their right to decide on whether they wanted to give life. He described the situation at the time as "horrible" and "the most humiliating, frightening prospect for women that you can imagine." Later, he established a network of 1,400 clergymen; he also helped women from other states get safe and affordable abortions after New York State legalised abortion.

One further social group that contributed to pro-choice activism were entrepreneurs. Joseph Sunnen, son of a coal miner, was a gifted inventor who developed valve-lifter tools, suffering severe burns and other injuries during experiments before his products eventually became successful. Sunnen (1897–1979) vowed that if he survived the accident, he would devote his activities to mankind; later, he passed on an incredible 50 per cent of his company's income to charity. The Sunnen Foundation contributed regularly to Catholics for a Free Choice to fund abortions and has supported other religious groups, earning the ire of the wider Catholic community. Sunnen's company also manufactured contraceptive foam; later, Johnson and Johnson took over the company.

Stewart R. Mott was a far more controversial philanthropist. Mott (1937–2008) used his inherited fortune to further a wide range of causes: from sex research to gay rights, legislative reform and arms control. Abortion was a cause close to his heart, because he believed the planet's major challenges were nuclear war and population explosion. Both eccentric and exhibitionistic – he lodged both on a Chinese junk on the Hudson and in a Manhattan penthouse with a garden full of exotic plants, while naming his sexual partners in his bulletins to the outside world – he was one of NARAL's early supporters and initiated the Friends of Family Planning, which united various pro-choice organisations.

Canada: Two Charismatic Jews

The Canadian experience with abortion is unique, consisting of a remarkably radical change from restrictive to reasonably permissive legislation. Initially, Canada resembled most of the other Western countries: abortion was banned under penalty of life imprisonment in 1869. A large number of illegal abortions took place for around a century, until the outspoken Chief Coroner of Toronto publicly attacked the legal system in the early 1960s.

Morton Shulman was by any standards an extraordinary man: after qualifying as a doctor, he entered politics as a member of the Conservative Party, became Chief Coroner and campaigned for a series of causes including the use of life jackets in small boats and of breathalysers.

As Chief Coroner, Shulman (1925–2000) shrewdly gained publicity for the consequences of illegal abortions by instructing coroners to carry out a public inquest after each abortion-caused death. The Criminal Law Amendment Act passed in 1969 ultimately implemented his recommendations. Birth control became no longer an offence, while abortion was allowed under stringent conditions such as when the health of the mother was deemed at risk by a three-doctor committee.

Shulman later became a politician, a highly successful stock-market dealer and a bestselling writer. He reacted to being diagnosed with Parkinson's by founding a company offering treatment for the disease. When he died, his daughter described him as "a lonely only child, a scrawny Jewish kid in a city with limited tolerance for Jews. He had no money, no looks, no athletic ability, no social graces and no connections. Girls laughed at him, in a series of rejections he never got over." Born a loser, Shulman had an inner drive that led him to become a winner, paired with indignation against injustice and sympathy for those maltreated. He enjoyed flirting with women, but also had great compassion with those facing the prospect of an illegal abortion.

Henry Morgenthaler was even more of a born loser and his inner drive focused entirely on the pro-choice issue. The very fact that he reached Canada alive is quite a miracle. Born in Poland of Jewish parents, Morgenthaler (1923–2013) together with his family was thrown into the Lodz ghetto. The Gestapo murdered his father, his mother died in Auschwitz and he himself barely survived the Dachau concentration camp. After briefly emigrating to the U.S. and to Belgium, he reached Canada in 1950, qualified as a doctor and soon became an expert for vasectomies and intrauterine devices.

Horrified by the human tragedies he was experiencing, Morgenthaler started performing illegal abortions while campaigning fiercely for the repeal of the restrictive laws, appearing before a federal committee as early as 1967. Prosecuted and persecuted for decades and jailed several times, the doctor then received support from feminist groups such as the Vancouver Women's Caucus and the Canadian Abortion Rights Action League. Finally, in 1988, the Supreme Court ruled in *R v. Morgentaler* that the Criminal Code was unconstitutional because it violated women's rights. By this time, an overwhelming majority of the population was pro-choice oriented. Like Shulman, Morgenthaler ultimately received official recognition by being awarded the Order of Canada in the face of protests by mostly Catholic celebrities.

Like Shulman, Morgenthaler had an outgoing combative personality and a distinct sense of his own importance. He openly admitted that he was proud of being finally recognised as a hero by the government and was branded a womaniser in a muckraking film, in which he admitted to infidelity. Sentences like "My God is a Goddess with golden breasts, dripping milk and honey" are of dubious political correctness. The characterisation "flawed saint" used by the journalist Margaret Wente well sums up his character.

The North American Abortion Backlash

Opposition to liberalising abortion has remained constant both in Canadian politics and in public life. Successive Conservative governments tried to pass restrictive abortion legislation. While unsuccessful at the federal level, states like Nova Scotia and New Brunswick have made operations outside hospitals illegal, cut funding and thus severed the lifelines of private abortion clinics. In 2014, the Morgenthaler clinic in Fredericton, the only private facility in New Brunswick, closed down.

Personal attacks on abortion practitioners frequently occurred. Morgenthaler received death threats and was assaulted. His clinics were firebombed and subjected to acid attacks. Though he survived, one of his colleagues, Dr Barnett Slepian, was shot to death. Other doctors started wearing bullet-proof vests after attempts were made to kill them.

The situation was even more drastic in the U.S. From the mid-1970s onwards, legalisation of abortion led to increasingly violent agitation. Activists ravaged clinics, threatening doctors and their helpers in an attempt to intimidate those practising the freedoms that the landmark *Roe v. Wade* case had brought.

David Gunn, a physician who carried out abortions in Alabama, Georgia and Florida, was murdered in 1993 by a Christian fundamentalist. In Pensacola, Florida, where Gunn was murdered, his successor John Britton was mortally attacked the following year by a former Presbyterian minister who had however been expelled from the Church in 1993.

While David Gunn (1946–93), who suffered from polio as a child, was a pure idealist, responding to the pleas of an abortion clinic in Columbus and then expanding his activities because of constant calls for help, John Britton's motives were more ambiguous. Personally opposed to abortion, he started doing operations after being penalised by the local authorities for wrongly prescribing drugs and after encountering strong financial difficulties. However, Britton (1925–94) was dedicated to his work and rejected the pretensions of the anti-abortionists to decide on the right to life of a foetus.

George Tiller, murdered as recently as 2009, resembled David Gunn in terms of aspirations, carrying on the tradition of his father, who had performed abortions in the 1950s and 1960s. Tiller (1941–2009), often persecuted by right-wing Republican State Attorneys, was known for slogans like "Trust Women."

While pro-life groups hastened to condemn these acts, there seems little doubt that a form of anti-abortion terrorism exists in the U.S., aided and abetted by religious extremism masquerading as morality. "Wanted" posters, demonstrations, hate mail and periodic death threats belong to the arsenal of a cross-section of the population that puts the rights of unborn children above the right to choice of the women conceiving the children.

Britain: Slow and Civilised Progress

Initial conditions in Britain resembled those in North America: abortion was criminalised in the early 19th century. Until then, abortion was permissible under Common Law before "quickening," meaning movement of the foetus. Lord Ellenborough's Act of 1803 equated abortion with shooting, stabbing and poisoning: the "malicious using of means to procure the miscarriage of women" was a felony.

The Offences Against the Person Act of 1861 was equally draconian with regard to women aborting: anyone found "administering to herself any poison or other noxious thing" was liable to a life sentence of penal servitude. This law was particularly degrading, because it treated a forced miscarriage as a form of homicide or assault.

Many male doctors in the early 20th century did abortions, both for material and idealistic reasons. If caught, as in the case of Dr Devi Sasun, there was draconian punishment; Sasun received a sentence of ten years' penal servitude. Others, like Dr Daniel Powell, were tried, but acquitted. The Infant Life Act of 1929 brought a slight liberalisation, permitting abortion in cases where birth would seriously endanger the mother's life.

Enlightened judges like Justice McCardie declared while passing judgement during abortion cases in 1930 and 1931 that the law needed amendment. McCardie refused to subject women seeking or performing abortions to the severe punishment prescribed by law. This however was a viewpoint governed more by eugenics than by humanitarian considerations. McCardie's speech at the Eugenic Society influenced both men and women to seek legislative change.

Many prominent feminists opposed abortion; these included a large cross-section of those who fought for suffrage. Despite the founding of the Abortion Law Reform Association (ALRA) in 1936 with overwhelmingly female membership, public support for abortion remained feeble. Contraception was far more in the public eye. In ALRA's founding year, Dr Laura Sanders-Bliss was sentenced to three years in prison for having performed five abortions.

However, one prominent case electrified public opinion. Dr Aleck Bourne defied the law in 1938 by operating on a 14-year-old girl who had been raped by several soldiers. Bourne (1886–1974) was well aware of the significance of his act; in fact, he informed the police of what he was doing, thus creating a test case. In court, he pleaded that termination was justified because of risk to the patient's physical and mental health. The Infant Life Act of 1929 did in fact provide a loophole in the case of a life threat to a pregnant woman. Though this was obviously not the case, Justice McNaghten ruled that doctors were justified in acting if convinced that birth of the child would render the woman "a physical and mental wreck." Like his colleague McCardie, McNaghten thus liberalised the law on his own initiative.

Ironically, Bourne later became a strident opponent of abortion for social reasons and a founding member of the Society for the Protection of Unborn Children, firmly opposing the liberal Abortion Bill of 1967. He was a humane doctor, not a human-rights expert, a highly qualified and respected gynaecologist with a first-class natural-sciences tripos from Cambridge and a long string of publications to his credit.

Regardless of his convictions, he had however redefined the issue. After the Bourne case, no gynaecologist had to fear prosecution if he performed an abortion for medical reasons. The McNaghten ruling reverberated not only across the British Isles; in Australia, it influenced several judicial rulings including one case in Queensland as late as 2010. A 21-year-old girl called Tegan Leach was acquitted from the charge of conducting an illegal abortion on herself in less than an hour by a jury, though the restrictive Queensland abortion law of 1899 had not been liberalised.

However, in social terms, the case changed little. A highly respected doctor won the case because he assured the court that the girl was "normal" and "moral"; her middle-class parents and her age were testimony to this. As ALRA's activists soon realised, abortion was still not acceptable as a matter of a woman's free choice. In addition, working-class women seldom had access to eloquent, well-placed doctors. In 1937, an Interdepartmental Committee on Abortion rejected social, economic or personal reasons, though the committee accepted the fact that most abortions occurred because of financial constraints.

Triumph of Doctors over Civil Society

In the U.S., a broad coalition of doctors, lawyers, journalists and priests united to lobby for liberalisation. In Britain, equally a civil society, medical experts ruled supreme and marginalised other groups. With the signal effect that abortion became a doctor's decision; the social aspects receded to the background.

One reason for this disparity lies in the passive attitude of Britain's Labour Party. In the U.S., as well as in European countries like Germany, abortion could count on support from the left. In Britain, the party repeatedly refused to address the issue; in the 1930s, even the women's section of Labour was oblivious to the need for new legislation. The same applied to the new Labour government under Harold Wilson in the mid-1960s. As a whole, the party failed to push the issue, though individual cabinet members were firm supporters of abortion.

This lethargy was however common to other political parties as well. A number of attempts were made in the 1950s and early 1960s to introduce Abortion Bills to the Houses of Commons and Lords. These were either withdrawn before the Second Reading, deferred or talked out of parliament.

Throughout this period, ALRA remained the predominant pressure group. Despite this, their membership remained restricted to a couple of hundred persons until the early 1960s.

Beyond this, most adherents were members or supporters of the Eugenic Society. One of ALRA's founders, Janet Chance, approved of compulsory abortion of the degenerate, rather like Marie Stopes. Her stockbroker husband Clinton, President of the Eugenic Society, funded ALRA in its early years.

ALRA was more intent on improving marital life than empowering women; it certainly did not approve of abortion on demand. The mind-sets of most members was conservative, with one signal exception: Glanville Williams. Williams (1911–97) was arguably *the* British legal thinker of the 20th century and a remarkably influential reformer. In *The Sanctity of Life and the Criminal Law*, published in 1958, he called out for humane laws governing birth, regardless of whether they involved contraception, sterilisation or abortion.

Williams was as much a Utilitarian as a Eugenicist; he called for laws that were both understandable and humane. One commentator called him "Jeremy Bentham's illegitimate child," while he was also considered to be a "kind of legal Asterix." The academic managed to belong to the Establishment, as an honoured member of various Commissions and Professor at University College London; simultaneously, he sympathised with the radical fringe, supporting a plethora of causes including abortion and euthanasia. As President of ALRA, he focused the organisation's drive for legal reform.

To gain greater respectability and to deflect attacks from pro-life activists, ALRA cultivated the medical profession, compromising some of its own policy goals such as social indicators. Thus, the British Medical Association (BMA) exerted a strong influence on the Abolition Act passed in 1967, despite the strong links between ALRA's extremely efficient parliamentary lobbyist Alastair Service and senior members of the Labour government including Home Secretary Roy Jenkins, not to speak of its early contacts with the Bill's architect, the young Liberal MP David Steel.

The medical profession's influence is apparent in the fundament of the Abortion Act: two doctors have to approve the termination of pregnancy and take decisions on issues pertaining to the patient's health. The initially proposed social clause was dropped when opposed by various medical associations; however, the proviso that abortion was acceptable if the "physical or mental health" of the woman concerned would be impaired by the child's birth, opened certain loopholes.

Steel (1938–), later Leader of the Liberal Party from 1976 to 1988, became an MP in 1964 and had early contacts with ALRA. After winning the ballot to enter a Private Member's Bill, Steel decided to select abortion as the issue at stake and inherited a Bill that had already been through the House of Lords. Steel contends: "We did not create abortion on request, we created a state of law where there is a balance between the right of the foetus to develop to full life and the right of the women to have what I would call in the biblical phrase 'abundant life'."

Steel also decries any feminist influence on the law: "We do not have a woman's right to choose in this country." This conforms to BMA's advice that the doctor's role was not to act according to women's wishes, but to recommend termination at his own discretion. Despite his close contacts with ALRA, Steel declared his particular pride in the fact that the retiring secretary of BMA had considered the act to be the greatest advance in social medical care during his career. As Kate Gleeson points out in her analysis of law reform in the U.K.: "Steel was enamoured of medical science, especially medical technology." However, one factor strongly favouring women in Britain was that women could abort up to 28 weeks after conception; the term was later reduced to 24 weeks, still longer than in most other countries.

Ironically, the House of Lords was less technocratic and closer to social reality. The Bills presented by Lord Lewis Silkin were strongly influenced by ALRA and had a strong social orientation, with extreme poverty figuring as much as a reason for abortion as rape or fetal abnormality. Silkin (1889–1972) was a remarkable political personality. Of Lithuanian Jewish origin, he rose from poor surroundings to study in Oxford, start his own company and officiate as deputy leader of the London County Council during World War Two, becoming a peer in 1950. Silkin was a born reformer, and after acting in favour of abolishing capital punishment, he welcomed abortion as a fresh issue for legal reform. After Steel adopted the issue, Silkin dropped his own Bill.

Britain has experienced its own backlashes. There have been a large number of unsuccessful attempts to repeal the law or to slice the termination period from 24 to 12 weeks. Significantly, opinion polls have shown that a larger percentage of women than men support curtailing the termination period, thus revising the common assumption that restrictions on abortion are a male prerogative or priority. Despite a series of Amendment Bills and constant campaigns, abortion protest has not so far exploded into violence as in the U.S.

Germany: Socialists and National Socialists

Germany is in many ways exceptional. The general climate for sexual issues has traditionally been more liberal than in the Anglo-Saxon countries. The famous sexologist Havelock Ellis for instance published his book *Sexual Inversion* first in Germany in 1896 after failing to find a British publisher. Discussion of homo- and transsexuality was highly uninhibited both before and after the First World War. Though this stopped abruptly when the National Socialists came to power in 1933, BC remained an issue that scientists and doctors pursued steadily and with excellent results.

German-speaking countries played a major role in the development of contraceptives. The Austrian physiologist Ludwig Haberland investigated the hormonal impact on menstruation at the beginning of the 20th century; in 1919, he discovered that hormones could regulate fertility. Like Pincus, Haberland (1885–1932) experienced a huge amount of opposition both from his medical colleagues and in the press. He developed the compound "Infecundin" for a Hungarian company, but committed suicide before the necessary pharmaceutical tests began. Djerassi acclaimed him as the father of the pill, but apart from that, he is largely forgotten. The same applies to his contemporary Emil Knauer, who discovered as early as 1890 substances later called "sexual hormones."

In Germany, a succession of Jewish doctors, mostly with socialist inclinations and closely connected to Margaret Sanger, spearheaded the movement for family planning. Sanger had visited Germany several times since 1920 and discovered a jelly produced in Friedrichshafen that served as a prototype for the substance used in her American clinics. Among her closest associates was Hans Lehfeldt, known for developing intrauterine devices (IUD) and a cervical cap. Lehfeldt (1899–1993) shared Sanger's belief that each woman needed treatment in a medical setting with attention paid to keeping accurate records, but differed from her in favouring a wide range of contraception devices including condoms and the "safe period." After emigrating to the U.S. in 1935, he opened a thriving private practice in Manhattan.

In common with many BC specialists, Lehfeldt was eugenically inclined, endorsing sterilisation as a means to exclude the "unfit" and "feeble-minded" from reproduction. He even endorsed the Nazi legislation of obligatory sterilisation of the insane, while Sanger, to her credit, had misgivings about the abuse of the law. Despite occasional frictions, he remained loyal to her until she died in 1966.

Among Lehfeldt's closest professional friends was Ernst Gräfenberg, best known for giving his name to the "G spot," the female erogenous zone. Gräfenberg (1881–1957) also invented the "Gräfenberg Ring," an intrauterine coil. He initially introduced

Lehfeldt to Sanger and had a thriving private practice in Berlin with high-level clients; he also had a strong social conscience and often consulted free of charge. As much a researcher as a practitioner, Gräfenberg served as Head of the Gynaecological Department of a Berlin hospital. Sacked by the Nazis in 1933, he continued with his private practice, disregarding Lehfeldt's warnings to leave the country. After he was imprisoned in 1938 for smuggling a stamp collection out of the country, Sanger helped him emigrate and, like Lehfeldt, he practised in New York after a short spell at Sanger's clinic.

More famous in his time than both Lehfeldt and Gräfenberg was Magnus Hirschfeld, often called the "Einstein of sex" for his innovative approach to sexual deviance. Beyond his pioneer work on homosexuality and his theory of the "third sex," Hirschfeld (1868–1935) was a firm supporter of BC and a greater feminist than his fellow doctors were. Proof of this is his close collaboration with Helene Stöcker, founder of the League for the Protection of Mothers. Writing in *Birth Control Review* in 1931, Hirschfeld declared himself opposed to abortion, while also rejecting punishment for the performance of abortion. He firmly believed in a woman's right over her own body.

Hirschfeld had socialist views, but remained a sex-researcher, whereas Julius Moses was both doctor and politician, serving as a member of the Reichstag from 1920 to 1932 and founding the Social Democratic medical association. Moses (1868–1942) agitated for abortion reform, which narrowly failed to be implemented in 1924. Here he differed strongly from Hirschfeld.

As early as 1912, the politicised doctor lectured on contraception methods and propagated a controversial "Gebärstreik," a childbearing strike destined to reduce births in proletarian circles. Here Moses clashed with feminists like Clara Zetkin and Rosa Luxemburg, who considered the strike to lack ideological focus. While they favoured a large proletarian population as the bedrock of revolution, Moses' motivation was to a greater degree humanistic. As a doctor, he was better acquainted with the poverty and distress in large working-class families. Arrested and deported by the Nazis, this remarkably ethical doctor died in the Theresienstadt concentration camp.

Ironically, scientists who were either members of the National Socialist Party or fellow travellers had a far stronger impact on developing the pill despite the Nazi emphasis on enlarging the Germanic population. Adolf Butenandt for instance, who, together with other professors, professed his allegiance to the new regime in November 1933, had already succeeded in isolating estrone, the female sex hormone. After a study visit to the U.S.A. sponsored by the Rockefeller Foundation, Butenandt (1903–95) declined a professorship in Harvard, preferring to continue his career in Germany. He became an N.S. party member in 1936, at a time when new members were no longer admitted, which demonstrates his status within the regime. Butenandt was in no way anti-Semitic; in fact, he apparently helped several Jews to escape oppression. However, he did collaborate with the regime.

Gaining the Nobel Prize in 1939 but unable to leave the country in order to receive it, Butenandt continued his distinguished career after the war with great insouciance, officiating as President of the highly prestigious research organisation Max Planck Gesellschaft from 1960 to 1972. Robert N. Proctor of Stanford University investigated his dubious role during the Third Reich, but Proctor's findings remain controversial.

Researchers of the pharmaceutical company Schering played a key role in contraception research. Among the company's pioneering products were Porgynon and Proluton. Schering scientists Erwin Schwenk and Friedrich Hildebrandt developed a synthesis of estradiol, the basis for modern hormone products, in 1934; four years later, Hans Inhoffen and Walter Hohlweg developed the world's first orally active estrogen. War destruction curtailed further research, but Schering was the first

European company to produce the pill. Introduced in 1961, Anovlar was marketed across the world.

Parallel to the scientists, "social hygiene" specialists contributed to the racial policies of the NS regime. Hans Harmsen never became a party member, but played an influential role in facilitating the sterilisation law and having it applied to the mentally retarded. His population concept served as a blueprint for Nazi policies.

Harmsen (1899–1989) held leading medical positions; while against euthanasia, he had nothing against anti-Semitism. Like Butenandt, he smoothly continued his career after the war and was uniquely influential as cofounder and president of Pro Familia, the German branch of Margaret Sanger's Planned Parenthood Federation. Harmsen was highly estimated by Sanger and other important international figures with whom he had already collaborated before 1933.

Ironically, socialist experts of the Weimar Republic period like Franz Gampe and Willy Karger, who both had impeccable moral credentials, were brushed aside in the post-war years. Harmsen remains an enigmatic figure; some post-war collaborators praised his standing-up for women's rights, and Pro Familia publicly disassociated itself from him as late as 1984 after details of his role in the Third Reich had leaked out.

Harmsen and others were more progressive in their attitudes to BC than large segments of the German population. A survey done in 1963 showed that 47% of all women (and 43% of all men) were against allowing the anti-baby pill; 41% of the women (45% of the men) were for it, while around 9% believed that it depended on the circumstances.

Abortion: An Ominous Section in the Penal Code

Abortion has always been a completely different issue in Germany. In his comprehensive analysis of regulations on abortion, *Abortion and Women's Legal Personhood in Germany,*

Jeremy Telman rightly points out that the country has "one of the world's most complex and confusing laws." This strongly contrasts with a generally enlightened approach to sexual issues and is often considered one of the residues in post-war Germany of the Cult of Motherhood propagated by the Nazi regime. In reality, the roots of the German abhorrence to abortion date back far earlier, to Martin Luther's family model and Johann Heinrich Pestalozzi's *Book for Mothers*. They are correspondingly strongly entrenched.

Prussia regulated abortion in 1851. Until then, the norms of the Catholic Church applied, whereby abortion only became criminal 80 days after birth. The criminal code adopted by united Germany 20 years later was both stringent and simple: abortion was a criminal offence, attempted abortion equally so.

The infamous Section 218 of the Imperial Penal Code forbade premature termination even in cases of mortal danger to the mother's life. This was as much an exercise in ethnonationalism as a clear role assignment to women as mothers. In the years before and during World War One, the need to produce more soldiers was the primary motivation of policies aimed against both abortion and contraception.

Pressure for change developed during the Weimar Republic in the context of the "new woman." However, Germany's Social Democratic Party (SPD) was as lukewarm in its support for abortion as Britain's Labour Party. If at all, family planning was important in the context of working-class poverty, not in terms of individual rights. Thus, Gustav Radbruch, arguably *the* German legal philosopher of the 20th century and Minister of Justice in several Weimar Republic cabinets, brought a bill to the Reichstag as early as 1920 that would have legalised abortion during the first three months. This bill met with strong opposition and was then withdrawn.

Radbruch (1878–1949) was an enlightened thinker well comparable to Granville Williams. He was responsible for legislation to humanise the criminal code, and also for a law passed in 1922 allowing women access to all legal professions. Radbruch cooperated with the new female parliamentarians and the leading women's associations, pushing through legislation against strong opposition from judges who believed that women, because of their "soul qualities," lacked the intelligence needed to act as judges or jurors. However, on Radbruch's list of priorities, abortion was a side issue, omitted in the draft for criminal-law reform he prepared in 1922. Sex-reform activists protested; however, the principal women's association BDF was against abortion. The moderate feminist women subscribed to the mantra of marriage and motherhood, later seeing women's responsibilities as maintaining the "biological substance of the people."

In Germany, there was a clear lack of a civil society with prominent individuals obeying their consciences and risking their careers to allow women to make a free choice as in the U.S. and to a certain degree in Britain. Radbruch openly declared himself against the "individualist idea… that everyone would be master of his/her body and have the right of self-determination." Intriguingly, the Communist Party (KPD) was the only political group in Weimar Germany to support women's individual rights unequivocally under the slogan "Your body belongs to you!" As Telman writes: "The KPD was thus in the odd position of defending the rights of its class enemies to abortion on demand." However, the Communists lacked the political influence to push through legislation. Modified in 1926, the law made abortion a misdemeanour rather than a penal offence, allowing doctors to act in cases of medical emergency.

Beyond suppressing other parties such as the SPD and the KPD, the National Socialist government made motherhood an ideal and strictly enforced the abortion law. While the SPD had emphasised responsibility to the community, the Nazis used a tribal term (Sippe). After the war, the strong Catholic affiliations of the ruling Christian Democrats (CDU) ensured that reform was sluggish, with a first reform in 1962 overtly promoting "medical indications," while giving leeway to abortions on social grounds. Legal abortions increased from around 3,000 in 1968 to 18,000 six years later. The new women's movement seized on the issue in a famous magazine campaign launched in 1971 modelled on a French initiative, with 375 prominent women declaring that they had had abortions. The Constitutional Court then struck down a bill passed in parliament that would have liberalised abortion. Progress has been tortuous at best.

In theory, § 218 remains in force and clearly states that abortion is illegal. However, since 1976, permission can be given after mandatory counselling and during the first 12 weeks of pregnancy. Thus, policies after reunification are more restrictive than they were in East Germany, where the socialist regime freely allowed abortion in the first trimester. Any review of abortion in Germany is bound to come to the bitter verdict: Where were the men and why did the women take so long to react?

France: Fighting Natal Nationalism

In political terms, the contrast between family planning in post-war Germany and France could hardly be greater. Germany showed the strong influence of former Nazi collaborators and fellow travellers. In France, leading figures belonged to the Resistance or faced persecution as Jews. They combatted the post-Vichy contamination of French society best described as a combination of Catholicism, conservatism and persistent natal nationalism.

Fears of depopulation persisted during the Third Republic, making birth control seem an absurd proposition. In 1851, France had the second-largest population of the major powers; in 1871, after its crushing defeat by the Prussian army, it ranked at number four, surpassed by newly united Germany. Vauban's famous epithet, "The greatness of kings is measured by the number of their subjects," rang particularly bitterly in the ears of a nation that had abruptly stopped being a monarchy and was progressively losing its preeminence in Europe.

Natal nationalism was correspondingly widespread. Among the lone figures who opposed it were Paul Robin, a Darwinian atheist who graduated from the elite École normale supérieure and was hounded out of France because of his progressive views on education. After spells in Belgium, Switzerland and Britain, Robin (1837–1912) returned to France in 1879, achieving a high position as inspector of primary education. Robin propagated BC both for Neo-Malthusian and humanistic reasons, seeing it as a means of emancipation for the working class. As opposed to Rousseau, he was a pedagogic feminist, insisting on strict equality between boys and girls. However, the Normalien remained a fringe figure.

In World War One, around 1.5 million young men died in combat. Politicians reacted by tightening the legal provisions against abortion and BC. In 1920, abortion became a criminal offence; equally, publicity for BC was illegal. Despite this, Jean Charles Isidor Dalsace, who first studied law before becoming a gynaecologist, opened France's first BC dispensary in 1935. Abraham Stone, a collaborator of Margaret Sanger, whom he had met on a trip to the U.S., influenced him.

Dalsace (1893–1970) could count on support from Henri Sellier, the mayor of Suresne, the Paris suburb in which the dispensary opened. Though he did not face prosecution, the opening cost Dalsace his job as Head of one of France's leading gynaecological laboratories. A militant pacifist and member of the Communist Party, Dalsace later became a major Resistance figure, his name figuring in Gestapo lists of suspects.

An anti-abortion police brigade was founded in 1937. Several years later, after the fall of France, the Vichy regime made abortion a crime warranting capital punishment. In 1943, two women were actually executed for performing abortions. Despite these draconian measures, the birth rate fell from 800,000 a year in 1920 to 600,000 in 1940. After the war however, France, like other European countries, experienced a baby boom. Despite this, estimates of the number of abortions ranged between 500,000 and one million per year; conservative estimates of mortal casualties from abortions were at around 10,000 a year.

Up to the mid-1950s, the politics of nationalism and social conservatism ruled out policy change. Then, Lagroua Weill-Hallé, a female gynaecologist, founded the "Happy Motherhood" association. The association later morphed into the French Movement for Family Planning (MFPF). Most of its supporters were women. However, the battle for legalising contraception was won almost single-handed by a man.

Lucien Neuwirth was by any accounts an extraordinary personality. He started life with a very close relationship to his mother and this led to a firm conviction that mothers should take the final decision on having children. During the Nazi invasion of France, Neuwirth (1924–2013) fled to England and joined de Gaulle's Forces Françaises Libres. There, he discovered methods of contraception that were illegal in France. Parachuted into the country and captured by the Nazis, he miraculously escaped death by a firing squad. Some British coins he happened to be carrying deflected the bullets from his heart.

Directly after the war, Neuwirth travelled to the U.S. and this increased his knowledge of contraceptives. As a young assistant-mayor in Saint-Étienne, he was confronted with the misery of women with unwanted children, in particular one woman who said, "Listen, I'm sick and tired of having a child each time my husband returns drunk." Another young woman committed suicide.

The law of 1920 declared any public discussion of abortion or BC illegal. Thus, when Happy Motherhood came into being, Neuwirth quickly made contact. As an MP for the Loire region freshly elected in 1958, he used his political contacts, in particular to de Gaulle, to agitate for a new law. The General hesitated; his strongly Catholic wife and premier minister Georges Pompidou were both staunch opponents. First attempts to pass legislation occurred in 1964 and 1965; then, at a private dinner in 1967, de Gaulle invited Neuwirth to present his arguments, finally agreeing that transmitting life ought to be a "lucid act" and asking his ministers to support legislation.

Conservatives in parliament were furious; Neuwirth became the target of juicy invectives such as "Fornication is rationalised by contraception" and "Birth control is an abominable exploitation of the animalist and swinish sides of the human spirit." They even called the reformer "Immaculate Contraception" and "infant's assassin." Conservative extremists insulted his wife and defaced his house with obscene graffiti; his daughter was forced to leave school because the parents of a pro-natal group protested. However, the Socialists supported legislation, proving themselves more progressive here than on the suffrage issue. François Mitterrand duly adopted the right to contraception as a part of his presidential campaign programme in 1965.

In December 1967, the "loi Neuwirth" legalising oral contraception finally passed parliament. The BC hero remained active in politics until 1981; he firmly supported Simone Veil, French Minister of Health from 1974 to 1979, in her efforts to have abortion legalised. The "loi Veil" legalising abortion was passed in 1974. In the incensed parliamentary debate, Neuwirth comforted her when she was in tears after one deputy called her a Nazi. In fact, she was of Jewish origin and had spent the war in a concentration camp.

In the year 2000, at the age of 76, Neuwirth, now in the Senate, was defending the distribution of morning-after pills free of charge to disadvantaged minors. Later, the parliamentarian said he was encountering the same arguments as in 1967. One observer emphasises his pragmatism; he put application before theory, obviously under Anglo-Saxon influence. He is arguably the most remarkable French profeminist ever to live.

One of Neuwirth's closest collaborators was the gynaecologist Pierre Simon. Forced because of his Jewish origins to go into hiding during the Nazi occupation of France, Simon (1925–2008) studied medicine with a clear interest in using it to transform society. Appalled by the horrifying conditions under which women gave birth, he publicly called the practitioners of the Ordre des Médecins, an organisation of doctors set up during the Vichy period, butchers. Simon joined a freemason group of Francophone gynaecologists that met in Switzerland in the early 1950s; like Neuwirth, he later gravitated to Happy Motherhood.

Neuwirth was an enlightened conservative, whereas Simon was a radical, travelling to Communist China in 1957 to acquaint himself on contraception methods used there. He later became the medical director of MFPF, quitting it in 1969 for ideological reasons. By then, he had prepared a series of studies and memoranda and joined the Ministry of Public Health for a distinguished career as a civil servant.

Parallel to Simon, who was active in Paris, doctors in other parts of France fought for contraception. In Grenoble, Henri Fabre started a local section of Happy Motherhood that was more strongly politicised and insisted on BC for all. Fabre (1920–2012) had participated in the Resistance and had been a member of the Communist Party. However, his motivation was mostly humanistic, prompted by dramatic cases like that of a woman who died because she was unable to obtain a therapeutic abortion. He pressed the point that even if a pregnant woman contracted German measles, which led in 95 per cent of all cases to deformation of the foetus, she would by existing law be forced to go abroad to get an abortion.

The first centre for family planning opened significantly enough not in Paris but in Grenoble. Fabre took sole judicial responsibility for the centre and faced opposition not only from the Ordre des Médecins and the Catholic Church but also from the Communist Party, who believed, like the German Communists, that the working class should develop strength by numbers. However, the clinic received unexpected support from priests and school superintendents. Within eight months, it served around 2,000 clients. In 1981, the National Council of the Ordre des Médecins admitted they had been mistaken in their opposition to his work. It was a late tribute to Fabre's courage and persistence.

Fabre was however not alone; he received moral support from fellow doctors, some of whom were equally active. Most prominent among them was Jacques Monod, Nobel Prize-winner for medicine and one of France's leading molecular biologists. The son of an American mother and a Huguenot father, Monod (1910–76) grew up free of Catholic norms. Interrupting his distinguished academic career to join the Resistance, he reached a high position as Chief of Operating Staff for the Forces Françaises de l'Intérieur, taking responsibility for the parachuting of weapons and supplies, as well as for sabotaging railway lines.

Monod was a profound atheist, seeing man as an accident of creation: "His destiny is nowhere spelled out, nor is his duty." He protested stridently against laws that stopped doctors from following their consciences and their professional duties, also arguing that the diffusion of scientific information was being obstructed. Together with his fellow Nobel Prize-winners André Lwoff and Francis Jacob, he presided over MFPF at an initial stage.

Support also came from childbirth specialists. Fernand Lamaze (1894–1957), well known in professional circles for his "method" of natural birth, had also served in the Resistance. Later he established the maternity wing of a medical centre financed by the trade unions for their members. His younger colleague, Pierre Vellay (1919–2007) first operated in 1952 using the Lamaze Method and was an advocate of women desiring abortion. He insisted on listening to women's authentic experiences, because, as a man, he felt he could only develop his feelings on the subject by listening to women's "indispensable" voices.

Men played an important role in legalising BC and abortion in France until the early 1970s. In 1971, 343 prominent French women published a manifesto claiming that they had aborted; this served as a model for the German campaign. Women's control over their own bodies became an intrinsic part of feminist ideology. Organisations like the Association Nationale pour l'Étude de l'Avortement, mostly dominated by male doctors, were correspondingly marginalised.

The Men's Share: How Large, How Important?

Men contributed to liberating women's bodies to varying degrees. In terms of abortion, they were at the forefront, particularly in the U.S.; on birth-control issues, they played an important, but not central role; while their role in eradicating or humanising prostitution was certainly more marginal and questionable.

Linda Greenhouse, a long-term *New York Times* journalist and lecturer at the Yale Law School, has pointed out that major anti-abortion initiatives derived not from women's-rights groups but from groups of doctors, judges and lawyers. "These were heavily, heavily [sic] male-dominated professional organisations that looked at the regime of criminal abortion laws that were driving women to back alleys..." Doctors were also in the forefront in Britain, Germany and France, but other groups like politicians, priests and journalists were equally active.

The same range of political persuasions exists: from Conservative and Liberal to Social Democrat and Communist. In addition, in personal terms, there were huge differences: extroverts and introverts, celibates and womanisers, intellectuals and men of action. No single male model emerges.

Individual men had paradoxical viewpoints, being for suffrage and against abortion or the other way round. This effectively means that they either believed in the power of women's minds or in the autonomy of their bodies, but only a minority believed in both. In addition, within the arena of bodily autonomy, they could be for birth control and against abortion. This of course was no male proclivity: the fact that the founding mother of BC, Margaret Sanger, was against abortion, speaks volumes.

Women's minds and bodies: an assessment of the diverse personalities in terms of their feminist persuasions reveals that many educationists were at best relational feminists. They viewed women not only as different but often also as predestined to specific roles as wives and mothers. A minority advocated complete equality, not considering it their business to determine what women should or should not learn.

Those fighting for abortion and birth control often belonged to this minority of individualistic feminists. They regarded women as persons with specific rights, most important of which was the right to take decisions on whether they wanted to procreate or not.

5

Behind Every Great Woman: Relatives, Friends, Allies

The men who embraced women's rights were not just fellow travellers helping to create the right conditions for modern feminism to develop. Rather, they were central participants, working together with women to create more 'perfect' selves and a more 'perfect' culture in which sexual discrimination might be minimized.
Arianne Chernock

She was the founding mother of modern feminism. A heroine, one of the first English women to revolt against a masculine establishment that consigned women to menial supporting roles. In the face of immense pressure, she asserted women's rights and assailed men's prerogatives.

All this is true. Yet, image and reality deviate in the case of Mary Wollstonecraft (1759–98) to a degree that is characteristic of many well-meaning assumptions relating to women's rights. Recent scholarship has relativised Wollstonecraft's lone, heroic role and put it into a progressive perspective.

The founding mother was in fact part of a group of radical men and women, religious dissenters who were mostly supporters of the French Revolution in the early phase. In philosophical terms, they were rationalists and utilitarians. In personal terms, they subscribed to warm friendships as equals. As Arianne Chernock points out in *Men and the Making of Modern British Feminism*, these men were not just "fellow travellers," but rather "central participants" in the struggle for women's rights.

Wollstonecraft's Comrades-in-Arms

Who were these central participants, what roles did they play and how can they be more closely classified? The inner core played diverse roles in Wollstonecraft's life as in those of other important women, from comrades-in-arms and followers to soul- and bed-mates, sparring partners and mentors.

Richard Price was a comrade-in-arms. Price (1723–91), leader of the Rational Dissenters and an influential priest, met Wollstonecraft in 1784, late in his life. Among his prominent friends were the American independence leaders John Quincy Adams and Benjamin Franklin; Price's *Observations on the Nature of Civil Liberty* was a defence of the American colonists.

Then Price fatefully preached in favour of the French Revolution in 1789, inciting Edmund Burke to publish his celebrated *Reflections on the Revolution in France*. This in turn prompted Wollstonecraft to write *A Vindication of the Rights of Man*. Neither pulled their punches; Burke attacked Price with strong language and Wollstonecraft demonstrated what would later be called her strong capacity to hate, accusing the author of sentimentality, narcissism and of buckling down to authority.

Both Price and Wollstonecraft were strong critics of society, seeing themselves as citizens of the world. Implicitly, this was also the common bond between the feminist and her publisher Joseph Johnson. Johnson (1738–1809) was a London bookseller who published the works of many radicals and dissenters including several women. One of his bestsellers was Price's *Observations on the Nature of Civil Liberty*.

In 1777, Johnson brought out an anonymous work attributed to Elizabeth Chudleigh, Duchess of Kingston, which informed women of their natural rights; this predestined him to publish Wollstonecraft's landmark *Vindication of the Rights of Women* 15 years later. Johnson was far more than Wollstonecraft's publisher; he supported her financially by publishing her first pamphlet and having her do translations of French and German texts. The publisher also provided moral support by including her in his circle of friends that regularly met for a weekly dinner.

Johnson was the elder brother she would have liked to have; she once wrote him, "You are my only friend – the only person I am intimate with. I never had a father, or a brother – you have been both to me..."

This is an obvious exaggeration; Wollstonecraft had intimate contacts with an entire group of men, including those to whom she was physically attracted: Henry Fuseli, Gilbert Ismay and William Godwin. Johnson supported a number of other needy authors; however, he sponsored Mary to an even greater extent, finding her housing, dealing with her creditors, helping her cope with bouts of depression.

By contrast, William Godwin (1756–1836) was more soulmate than mentor. He belonged to the dissenting community and his influential book *An Enquiry concerning Political Justice* was published in 1793. Godwin was a philosophical anarchist, who saw government as a corrupting element. Fittingly, he met Wollstonecraft at a dinner given by Johnson to honour the famous radical Thomas Paine. Both were unimpressed with each other at first sight, but later became intimate. Despite marrying later, they remained independent partners, residing in adjacent houses and often communicating through letters.

After Wollstonecraft's premature death, her husband did her a serious disservice by publishing the *Memoirs of the Author of a Vindication of the Rights of Women*, a frank biography relating her love affairs, pregnancies and suicide attempts that shocked the public and ruined her reputation well into the Victorian period. Robert Southey accused him of "stripping his dead wife naked," but Wollstonecraft's unorthodox views on love and marriage were already well known and considered objectionable. This led to disgusting insults from both men and women: Horace Walpole infamously called her a "hyena in petticoats" while Hannah More refused to even read the *Vindication* because she considered the title alone to be absurd.

Posthumously, Wollstonecraft has been both deified and

maligned, though more for her viewpoints than for her lifestyle. Those in the feminist movement who have made an icon of her did her a disservice for this precise reason; icons can be worshiped or torn down. Storybook heroism rarely survives criticism.

Torn out of context, her referring to women as spaniels or toys can seem misogynistic, though in fact Wollstonecraft clearly identifies women as victims of poor education. Her condemnation of the market women of Paris, who forced themselves entry into the palace to put forward their complaints, as being unwomanly is more difficult to justify and perhaps illustrates that the lady, despite her radical tendencies, had an instinctive respect for royalty and for due decorum.

However, accusations of her having given birth to "feminist misogyny" and of being silly, egotistical, envious and meddling are more denunciations than judicious appraisals of her life and work, of her courage, fortitude and idealism. Similarly, the important part played by her network of friends and helpers, among others by poets like Shelley, Blake and Wordsworth, has been obliterated by the general heat of argument. In fact, her interactions with men on a whole range of levels are characteristic of a broad cross-section of feminists, both in the 18th and 19th centuries.

Enlightened Thoughts, Equivalent Relationships?

In many ways, Mary Hays was Wollstonecraft's successor, a torchbearer for women's rights. Hays (1759–1843) was inspired by the *Vindication* to write her *Appeal to the Men of Great Britain on Behalf of Women* in 1798, the year of Wollstonecraft's death. Reading the *Vindication* led her to contact Joseph Johnson, who guided her intellectually while also supporting her in material terms. Her *Appeal* reveals how women are socially and culturally constricted and is thus more a precursor of gender studies than Wollstonecraft's *Vindication* was.

Like Wollstonecraft, with whom she later became friends, Hays had the courage of her convictions, moving out of her mother's home to live as a single woman in London. Like the other Mary, Hays was forthright about her physical needs. After her teenage heartthrob John Eccles prematurely died, she became close to the Baptist teacher Robert Robinson and to the Cambridge mathematician and Unitarian William Frend, for whom she expressed unrequited love.

All these men were both friends and mentors, as Eleanor Ty writes in her short biography of Hays. She expressed her feelings for Frend in the novel *Emma Courtney*, that reflects the author's travails as a single woman. Hays moved in Wollstonecraft's circles, later becoming friends with Godwin, who also served as an intellectual guide. Like Wollstonecraft, she was vilified as an "unsexed female," the term deriving from a poem by Reverend Richard Polwhele. The Scotch novelist Elizabeth Hamilton, who caricatured Hays in *Memoirs of Modern Philosophers* as being a man-chaser with an insatiable appetite, notably deepened this theme.

This was typical of a conservative backlash that united men and women in their disapproval of female independence. "Loyalists" like Burke, supported by a large cross-section of conservative women including Hamilton, Anna Barbauld and Hannah More, attacked the English "Jacobins," to whom both Wollstonecraft and Hays belonged.

Hays later pursued respectability by publishing six volumes of *Female Biographies* covering 294 illustrious women, signally omitting Wollstonecraft from the list of women whose lives she described. Despite mostly male support, she was isolated in the context of a political climate that reacted to the French Revolution by attacking and partially suppressing progressive views.

The third of the three Marys, the actress and poet Mary Robinson, provided a stark contrast. While Wollstonecraft and Hays could be decried as lustful bluestockings, Robinson was a sensuous beauty whose portrait was painted by leading artists like Thomas Gainsborough and Joshua Reynolds. They moved in intellectual circles; she by contrast was prominent in the theatre world and at court, becoming George IV's mistress in his early years, before he acceded to the throne. She had affairs both with noblemen and with prominent politicians like Charles James Fox.

After an unhappy childhood and early adulthood – her father deserted the family, her husband, the philanderer Thomas Robinson, married her under false pretences and was gaoled for living chronically beyond his means – Mary (1757–1800) found a powerful mentor and promoter in the legendary actor David Garrick. Garrick supported both actresses and women-playwrights like Hannah More and Hannah Cowley. His intentions were decidedly honourable, as were those of the famous playwright and impresario Richard Brinsley Sheridan, who made a star out of Robinson. Both became lifelong allies and served as her mentors.

Her portraitist Reynolds equally became a trustworthy friend; the same applies to Godwin and the poet Coleridge, who called her "a woman of undoubted Genius." This applied to Robinson's later career as a celebrated poet. Detractors and caricaturists focused on her private life, though she was as progressive in her views as Wollstonecraft and a strident supporter of the French Revolution.

One year after Wollstonecraft's death, the former actress published *Thoughts on the Condition of Women, and on the Injustice of Mental Subordination*. Here, Robinson particularly revolts against the placing of "women's mind in the subordinate ranks of intellectual sociability." This was the complaint of a highly attractive woman that men in general refused to take her mental powers seriously; it however in no way applied to her circle of male friends and mentors.

In many ways, Catherine Macaulay enjoyed privileges denied

to the three Marys. Though her wealthy father neglected her education, she had access to his extensive library and self-educated herself in Greek and Roman history, later writing a remarkable eight-volume *History of England*. Though treated condescendingly as "our fair Historian," Macaulay (1731–91) gained a formidable reputation in both Britain and the United States.

Catherine's great ally and supporter was her husband, Dr George Macaulay. Fifteen years her senior, he was remarkably intelligent, versatile and good-willed. The scion of an established Edinburgh family, he was a highly qualified surgeon with a double doctorate from the University of Padova. Beyond this, George (1716–66) had strong philosophical interests and was an accomplished classicist, with a mastery of modern European languages.

Macaulay was a great philanthropist, who dedicated his life to charity, serving as a surgeon in the first English hospital dedicated to obstetrical services for poor women. As his biographers James Wyatt Cook and Barbara Collier Cook point out in their well titled book *Man-midwife, Male Feminist*: "Perhaps most notably, in a place and time characterised by rampant misogyny, Macaulay displayed a highly unusual sympathy for and empathy with women." Catherine certainly profited from this empathy, though they were married for only six years before he died in 1766.

Like Mary Wollstonecraft and Mary Hays, Catherine Macaulay moved in supportive radical circles and for a time ran her own salon. By all accounts, she was formidably rational, with a domineering streak in her personality. For health reasons, she shifted from London to Bath in 1774, living at the house of Reverend Thomas Wilson, who was 28 years her senior. He was infatuated with her and, as was the case with her father, she enjoyed the use of an extensive library. Then, at the age of 47, she announced her marriage to a 21-year-old ship's mate, scandalising society and ruining her reputation. Despite this, in France and the U.S. she was feted as a celebrity, and her marriage was by all accounts harmonious and lasted until her death.

More clearly than the three Marys, Catherine was a leader; while her first husband George Macaulay was in many ways a fellow traveller, Thomas Wilson and her second husband, William Graham, were clearly followers. Her *Letters on Education*, published in 1790, see no intellectual differences between the sexes, those that existed being clearly a product of the triviality of female education. Catherine favoured co-education and her observations on how social and cultural factors result in sexual differences parallel Mary Hays' obscrvations. Wollstonecraft roundly called her "the woman of the greatest abilities that this country has ever produced" and her ideas on education reveal Macaulay's influence.

Here there are clear parallels to the life and works of Margaret Lucas Cavendish, who lived a century earlier. Margaret (1623–73) equally came from wealthy surroundings, was poorly educated but lucky in having a scholarly brother, John, with whom she could converse on law, philosophy and above all natural science. Exiled as a royalist after the downfall of Charles I, she married William Cavendish, Duke of Newcastle, 30 years her senior, in 1645 in Paris, and strongly profited from his material and moral support. In Amsterdam, where they emigrated to, the "Cavendish Circle" includes Hobbes and Descartes.

Margaret had a reputation for being both outspoken and eccentric, arguing that theology would not stand the test of scientific inquiry. Inevitably, she made enemies; Samuel Pepys called her a "mad, conceited, ridiculous woman," while Dorothy Osborne found it ridiculous that she wrote books. However, the Duke stood by his wife and responded to criticism of her works by pointing out that her only crime was being a woman and thus entrenching upon "the male prerogative."

Margaret Cavendish's great triumph was an invitation to attend a meeting of the Royal Society, which her brother John had helped found. Her philosophical materialism was in tune with the Zeitgeist and, fittingly, she was buried in Westminster Abbey.

Conservative Women and their Allies

Were Wollstonecraft's female adversaries, those with conservative views on a woman's role in society, unmarried women and virtuous housewives? To a certain degree, yes. Elizabeth Hamilton (1758–1816), who had made fun of Hays in her *Memoirs of Modern Philosophers* while arguing that a woman's role was in the home, does not seem to have had a serious relationship with a man during her lifetime. After being close to her elder brother, she then became friends with the clergyman George Gregory and his wife, living with one of her aunts in Scotland for a long period. Though unmarried, she insisted on being called Mrs Hamilton.

Anna Laetitia Barbauld (1743–1825), though married, similarly shows little evidence of having had productive rapports with men. Barbauld's father gave her an excellent education and she reportedly had a remarkably equal relationship with her husband Rochemont, who however later became insane. Though a rational dissenter, she strongly opposed the views of Wollstonecraft and Macaulay on education. Like Rousseau, she believed that girls only needed a "general tincture of knowledge to make them agreeable companions to a man of sense."

Though conservative in this respect, Barbauld was highly influential both as a writer and as the editor of Samuel Richardson and other prominent authors. Her relationship to Wollstonecraft was ambiguous, a mixture of personal sympathy and ideological antipathy. In her poem *The Rights of Woman*, she writes:

Then, then, abandon each ambitious thought,
Conquest or rule thy heart shall feebly move,
In Nature's school, by her soft maxims taught,
That separate rights are lost in mutual love.

Separate rights lost in mutual love: this kind of repressive idealism characterised entire generations of women, including reformers like Barbauld. As a rational dissenter, Anna was predestined for progressive ideas; however, they apparently did not apply to her own sex.

A similar duality characterises Hannah More. She was on the one hand a playwright supported by Garrick and moved in the rarefied circles of Edmund Burke and Joshua Reynolds. Beyond that, More (1745–1833) firmly opposed slavery and supported William Wilberforce, who became a friend. Her *Strictures on the Modern System of Female Education* condemned the triviality of what girls were taught, while accepting their roles as wives and mothers. On the other hand, More was an evangelical moralist with strong views on how to combat the kind of sedition that Thomas Paine and the French Revolution presented. Her Christian morality stories, which sold in millions of copies, united Christian qualities like humility and trust both in God and in the kindness of the gentry with rabid anti-French feelings. Moreover, even in her *Strictures,* she pleaded for an education that could transform women into moral examples.

Despite her conservative views, Hannah had equal relationships with men; her company was appreciated by personalities as diverse as Dr Johnson and Horace Walpole. Among the children who visited her towards the end of her life were Gladstone and Macaulay. However, she experienced a traumatic engagement for six years to a rich landowner called William Turner, who then backed down, compensating for this by paying her an annuity for the rest of her life.

Literary Luminaries

Anne Stott's biography of Hannah More is fittingly entitled *The First Victorian*. Indeed, Moore's sense of propriety, despite or rather in combination with great productivity, characterises predominant attitudes during the "long" 19th century. According to the Marxist historian Eric Hobsbawm, this century covered the period from the French Revolution until the outbreak of World War One. In Britain, the Victorian era is certainly the apogee of this period, in which a new generation of women's-rights activists fought against the forces of middle-class moralism using mass media and organising campaigns.

Ironically, Wollstonecraft's impact was a lot stronger on literary women than on those fighting for common causes like education and social equality. Some commentators have found parallels to Jane Austen (1775–1817), who in her novels vividly portrayed the tight corset that middle-class women endured. Miriam Ascarelli sees "a feminist connection" in the way both Wollstonecraft and Austen portrayed women's role in society.

Unlike Wollstonecraft, Austen lived a highly secluded life; her male support was clearly familial. Blessed with a father who believed in her talent and tried to have her works published, she was equally fortunate in having a brother who followed his father's example. Henry, a banker by profession, effectively became Jane's agent and finally succeeded in having *Sense and Sensibility* published. After becoming bankrupt, he took orders and preached at the village church in Chawton, where Jane lived. His biographical sketch of Jane after she died did less damage than Godwin's stark portrayal of Wollstonecraft. However, he misrepresented his sister as a pious Christian and a sweet soul, leaving out the spicy burlesques she wrote as a young girl, her brushes with publishers and other flesh-and-blood aspects.

The link between Wollstonecraft and George Eliot is far more manifest. Eliot was arguably one of the most emancipated women of the 19th century, though recent scholarship has emphasised her emotional dependence on various lovers. Like Mary W, George E (1819–80) moved in radical circles, being close to a group of men who respected and liked her for what she was, not for what they thought women ought to be. This allowed her to live a remarkably free life in the supposedly stifling Victorian age.

Starting life under her father's influence as a devout Christian, Eliot later became an agnostic. On her journey away from religion, Charles Hennell, a kind of spiritual mentor, influenced her. Later, she lived for a time with Hennell's father-in-law, R. H. Brabant, an amateur theologist, until Brabant's jealous wife forced her to leave the house.

Eliot experienced the same kind of humiliation soon after. She had translated a German rationalist treatise by David Friedrich Strauss on the life of Jesus and the publisher, John Chapman, invited her to write for the magazine *The Westminster Review*, which he later purchased. Soon after, she started living in the Chapman household. This was a disastrous thing to do since Chapman, a remarkable seducer, already had a mistress on the premises, his children's governess, who also served as housekeeper. The resident ladies, Chapman's wife and mistress, united in getting Eliot evicted. Later, she edited the *Review* and returned to the house, though she apparently had no sexual relationship with the publisher.

John Chapman (1821–94) was a jack of many trades: first apprenticed to a watchmaker, he then studied medicine and later became a bookseller. His circle of friends included Mazzini and Karl Marx. Among the authors he published were luminaries like John Stuart Mill, Herbert Spencer and Thomas Huxley. He promoted them, as he did Eliot. Chapman is an excellent example of male duality: a man of great progressive principles, campaigning for the liberalisation of divorce laws and supporting the reform of education and property rights for women. At the same time, he not only sexually exploited women but also allowed Eliot to do the hard work of editing the *Review* while he gathered the laurels as its publisher.

George E found an erotic soulmate in George Henry Lewes, equally a jack of many trades, ranging from medical and commercial projects to acting; he later became a noted philosopher and literary critic. Lewes (1817–78) had an open marriage with Agnes Jervis, who had affairs with other men. In 1854, he and Eliot started living together.

Like Eliot, he was a Germanophile and wrote an acclaimed *Life of Goethe*. Moreover, like Eliot, he was reputed to be distinctly ugly; his friends variously referred to him as an "ape" and as the "ugliest man in London," while Eliot was known to have called herself "a withered cabbage in a flower garden." Lewes became Eliot's devoted companion, shielding her from literary and social criticism.

Parallel to this, Eliot found a kind of Platonic soulmate in the biologist philosopher Herbert Spencer, who coined the phrase "survival of the fittest." Spencer (1820–1903) visited Chapman's Friday-night soirées and by 1852, Eliot referred to her "deliciously calm new friendship" and "delightful comradery" with him. She took a maternal interest in the philosopher, even attempting to find him a female partner. Though they were very close and Spencer himself described the friendship as "intimate," her true love was Lewes. Reports that Spencer rejected her because, according to his own biological theories, women's natural function was to be beautiful and Eliot manifestly was not, relativise his physical interest in her. Spencer later reneged on his early feminist tendencies and became the Social Darwinist that history remembers him as being. However, his estimation of Eliot is evident from the term he used to describe her: "a female Shakespeare."

After Lewes's death in 1878, Eliot again scandalised society by marrying the American banker John Cross, her long-time business advisor and confidant. Initially, she had been shattered and became a recluse, not even attending Lewes' funeral. Cross asked for her hand three times until Eliot finally married him in 1880, the year of her death.

Like Wollstonecraft, Eliot was encouraged and supported by men who could hardly be more diverse. This perhaps tempered her feminism; one sign is that the first edition of her novel *Middlemarch* ended with an appeal for women's rights, while later editions broadened the tenor to include all groups of exploited human beings.

Cause Célèbre: Caroline Norton and the Rights to Custody and Divorce

Caroline Norton was an unlikely suspect, pushed into her pivotal role as the prime reformer of the rights of married women because she privately suffered under the existing laws. The granddaughter of the playwright Richard Brinsley Sheridan had married George Norton under pressure from her mother and for financial reasons. Norton turned out to be lazy, drunk and violent, injuring her severely on various occasions. Beyond that, their political views diverged: he was a dyed-in-the-wool Tory, she a Whig with a strong stake in social reform.

A beautiful socialite, Caroline (1808–77) had illustrious friends in politics and the arts. Benjamin Disraeli, Mary Shelley, Edward Bulwer-Lytton and Fanny Kemble belonged to her circle, as did the Home Secretary Lord Melbourne. George Norton first instigated his wife to use her influence with Melbourne to get him a magistrate's post and then tried to blackmail the politician when he became Prime Minister in 1835, insinuating that Melbourne was having an affair with Caroline. He sued Melbourne for adultery and, after a clear defeat in court, retaliated by denying Caroline access to her three children.

English Common Law grossly discriminated against married women well into the 20th century. Single women could own property and enter into contracts, while married women's rights merged with those of their husbands. Male prerogatives included child custody, so George was perfectly within his rights when he refused her access to the family home. Caroline reacted by publishing pamphlets on the natural claims of mothers to their children and enlisted powerful supporters to change the law.

Thomas Talfourd was one of Caroline's staunch allies. Talfourd (1795–1854) was a barrister with a keen sense of justice, condemning the Peterloo massacre and speaking out against the slave trade. He also pleaded for universal male suffrage. Talfourd was equally a playwright and a great friend of Charles Dickens, who dedicated the *Pickwick Papers* to him. He reacted particularly sympathetically to Caroline Norton's cause because, as a barrister, he had won the case of a father claiming custody of his child, though the court recognised at the time that the mother had a stronger moral claim to custody. The barrister was thus sensitised to the gulf between the letter of the law and moral justice.

Talfourd introduced the Infant Custody bill to the House of Commons. It passed the Commons and then failed by a narrow majority in the House of Lords. One of the bill's most fervent supporters was Lord Lyndhurst, who attacked the manifest injustice of a system that debarred women from contact to their offspring. When the bill was defeated in the Lords, he signed a protest together with his ally, Baron Holland, which eloquently claimed that "nature and reason point out the mother as the proper guardian of her infant child."

Lyndhurst (1772–1863) was like Talfourd a brilliant thinker, leaving Cambridge with a mathematical tripos. Later called to the bar, he defended Luddite protesters successfully and was a superb lawyer, lucid and precise in his presentation of arguments. He played senior roles in public life as solicitor- and attorney-general, later becoming Chancellor of the Exchequer during several administrations.

Infant Custody finally became an Act of Parliament in 1839,

allowing women not convicted of adultery custody of children under seven and access to older ones. This was generally perceived as a triumph for Caroline, who then developed into a literary figure, publishing a succession of poems and plays. She later clashed with her husband on financial grounds: he demanded that she hand over to him a small legacy she had inherited on the death of Lord Melbourne; when she refused, he declined to continue to pay for the upbringing of their sons.

This instigated Caroline to campaign for a reform of the divorce laws. In 1856, the issue came up in parliament and again Lord Lyndhurst, though over the age of 80 at the time, eloquently and ably argued the case, frequently quoting from Caroline's pamphlets on the subject. In 1857, the Matrimonial Causes Act was adopted. It allowed divorces to be settled by secular courts instead of by an act of parliament; equally important was the fact that divorced women could keep their income. However, adultery remained the sole legitimate ground for divorce and while men could easily plead for a divorce, women still had to prove gross misconduct such as bigamy, rape or cruelty.

Despite these remarkable achievements, Caroline remained curiously detached from the mainstream of women's-rights protest. Early feminists, including Lydia Becker and Harriet Martineau, had formed the Women's Committee that worked closely with the Law Amendment Society of Lord Brougham. They too campaigned for divorce reform and Brougham commented on one of Caroline's letters to Queen Victoria, admiringly calling it "as clever a thing as ever was written" and stating that "it has produced great good." Remarkably, despite her scandalous reputation, Norton had personal contact to the Queen and to a broad cross-section of the aristocracy.

She not only moved in more rarefied circles than her middle-class contemporaries of the Women's Committee; she also made no secret of the fact that she preferred the company of men to that of women and considered men to be the superior sex. In 1838, she wrote a letter to *The Times* claiming: "I never pretended to the wild and ridiculous doctrine of equality." Despite this, she is a precursor of the Second-Wave Feminists: she made the personal political in the sense that she dealt with her predicament as wife and mother in a public way that led to lasting reform.

Henry Brougham by contrast fervently believed in women's rights. Like Talfourd and Lyndhurst, he was a lawyer with a keen sense of justice, successfully defending 38 weavers in Manchester. They had been arrested for trying to found a trade union. Brougham (1778–1868) later became one of the leading parliamentary radicals, campaigning strongly against the slave trade. The Law Amendment Society he founded in 1844 became the epicentre of legal reform. Thus, Brougham was predestined for his role in campaigning for the Matrimonial Causes Act.

In private terms, he was no angel. Often accused of being vain and selfish, he was also a philanderer, having affairs with various women. As a client of Harriet Wilson, a celebrated courtesan, he was blackmailed by her when she published her memoirs, fearing public disgrace as Lord Chancellor if she revealed his name. Here, he was in very good company; Wilson's lovers included the Duke of Wellington, Lord Palmerston and in fact George IV. Brougham cleverly offered to be her legal advisor beyond paying her an annuity; she responded by publicly praising him as a man of great talents, motivated solely by "the spirit of philanthropy." This mixture of noble public and tawdry private demeanour contrasts strongly with Caroline's clarity and honesty. Brougham is in the final reckoning a recognisably Victorian figure, while Caroline seems closer to Regency mores.

Victorian Mainstream Respectability

While Wollstonecraft, Eliot and Norton were all in their own ways social outlaws who defied convention, the Victorian mainstream reformers were profoundly respectable. This corresponded with a professionalisation of the women's-rights movements, away from flamboyant individuals and towards sober organisers. It also corresponded with the real world of economic expansion and modern media. Salons and in-groups automatically became less relevant than mass-media campaigns and committee decisions.

Given the respectability that distinguished feminist luminaries like Millicent Fawcett and Josephine Butler, it is hardly surprising that fathers, husbands and brothers played larger roles in their lives than soulmates and lovers. Fawcett's father was a successful businessman and she inherited from him a sense of enterprise, a liberal mind-set and a lack of snobbishness that did not however include a real sense of social justice. Her highly intelligent and congenial husband Henry, who, despite being blind, became a Cambridge don and a Liberal MP, equally influenced her. Later, Gladstone made him Postmaster General and Henry (1833–84) used his new position to expand female employment, while getting an official reprimand for his refusal to oppose a women's suffrage amendment in parliament.

Dame Millicent Garrett Fawcett (1847–1929) became a convert to the suffrage cause after hearing John Stuart Mill speak on the issue. He became her mentor and introduced her to her husband. She remained a moderate suffrage campaigner throughout her life and the National Union of Women's Suffrage Societies (NUWSS) that she led had many pacifist supporters. The influence of her energetic, congenial father and her enlightened husband, both converts to Gladstonian Liberalism, are as apparent as the influence of the fiery radical Richard Pankhurst on his wife and daughter, who ran the rival WSPU suffragette organisation.

Millicent and her husband both sympathised with the campaign against the Contagious Diseases Act; however, they reserved their energies for suffrage agitation. Josephine Butler

(1828–1906) on the other hand devoted her life to the Abolitionist cause and equally derived great sustenance from her father and husband. While Millicent's father was a self-made man, Josephine's came from a Whig dynasty and belonged to the landed gentry. He combined this with remarkably enlightened views as a strident opponent of slavery, a proponent of Catholic Emancipation, of free trade and, last but certainly not least, as an active supporter of women's rights. He was also a devoted husband and had an equal relationship with his wife, who advised him on business issues.

Similarly, her husband Canon George Butler (1819–90) was of great support. A brilliant scholar, later Principal of a College, he not only provided moral support to his wife but voiced progressive views on subjects like women's education. This was certainly not normal in Oxford, where Josephine Butler experienced a great amount of misogyny during the period when her husband worked as examiner of schools at Oxford University.

A remarkably humble man, George devoted his life to supporting Josephine's abolition campaign, seriously annoying his seniors in the Church of England in the process. He was however equally as devout as Josephine's father. Beyond that, he welcomed rescued prostitutes to their home, reading to and praying with the women. Josephine was greatly devoted to both men and wrote biographies of their lives when they died. By contrast, she scarcely mentioned the roles her mother and sister played. The same applies to her aunt Margaretta, who was a clear critic of discrimination against women. Like Millicent Fawcett, Josephine Butler clearly identified with the public persona of the men in her family.

George could well serve as a paragon for the self-effacing spouse. Before they married, he said it would be "undue presumption" on his part "to suggest anything to you in regard to your life and duties." Later he went as far as saying that he might be able to help her in terms of physical strength and if he could, "depend on it I will do so. In all other matters I think you are more capable of giving me aid than of borrowing it."

This kind of gender interaction was certainly not the case with all Victorian feminists. Pioneer educationist Emily Davies (1830–1921) is a contrary example. Her father John, a clergyman and schoolmaster, clearly discriminated against his daughters while sending his sons to public schools and university. He was apparently narrow-minded and instable, suffering repeatedly from nervous breakdowns. Her mother was supportive, though she constantly tried to conform to the role of clergyman's spouse.

Emily experienced discrimination first-hand at an early age; her father excluded girls from the school under his jurisdiction, openly professing that this would reduce standards. Later she was one of Girton College's cofounders and was active as a suffragist, collaborating here with John Stuart Mill. Her social contacts were mostly with women, though several men joined the executive committee to raise funds for a women's college in Cambridge, eventually called Girton. Davies' personality is described as abrasive and uncompromising; she had frequent clashes with men and women alike.

Suffragist Frances Power Cobbe was far more vehement in her assertion of feminine identity. An avowed lesbian, she lived with a sculptor, Mary Lloyd, for many years. When the patron saint of women's rights John Stuart Mill died, she wrote that he was one of two or three men whom she could love and honour "as if they were good women."

Frances (1882–1904) did not directly dislike men, but resented their power. Her father Charles belonged to the landed gentry in Ireland and the family was part of the Anglo-Irish establishment. As the only girl with four brothers, her education was rudimentary and she rebelled at an early age against the role of a young lady, going through both religious and psychic crises. Her father banished Frances to her brother's countryside farm after she made her deist views known.

After his death, Cobbe became financially independent and travelled widely to Southern Europe and the Near East, doing highly unconventional things like camping alone in the desert. Later she felt the need to help others and first did social work, then gravitated to suffrage, where she also created a stir by chairing meetings.

Graced with a very clear mind, she put women's discrimination into context as a form of persecution "of every uprising race or class or order." Cobbe published widely in mainstream media, which led to her being marginalised in feminist studies. Her style of writing is both forthright and imaginative. One of her articles on the discrimination of married women is characteristically entitled *Criminals, Idiots, Women and Minors: Is the Classification Sound?*

Frances apparently inherited from her father what an obituary described as "a very strong will, a masterful and sometimes imperious disposition and a somewhat impatient and fiery temper." This made her a highly effective activist though not a particularly likeable person.

Less openly feminist but equally effective and fearsome was the social reformer Octavia Hill, who has gained lasting fame as cofounder of the National Trust. She symbolises Victorian individualistic philanthropy as opposed to the social collectivism that later predominated. Octavia's father contrasts with Frances': a corn merchant and social Utopian in the Owenite mould, he later went bankrupt and had a nervous breakdown. The girl's maternal grandfather Dr Southwood Smith, an immensely active health reformer, had a strong influence on her and provided the family with financial and moral support.

Hill (1838–1912) was in common with many social reformers deeply influenced by F.D. Maurice's Christian socialism. He was also her employer when she worked as a secretary for the women's courses at the Working Men's College. The critic John Ruskin provided her with both a livelihood and a vocation by allowing her to manage his social-housing scheme. Both were strong influences on her. However, the concept and management of the housing, which soon amounted to 30 enterprises with 3,000 tenants, was almost entirely her achievement.

Octavia was a typically Victorian blend of the stern and the benevolent. The Octavia Hill System, as it was later called, was designed, as Lord Salisbury put it, "to improve the tenants with the tenements." She also had the vision to realise that the poor needed open spaces as much as sanitised housing. Here were the germs of the National Trust.

In feminist terms, the housing reformer was an odd mixture: against suffrage, because she believed in separate spheres for men and women, but for women's education and for married women's property. Octavia's housing projects relied entirely on female staff; Hill was of the opinion that only women were qualified. Her reasoning seems as clichéd as that of the men arguing against employing women: "Ladies must do it, for it is detailed work; ladies must do it, for it is household work; it needs moreover persistent patience, gentleness, hope."

Whatever her opinion of ladies was, Miss Octavia herself was the opposite of gentle, often being described as ruthless and dictatorial. Archbishop Temple once remarked after debating an issue with her that he had never had "such a beating" in his whole life. On the other hand, she was highly dedicated, working herself mercilessly until she collapsed. Moreover, while her reliance on self-initiative and her refusal to countenance state subsidies seemed absurdly old-fashioned during the heyday of the welfare state, they have gained relevance in the context of Thatcherist values. There seems little doubt that Miss Hill would have been a firm supporter of Mrs Thatcher, both being remarkably successful, strong-minded women who triumphed under adverse conditions.

Is it a coincidence that the happily married Fawcett and Butler had harmonious personalities and united diverse groups of men and women, while the single women Davies, Cobbe and Hill proved to be difficult in their personal dealings? Did the influence of fathers and husbands mellow personalities and encourage cohesion? The evidence suggests this.

Bloomsbury Connections

Virginia Woolf belonged not only in temporal terms to a new generation; her viewpoints and lifestyle were diametrically different from those of the Victorian reformers, though she did report meeting and being impressed by Octavia Hill. Woolf (1882–1941) was far closer to George Eliot, whom she analysed in a perceptive essay, deconstructing "the late Victorian version of a deluded woman who held phantom sway over subjects even more deluded than herself" and calling her "the pride and paragon of all her sex."

Woolf's feminism has been subject to much analysis. Like Emily Davies, she strongly resented having to stay at home while her brothers went to public schools and later to university, rightly blaming her father for this. Despite that, she profited not only from his library, but also from his broad intellectual interests. Fortunately, the broad circle of acquaintances that her brother Thoby had acquired at Cambridge became common friends. The humiliating dependency of women clearly motivated Woolf to write *A Room of One's Own*. She also however discerned that men of her class were forced into stiff moulds, "that great patriarchal machine."

Woolf firmly belonged to upper middle-class circles; her themes were women's access to professions like law, medicine and higher academia. She was ambivalent about women being philanthropists and social activists, as her biographer Hermione Lee points out, and avoided themes like poverty or social misery. In intellectual terms, she was far closer to the other, mostly male, members of the Bloomsbury set, to Lytton Strachey and E.M. Forster, to John Maynard Keynes and Clive Bell and above all to her later husband Leonard Woolf.

As a Jew from a relatively poor family, Leonard (1880–1969) was a social outsider. He was Virginia's devoted companion, not her lover. In fact, she had told him in no uncertain terms that she felt no physical attraction for him whatsoever. Women, in particular Vita Sackville-West, aroused the writer. However, it was Leonard who nursed her during her manic-depressive periods and who patiently endured her problematic personality.

Leonard is well comparable to George Lewes, who played a similarly therapeutic role in Eliot's life. Both men protected the frail personalities of their spouses. It appears that Virginia would never have been able to write her books without Leonard's stalwart support; in a very sensitive way, he found fulfilment in serving her.

America's Wollstonecraft

Margaret Fuller is often compared with Mary Wollstonecraft. Indeed, her immediate impact on America's feminists far surpassed Wollstonecraft's in Britain, while her lifestyle was equally colourful and her character at least as multifaceted. Her pioneering book *Woman in the Nineteenth Century* was celebrated as a masterpiece and for the first generation of suffragists, including Susan B. Anthony and Elizabeth Cady Stanton, Margaret was an inspirational figure. Her demands were not only for equal education but also for open employment; why for instance should a woman not be a sea captain?

Beyond this, Fuller (1810–50) was the first woman to do a variety of things: conduct research in the Harvard Library, become editor of an intellectual journal, Ralph Waldo Emerson's *Dial*, then be the first literary editor of a national newspaper, Horace Greeley's *New York Tribune*, and after that the newspaper's first female foreign correspondent.

Graced with supreme self-confidence – she once proclaimed that she had met everyone worth meeting in America and found no intellect comparable to her own – she was very much the product of her father's exacting education. When studying at Harvard, Timothy Fuller came under the influence of Wollstonecraft's *Vindication* and treated his daughter like a gifted boy, spurring her on with the motto: "Mediocrity is obscurity."

She learned to read and write at the age of three and was studying Latin at the age of five, rather like John Stuart Mill. Similar to Mill, she was a victim of her own precocity, suffering from nightmares and somnambulism. However, it made her the intellectual match of any man she met. Fuller herself considered this her masculine side, which contrasted vividly with her emotional vulnerability.

Margaret was well aware of these conflicting parts of her personality. Her often-quoted sentence "There is no wholly masculine man, no purely feminine woman" makes her the godmother of gender studies. She negated complete masculinity and femininity; all individuals were a product of both. Her search for complete closeness and intimacy proved too strenuous for the many men who were drawn to her because of her cerebral charm.

Her husband by contrast, Count Giovanni Orsoli, ten years younger than her, was by all accounts a decent person, but not her intellectual equal. She met him after moving to Europe as Greeley's foreign correspondent and after an intense relationship with the Polish nationalist poet Adam Mickiewicz, who confronted her with an emotional desire she had completely missed in Emerson. A follower of the philosopher of Italian unification Giovanni Mazzini, Orsoli was an ardent republican and served in the city guard during the siege of Rome. After the French forces recaptured the city, Fuller and he fled together with their newly born child and emigrated to the U.S. If all three of them had not tragically died of shipwreck near the coast of New Jersey, her life might have taken a different direction.

Emerson and Greeley both played important roles in her life. The transcendentalist philosopher was her intellectual idol and

Fuller yearned for an intimacy that Emerson was neither able to nor desirous of providing. In theory, Ralph Waldo (1803–82), like Margaret, questioned the efficacy of monogamous marriage for geniuses and preached free love; in practice, he was happy to remain with his second wife and four children. Emerson exploited her materially more than emotionally: Fuller never received the promised payment for her editorial work, though this was also the outcome of the financial problems suffered by the *Dial*.

Greeley (1811–72) by contrast was more her promoter than her mentor. Though unhappily married, Horace was not physically attracted to Margaret, with whom he clashed on various issues. Despite this, Greeley admired her wits and invited her to stay at his countryside home, perhaps to liven up "Castle Doleful," as he called it.

The newspaper magnate was a true liberal supporting a corona of enlightened causes like abolition of slavery and capital punishment; he was quickly convinced of the need for gender equality. Greeley however accused Fuller of not being consequent, of wanting complete equality while also expecting deference as a woman.

Greeley was Fuller's sparring partner in an equal relationship, despite the fact that he was also her boss. Their "friendly antagonism," as he described it, is quite exceptional. There is no record of Fuller having had any contacts of the same quality with women, though she did mix with a number of talented women both in her Transcendentalist phase and in the social work she conducted with female prisoners in Sing Sing.

Greeley praised her championing the causes of prostitutes, Native and African Americans. Here, they were kindred spirits. However, unlike Wollstonecraft, who rather disdained women in social contact, preferring to mix with men, Fuller believed that "women are the best helpers of one another." Thus, she had a stronger sense of gender solidarity.

Suffrage Stalwarts

Fuller might have been an idol for Lucretia Mott, Elizabeth Cady Stanton and other women's-rights activists, but they certainly did not emulate in any way her lifestyle, remaining as virtuous as their British colleagues. Both Lucretia Mott (1793–1880) and her husband James were avid abolitionists; they travelled to the Anti-Slavery Convention in London, where James participated, while Lucretia was as a woman barred from the proceedings, though she had, together with her husband, co-founded the American Anti-Slavery Society and spoken at an initial meeting in Philadelphia.

Lucretia Mott had met Elizabeth Cady Stanton in London and collaborated with her in organising the famous Seneca Falls Convention, though she was initially opposed to female suffrage. James (1788–1868) was a firm supporter of his wife and chaired the Convention on the opening day, the first and last time that a man officiated at an event of this kind. Lucretia served initially as Stanton's mentor and later tried to pacify the rivalling suffrage groups.

Stanton (1815–1902) resembled Millicent Fawcett in the sense that her father, husband and cousin were important influences. Her father Daniel Cady (1773–1859) was a distinguished lawyer, judge and congressional representative. His strict Scottish Presbyterian upbringing can well be compared to Margaret Fuller's intellectual initiation through her father. Elizabeth had the opportunity of attending a Female Seminary and studying Greek privately. Her father encouraged her to participate in legal discussions with his students, who frequently visited them. However, she was also aware that he valued sons more than daughters.

Daniel thoroughly disapproved of Elizabeth's husband Henry, a dyed-in-the-wool reformer and abolitionist. Characteristically, they spent their honeymoon visiting the World Anti-Slavery Convention in London, where Henry represented the American branch. Penniless because he devoted all his time and energy to political causes, Henry then agreed to study law with his father-in-law, but continued his work in the anti-slavery movement. Frederick Douglass, the former slave who gave vital support to Elizabeth's call for women's suffrage, once called Henry "unquestionably the best orator in the anti-slavery movement."

Henry Stanton (1805–87) was a devoted spouse who supported his wife unreservedly in moral terms. However, the upbringing of their seven children was almost solely in her hands. This was one of the reasons why Elizabeth was bound to her home in Rochester. By contrast, her ally Susan B. Anthony travelled widely on the suffrage mission. Susan received a greater degree of material support from her father and notably from her remarkable cousin, Gerrit Smith.

Gerrit Smith (1797–1874) was an even more vehement abolitionist than Henry. He was one of the Secret Six, the wealthy Northern anti-slavery activists who had supported John Brown's famous abortive raid. Consequently, Smith faced prosecution and the prospect of being hanged, as Brown was. He suffered a nervous breakdown, but continued his reforming activities.

Smith funded women's suffrage among many other causes; he was one of the country's leading philanthropists. His daughter Elizabeth Smith Miller, a leading suffragist, and Susan B. Anthony were constantly pressing him to support the cause. The reformer had a very clear view of the issue of women's dependency on men; they needed rights in his opinion, not privileges and concessions, which were "always revocable and always uncertain." He saw no "characteristic delicacy" in women, balancing "characteristic coarseness" in men, but believed that both sexes had the same nature.

Smith also intriguingly backed efforts to reform women's attire, because that would extinguish conventional ideas of chivalry and gallantry. His daughter Elizabeth (1822–1911) was one of the first to adopt the trouser-skirt combination – Turkish-style pantaloons, combined with a knee-length skirt – later known as Bloomers. She created a thorough scandal when wearing these at the famous Seneca Falls convention. Both her father and her husband Charles Dudley Miller supported her sartorial activities and her political views.

As in Britain, suffragette militants like Alice Paul and Lucy Burns, both of whom had female rather than male role models, later supplanted moderate suffragists like Stanton and Anthony. Both came from comfortable surroundings, but while Paul belonged to the WASP patricians, Burns was of Irish-Catholic extraction. Paul's (1885–1977) maternal and paternal roots reached back to John Winthrop and William Penn. Her father William, a successful businessman, lived on a working farm called Paulsdale. As Quakers, the Pauls firmly believed in gender equality and Paul's father supported her education. It started in Swarthmore College, a co-educational school founded by her maternal grandfather, where her mother Tacie had studied.

Her father firmly believed in her and once said, "Well, when there is a job to be done, I bank on Alice." Despite this, her mother Tacie was a stronger influence. As a committed suffragist, she took her daughter at an early age to meetings of the Suffrage Association and thus introduced her to the issue. Further influences within the Quaker community were Lucretia Mott and Susan B. Anthony. While in England to continue her studies, Paul soon made contact with the Pankhursts and adopted their militant tactics after returning to the U.S.

Lucy Burns (1879–1966) equally profited from her father's support. Edward Burns financed his daughter's extensive education in the U.S., where she attended Vassar College and also Columbia and Yale University. After further studies in Germany, Burns moved to Britain and then came under the influence of the Pankhursts, making the acquaintance of Paul at a police station. They became inseparable partners for their cause, like Stanton and Anthony, with Paul however in the driver's seat.

Like the Pankhursts, the American suffragettes were conservative at heart, forced into militancy by the need to fight effectively for the vote. Their progressive attitudes on suffrage contrasted starkly with a lack of interest in other gender issues or in racial or social reform. This was however equally true of some of the suffragists. Carrie Chapman Catt, who took over leadership of NAWSA from Susan B. Anthony, catered to populist sentiments when campaigning in conservative states. She accused the government of giving the vote to the "murderous Sioux" and "the slums," once pointing out: "White supremacy will be strengthened, not weakened, by women's suffrage." However, decades later, Catt (1859–1947) protested against fascism in Germany, organising a Protest Committee. Like Stanton, she could rely on firm support from her husband George, a rich engineer.

More than four decades later, Alice Paul played a major role in having the word "sex" inserted into the Civil Rights Act of 1964, originally designed to end discrimination against Black Americans. Her ally in the House of Representatives was an influential Virginia Democrat, who made no secret of his racist tendencies. Howard W. Smith had led a conservative coalition against Roosevelt's New Deal back in the 1930s and was a strong opponent of racial integration.

As Chairman of the House Committee on Rules between 1955 and 1967, Smith (1883–1976) had immense power over legislation and used it to block civil-rights initiatives. Simultaneously, he had close contacts to Alice Paul's National Woman's Party (NWP) and used the "sex" amendment in an attempt to sabotage the Civil Rights Act, arguing that legislation to protect blacks would discriminate against white women, who, unlike their black counterparts, would lack legal protection. Though his obstructive tactics finally failed, Smith's cynicism was apparent; while pleading for the amendment, he made jokes about women's "right to a nice husband and a family," reaping collective mirth in the House.

However, Smith supported NWP not only for opportunistic reasons. He had been for decades a strong supporter of the Equal Rights Amendment, since this was purely gender-based. Thus, he was both a feminist and a racist, proving once more that support for women's rights is not necessarily a humanistic enterprise.

From the Beechers to Greenwich Village

The Beechers were one of 19th-century America's stellar families, even if Harriet Beecher Stowe as the author of *Uncle Tom's Cabin* is the only name that comes to mind today. In fact, Harriet's sisters were more profound feminists and reformers. Her elder sister Catharine was a pioneer of women's education, while her younger sister Isabella was a prominent suffragist.

Their father Lyman (1775–1863) was a formative influence on the entire family. A Calvinist preacher with anti-Catholic convictions, he encouraged his daughters to assert themselves at an early age. Their upbringing was strict: regular prayer meetings, no dancing or theatre. This seems to have focused their energies on reform of all kinds. However, Lyman was against women becoming priests.

Their brother Henry Ward Beecher (1813–87) was also a clergyman and had a strong influence, particularly on Harriet. More whole-heartedly than his father, he embraced issues like suffrage, anti-slavery and temperance. However, his social conscience was underdeveloped: during a railroad strike, he preached strongly against the workers, declaring in one sermon that "man cannot live by bread alone, but the man who cannot live on bread and water is not fit to live."

Starting life as a slow-witted child with a stammer, he grew to become one of America's leading orators, feted by such diverse figures as Abraham Lincoln and Ralph Waldo Emerson. During the Civil War, he organised the smuggling of guns to those fighting slavery; the crates were labelled as bibles with the guns being later known as "Beecher's Bibles."

Henry's endorsement of suffrage, while firm, was a side issue. His role in the Civil War was so important that when Federal forces retook Fort Sumter, Lincoln chose Beecher to speak at the commemoration. When he died, the black commander of a garrison post and a former Confederate general walked arm-in-arm in the funeral procession. Despite this, he was, in Debby Applegate's words, "a notoriously paradoxical figure." Liberal opinions contrasted with conservative value judgments; warm-hearted in private, he preached with excessive vigour, stamping his foot and railing at all and sundry.

Isabella Beecher's husband John Hooker, while less prominent, offered more tangible support for women's rights. Also an abolitionist, he later fervently supported his wife's suffrage activities at the side of Stanton and Anthony, also writing a pamphlet, *The Bible and Woman Suffrage,* that the Connecticut Woman Suffrage Association distributed. This was by no means the norm in the family; Catherine rejected the idea of suffrage for women, while Harriet's attitude was more ambiguous.

The Beechers were a family of virtuous reformers, well identifiable as belonging to the 19th century. Henry's sex scandal – he was accused of practising free love, being later acquitted in court – was a singular exception. The Greenwich Village set, by contrast, corresponds well to Bloomsbury, though its members were not as upper class as Virginia Woolf and consorts.

Among its prominent members was Marie Jenny Howe, who founded the Heterodoxy Club, a group of 25 women committed to individualistic feminist ideals like self-development. Personal relationships and lifestyles were paramount; individual members like Marie however also pursued public issues like suffrage.

Marie's husband, social reformer Frederic C. Howe (1867–1940), was a reluctant convert to these ideals, once confessing: "As to women, I followed the changing mores. I spoke for women's suffrage without much wanting it. And I urged freedom for women without liking it." As Commissioner of Immigration in New York, he played an important public role in the city as a defender of civil liberties. However, his support for feminist goals was lukewarm, largely dutiful rather than felt.

Floyd Dell (1887–1969) by contrast was taken by charismatic women, some of whom he described in *Women as World Builders*, a work which sympathises with the "hell-raising" tendencies of militant, privileged women, while condescending to those women organising salons. He married his unconventional wife Margery Currey at a ceremony presided over by a Rabbi, though neither of them was Jewish. After various love affairs, they divorced and Dell moved to New York, quickly becoming a Greenwich Village insider, having affairs with talented women like the poet Edna St. Vincent Millay and later marrying the avowed feminist B. Marie Gage.

Dell was a prominent left-wing writer and editor of the magazine *The Masses*. In an article published there in 1914, Dell proclaimed, "Feminism is going to make it possible for the first time for men to be free." This made him far more convincing than Frederic Howe and indeed, Dell symbolised urbane, enlightened attitudes that flourished in New York.

Germany: Enlightenment Figures

Fathers and husbands were the natural allies of several German women during the Age of Enlightenment. Dorothea Christiane Erxleben (1715–62) for instance was the daughter of a highly progressive doctor, who personally taught her natural sciences and medicine, taking her on visits to his patients and generally treating her exactly like her brother. Beyond this, the Head of the local council school in her hometown Quedlinburg recognised her talent and personally taught her.

Later, she even treated patients independently on her father's behalf, continuing to do this after her marriage to a Protestant priest and the birth of her four children. At the age of 39, she did her doctorate and continued to practise for the rest of her short life. Dorothea was by all accounts not only highly intelligent, but also extremely self-assured, reacting to prejudices against her professional work with a pamphlet that analysed the reasons why the female sex was kept from higher studies.

Similarly, Sophie von La Roche, Germany's first female novelist, derived strong support from her father, as well as from her famous cousin Christoph Martin Wieland and from other mentors. Sophie's father taught her to read by the age of three and gave her a broad-based education, while her first fiancé Giovanni Ludovico Bianconi taught her Italian literature and history among other subjects.

She was also engaged for a time to Christoph Martin Wieland, founder of the literary circle in Weimar that later included Goethe and Schiller, the country's greatest writers. Sophie (1730–1807) instigated him to become an author and he was at least initially grateful. She ran a salon visited by the literary elite and served as a model for her granddaughters, several of whom became writers themselves.

Amalia Holst's father was a Prussian bureaucrat who separated from his wife and kept custody of his child. He educated Amalia (1758–1829) to extremely high standards and firmly believed that it was eminently useful for the female sex to receive a proper education. Arrested for the alleged embezzlement of official funds, Holst died in prison, while Amalia married a lawyer and ran a school with him. They apparently had an excellent working relationship, though they lived separately.

Amalia had a clear head on her shoulders, firmly condemning the reactionary pedagogic views of Rousseau, while greatly praising Hippel's progressive viewpoints. Her essay *On Woman's Destiny for Higher Education* clearly makes the case for educational equality and some consider her Germany's Wollstonecraft. The comparison seems exaggerated, but she certainly followed Hippel's example in terms of egalitarian ideas.

A Cautious Pioneer Attracts Masculine Supporters

Louise Otto-Peters was every bit as influential as Wollstonecraft and Fuller, though a hugely different kind of person. She founded Germany's women's-rights movement, uniting respectability with moderate demands. Like Fuller, she had a strong social conscience and the plight of the country's factory workers shocked her. However, unlike the charismatic American, Otto-Peters (1819–95) believed in steady work and good organisation. Unsurprisingly, the male support she marshalled resembled that of mainstream Anglo-Saxon suffragists.

Louise grew up under privileged conditions as the daughter of a judge. Her father firmly believed in mental equality and expected his daughters to participate in discussions of cultural and political issues during dinner. Unfortunately, both parents died when she was 16 years old, forcing her to seek a living.

Discovering that she had a talent for writing, she first wrote novels, then approached Robert Blum (1807–48), the radical journalist and politician later to become a martyr of the 1848 revolution after he was executed in Vienna. Blum published her articles on women's rights and encouraged her to pursue her goals for educational reform. The journalist was a charismatic self-made man, who rose from poor surroundings; he also was a ladies' man who had a number of affairs despite getting married in 1840. Blum demanded that women participate to a greater degree in public life. Hence, his support for Peters harmonised with his general beliefs.

Otto then founded a newspaper for women (*Frauen-Zeitung*); the authorities in Saxony reacted with a "Lex Otto," barring women from becoming publishers. In the context of her journalistic work, Louise Otto became acquainted with August Peters, a political journalist jailed for his participation in the revolution. They became engaged in prison and married after his release. Like Otto, Peters (1817–64) had written novels; he was also deeply humanistic. They cooperated in publishing a newspaper and supported each other until his premature death.

Shortly after his death, Louise played a major role in founding Germany's first Women's Society (Allgemeiner deutscher Frauenverein, ADF). Several men were instrumental in the early phase of ADF, which concentrated on better education and more working rights for women. Philipp Anton Korn was in fact the initiator of the Society and drafted the minutes of the first conference in 1865. A former Captain of the Hungarian Revolutionary Army, Korn apparently dominated the proceedings until Otto and her female allies passed a resolution barring men from becoming members of ADF. Other collaborators were a Professor of Zoology and former revolutionary called Emil Adolf Roßmäßler and the publisher Ludwig Eckardt, for whom Otto worked as a journalist.

Otto had the gift of finding supporters from various social milieus, possibly because she had a retiring manner and was a poor public speaker. The story goes that when ADF held its first meeting, she asked Eckardt to hold the opening speech. Whereupon he apparently declined with a smile, pointing out that since this was a woman's cause, women should be in the forefront. It is hard to imagine Wollstonecraft or Fuller asking for this kind of assistance. However, the real reason seems to be less timidity than a lack of rhetorical finesse; Otto spoke with a strong Saxon accent and had a weak voice.

Emily Kempin and the Fight for Civil Rights

When the German Civil Code (BGB) finally came into being in 1900 and ended the particularism of Roman law, Napoleonic Code and regional civil legislation, it gained fame across the world as the best law of its kind. Russia and the Scandinavian countries adopted the code; other countries oriented their legislation towards the German model.

One particularly controversial area was family law. As in Anglo-Saxon common law and the French Code Civil, BGB was grossly discriminatory against women. They did not exist as economic subjects; their husbands could dispose over their income. This disparity became a key issue for ADF after two professors, Hermann von Leonhardi (1809–75) and Karl David August Röder (1806–79), spoke at the Women's Congress in 1869. Röder in particular came out for equal rights, criticising the French Revolution's Declaration of the Rights of Man and of Citizens for unjustly ignoring the rights of women.

A number of other jurists followed suit, in particular Ludwig Wachler (1835–1908), who published a pamphlet on the legal position of women in the same year as the Women's Congress. By contrast to Röder's humanistic viewpoint, the practicing judge Wachler is more of a legalist, insisting that women had inalienable rights as legal subjects (rather than objects, which was their status at the time). Other judges like Julius Weil shared his views.

The discussion gained momentum when different drafts of the proposed Civil Code started to circulate. Otto Bähr (1817–95), both judge and parliamentarian, criticised men's administrative authority over their wives' property. By far the most stringent criticism came however from two remarkable personalities who were close friends: Carl Bulling and Ludwig Bamberger.

Bulling (1822–1909) was a mixture of underdog and establishment man. His father was a minor public official who relinquished his position after being accused of sodomy and then became penniless because he did not receive a pension. Carl himself was only able to continue his studies because a friend's parents supported him. Heinrich von Lengerke was a fellow student and pitied Carl, forced to work for his father after he failed to achieve a state position. Lengerke informed his parents of Carl's hypochondriac tendencies and, indeed, he was repeatedly compelled to postpone his exams for health reasons.

After qualifying as a lawyer, Bulling finally managed to enter state service and his career progressed smoothly until he irritated his superiors by deciding to marry a waitress. Banished to a provincial post as a minor judge, he later experienced severe financial difficulties because his wife became a mental patient in various sanatoriums. By all accounts, Carl easily made enemies; he did however have a strong sense of justice, which led him to demand greater rights for illegitimate children. This corresponded with the viewpoints of a broad cross-section of the women's movement and Bullinger became the legal advisor of the Women's Welfare Association (Verein Frauenwohl).

The Head of the Association praised Carl for the "love and dedication" he had shown in dealing with a subject that most men and in fact women found distasteful. Bulling then published an influential pamphlet on the Civil Code, which attacked the custodianship of married women's property by men. According to him, wives were neither in need of help nor unable to conduct their own affairs.

Bulling was not only close to the women's movement; he had a prominent friend who openly supported his views and thus gave them more publicity. Ludwig Bamberger (1823–99) was one of Germany's leading parliamentarians and a liberal opponent of Bismarck. He was condemned to death for his role in the 1848 revolution and lived for decades abroad, at one stage working at the bank of his uncle in London. Though he thoroughly disliked his role as banker, he was later one of the founders of Deutsche Bank, Germany's leading financial institute.

Bamberger, who came back to Germany in the 1860s and played influential roles as advisor to both Bismarck and the Kaiser, later became a prominent publicist after leaving parliament. In this role, he supported Bulling's viewpoints and praised him as a "humane jurist."

This was the extended prologue to Emilie Kempin's arrival on stage as the masterful draughtsman of exceptions to the generally discriminatory code. Kempin (1853–1901), wife of a Swiss priest, was well on her way into domesticity as mother of three children when her husband seemed in danger of losing his job. This stimulated her to finish school and study law at Zurich University. When she achieved her doctorate with distinction, she was the first woman in Europe with a legal degree. The authorities refused however to allow her to practise and after her case was dismissed by the Supreme Court, she immigrated to New York with her family, starting the country's first Women's Legal College. Her husband was unable to adjust to the American Way of Life and returned to Switzerland with two of their children.

Despite her success in the U.S., she followed him back to Europe and started a Women's Legal Counselling Office, which provided free advice. Constantly in financial difficulties and disappointed by the discriminatory treatment she was experiencing in Switzerland, she separated from her husband, moving then to Berlin, where she was soon in the epicentre of the controversy on the Civil Code.

On behalf of ADF, she published a book on the legal position of women in Germany. Left-wing members of the feminist movement accused her of writing in a dry style, while Kempin flatly pointed out that it was worthless to lament the unfairness of the existing laws. She also wrote that most German women were not interested in emancipating themselves from their husbands; they rather saw their greatest virtue in being devoted to the men in their lives.

A brilliant lawyer rather than a feminist, Kempin concentrated on mitigating the patriarchal sections on family law in the Code and on highlighting the potential of individual provisions like contractual separation of property. Here, she had a great ally in Carl Ferdinand von Stumm-Halberg, one of Germany's leading industrialists.

Historians are still uncertain what motivated the highly conservative patriarch Stumm, an embittered opponent of the Social Democrat Party (SPD), to join the mostly left-wing agitation led by SPD leader August Bebel for Civil Code reform. Stumm (1836–1901) was a steel magnate whose ambitions extended further. For three decades, he was a member of parliament; he was also a friend of Kaiser Wilhelm and a generous patron of the Protestant Church.

Like Bismarck, he was against trade unions but in favour of social insurance; he was a highly humane employer, motivated by a Protestant Ethic that was both stern and progressive. On the one hand, Stumm built housing, hospitals and churches for the workers. On the other hand, employees who wanted to marry had to ask his wife's permission; if she refused to approve, they were faced with the choice of either remaining single or leaving the company. By all accounts, he had a happy and very egalitarian relationship with his wife; one reason for his support of family-law reform could have resided in the fact that he wanted his four daughters to inherit his fortune regardless of whether or not they married.

As member of a commission set up to discuss the text of the Civil Code, Stumm used his position to introduce modifications drafted by Kempin. Of the 32 suggested changes concerning female custodianship and property, five were adopted. Stumm was quick to point out that he was not supporting women's emancipation; rather, he wanted to correct specific injustices that affected women as heirs, employees and entrepreneurs. Kempin had similarly specific views, which made them ideal collaborators.

Simultaneously, the partnership further isolated Kempin from the women's movement. Attacked as a traitor to the cause and in great material straits, she suffered from schizophrenia, then had a nervous breakdown and landed in a lunatic asylum in Basel, later dying of cervical cancer.

Husbands as Helpers

Men who were entirely convinced of the equality of the sexes increasingly supported the next generation of feminists. This applied as much to Auguste Kirchhoff as to Minna Cauer.

Auguste (1867–1940) married a successful judge and senator, Dr Heinrich Kirchhoff, and lived for a while the life of a comfortably situated mother of three daughters and two sons, inviting artists to her home and giving music lessons. She then became active in a Suffrage Association and was one of the very few women to oppose the First World War.

Her husband had the courage to endorse her views and was a confirmed liberal. His reputation as one of the leading citizens of the hanseatic city of Bremen protected his wife against public indignation after she travelled to the International Women's Peace Conference in The Hague in 1915. Heinrich was also of great practical assistance, giving the children their breakfasts when Auguste hurried to her political meetings. When he died in 1929, she collapsed and had a nervous breakdown.

Minna Cauer (1841–1922) was fortunate in having a father who spurred her on to express her own viewpoints, and a husband who was exemplary in both his liberal viewpoints and his unconditional support. Her father was an unconventional priest who constantly got into trouble with his superiors and he instigated Minna to assert herself and to develop a spirit of contradiction that served her well when she founded the Women's Welfare Association in Berlin in 1888.

She was one of the leading radicals in the women's movement. After her first husband died in a lunatic asylum, she became a teacher and then married a colleague, Eduard Cauer. Eduard was a liberal thinker who attacked the anti-Semitic court chaplain Adolf Stoecker. He also firmly believed that women were men's equals and wrote in his diary, "Women's history is yet to be written; it has to be written and it will demand lifelong commitment." Minna became a widow for the second time when he died in 1881 and continued her mission to achieve political rights for women, also cofounding the first Association for Women's Suffrage in Germany.

Husbands as Soulmates and Philanderers

Eduard Cauer and Heinrich Kirchhoff could serve as role models for many modern liberal men. Other spouses of feminists evinced a greater duality: they firmly supported their wives while simultaneously having affairs with other women. They acted as philanderers with the tacit consent and indeed encouragement of their wives, who displayed an emotional dependency at odds with their self-assured public image.

Bertha von Suttner for instance was one of the most influential women of her era. She was the first woman to win the Nobel Peace Prize and her pacifist book *Lay Down Your Arms!* was widely translated and highly acclaimed. Suttner (1843–1914) was the impoverished daughter of an Austrian general and worked as a governess in the Suttner household, falling in love with her later husband Arthur, whose parents disinherited him after they eloped. They lived precariously in Russia until Arthur's parents were reconciled to their marriage and they could then return to the family home.

Arthur von Suttner (1850-1902) thoroughly respected and supported his wife, who had worked briefly for Alfred Nobel in Paris and influenced him to endow a prize for those contributing to peace in the world. Nobel financed her lecturing trips, while her husband accompanied her and shared her outspoken philosemitic views, founding an association to fight against the endemic anti-Semitism in Austria. In the final years of her life, Bertha had close contacts to the international women's movement, though she declined leadership of the World Federation of Women.

Long before this, Arthur had an intimate relationship with his niece Marie; simultaneously, Marie was a close friend of Bertha.

When Marie published an autobiographic novel in 1898, she dedicated it to her "dear aunt and teacher Bertha." This ménage à trois continued until Arthur died in 1902. Bertha was apparently jealous, but did not do anything to change the situation.

The relationship between Max and Marianne Weber was even more complex. Max Weber (1864–1920), the famous sociologist who wrote the profoundly influential classic *The Protestant Ethic and the Spirit of Capitalism*, was a bundle of contradictions: a liberal with strong nationalistic tendencies, a rationalist always on the verge of nervous breakdowns – and a committed feminist with both paternalistic and sadomasochistic impulses.

Marianne (1870–1954) lost her mother at an early age and had a psychically disturbed father, two of whose brothers later landed in lunatic asylums. These early experiences were valuable, because they helped her deal with Max's emotional outbreaks and depressive phases. Max insisted on having a relationship with her on equal terms and wrote to her, "Our relationship is between free and equal partners."

When Max became a professor in Heidelberg, Marianne started an association that propagated "modern ideals for women" and fought for educational reform. The free-love movement was very much en vogue in Heidelberg at the turn of the century and Marianne belonged to its opponents, arguing that women's rights were better protected if they were married.

However, her good friend Else von Richthofen, the first woman to become a factory inspector in the state of Baden, was briefly engaged to Max Weber's brother Alfred, before marrying the economist Edgar Jaffé, while also having a son from Otto Gross, the great protagonist of free love. Max had been her teacher at the university and she did her doctorate under his surveillance. Later, Else (1874–1973) had a passionate relationship with Max Weber, in which she played domina. Marianne was not only aware of this sadomasochistic episode; she seems to have encouraged it in the interests of her husband's health.

Max openly supported his wife's feminist activities and criticised traditional women for their narrow attitudes. In 1919, Marianne held the important position of President of BDF; when her husband died in 1920, she had a nervous breakdown and resigned her position. She then dedicated the rest of her life to editing his work and wrote his biography.

Parallel to Else Jaffé, Max had a relationship with the Swiss pianist Minna Tobler (1880–1967) after they visited Wagner's romantic opera *Tristan und Isolde* in Munich. Marianne, also present at the performance, encouraged this relationship as well, never feeling threatened in her role as wife and comrade-in-arms. Tobelchen was for Weber more of a daughter and follower, while Else became his master in his final years. The three women remained close friends until the ends of their respective lives; Tobler and Jaffé even spent their last years in the same old-people's home.

Revolutionary Convictions, Bourgeois Sensibilities

Rosa Luxemburg and Clara Zetkin are icons of revolutionary Europe. One died as a martyr in the revolutionary period after the First World War, the other as an exile in Russia shortly after the Nazis came to power. Both had unhappy but fulfilling relationships with men and displayed a private vulnerability that contrasted with their robust public images.

Luxemburg (1871–1919) was a leftist Social Democrat who welcomed the October Revolution while disagreeing with Lenin's centralism. When the war ended, she was one of the cofounders of Germany's Communist Party and participated in the Spartacist uprising; members of a cavalry division then assassinated her in Berlin. While not overtly a feminist, she believed, like Clara Zetkin, that the woman question was an inseparable part of socialist endeavour.

For more than 15 years, Luxemburg had an intimate

relationship with Leo Jogiches, a rich Lithuanian socialist who also disagreed with Lenin in ideological terms. After meeting in Zurich in 1890, they became secret lovers and political collaborators. Jogiches (1867–1919) saw himself as Rosa's mentor, while she was clearly in love with him and constantly strived for a closeness that he neither needed nor desired. Luxemburg was very much the supplicant, constantly rebelling against his dispassionate attitude and then accepting it, until they terminated the affair, while continuing their political collaboration until her death.

Jogiches was very much her teacher, correcting her doctorate, criticising her for both her behaviour and her way of working. He himself never took an academic degree and was happy to play a background role, pulling the strings in various Communist groups in Central and Eastern Europe. Leo rejected her wish to have a child and her dream of combining political idealism with private happiness. However, when she separated from him in 1907 because she became close to Clara Zetkin's son Konstantin, he made great efforts to regain her sympathies and they remained in close contact.

At first sight, Clara Zetkin's relationship to Friedrich Zundel was the exact opposite: she was the intellectual leader, he the follower. However, in emotional terms, she depended tremendously on him and suffered greatly after their marriage floundered during the First World War, consenting to a divorce as late as 1927.

Clara (1857–1933) became a feminist early in her life when studying to become a teacher in Leipzig. As early as 1889, she advocated a proletarian woman's movement at the second International Congress in Paris. After living for a while with the Russian revolutionary Osip Zetkin in Paris, she returned to Germany after his premature death. Though never married since Clara believed in open relationships, she adopted his name.

Moving to Stuttgart, where she edited a socialist women's

magazine, she then met the painter Friedrich Zundel (1875–1948). After participating in a strike at the Art Academy, he had been relegated. Clara helped Zundel find an apartment and a studio; they soon became lovers and married in 1899, surprising her progressive friends, who assumed she wanted to conform to social norms. Party leader August Bebel was against the marriage; Clara's progressive friends considered Friedrich to be more of a dreamer than a fighter. She was 18 years older and clearly far more intelligent.

Zundel gradually achieved success as a painter and portraitist, gaining lucrative contacts from rich clients like Robert Bosch, founder of the precision mechanics company. The couple lived in a luxurious villa outside Stuttgart and Friedrich took care of the household chores. Zundel also took care of Clara when she was sick and exhausted; he even turned down a professorship at the prestigious Munich Art Academy, wanting to remain with her.

During the First World War, the couple drifted apart, both politically and personally. Friedrich was against the leftist tendencies of his wife; he also had a love affair with Robert Bosch's daughter Paula, whom he married in 1928. Clara was very much the impatient ideological activist, criticising him in a letter to Rosa Luxemburg for getting sick in November 1918, at a crucial moment directly after the war ended. It seems likely that she also disapproved of the increasingly mystical-mythological quality in his painting. History is rich in stories of powerful men inflicting themselves on sensitive women; here, the tables are turned.

"Men and Women Are Equal before the Law"

In retrospect, it seems implausible that one intrepid, enterprising woman was responsible for a clause in Germany's constitution of 1948 that established complete equality between men and women. Elisabeth Selbert, one of four female members of the

Constitutional Council, rebelled against plans to revert to the Weimar Constitution, which vaguely spoke of men and women having "the same civil rights and duties."

Selbert (1896–1986) insisted on equality in all areas and after campaigning fiercely in the early years after the Second World War – when women were in the majority and had a great sense of self-assurance, having taken over masculine working roles during the war – she succeeded in forcing the Council to adopt the law. Her threat to torpedo the Constitution (Grundgesetz) by calling on women to vote against it made her profoundly unpopular in her own Social Democratic Party (SPD) as well. She ended her career as a member of state parliament in Hessen, far below her own potential, but with a deep sense of gratification at her achievement.

Selbert always made a point of insisting that she was no feminist; she simply believed in the elementary principle of equal rights. One reason why her commitment seems purely rationalistic was that the men in her life supported her to a remarkable degree. Her grandfather quickly discovered her intellectual capacities and gave her books to read, much to the annoyance of her mother.

Her future husband, Adam Selbert, introduced her to politics, while Philipp Scheidemann, the first Chancellor of the Weimar Republic, at the time Lord Mayer of her hometown Kassel, encouraged her to take an active role in the SPD. Elisabeth was under no illusions as to the fact that despite having gained suffrage after the Great War, women were subject to discrimination in many spheres. "We are only equal on paper," she said as early as 1920.

She then finished her schooling and studied at university; her husband and other relatives took care of her two children. Ultimately, she did a doctorate in law, and when the Nazis came to power she gained permission to act as a lawyer in a higher court. New regulations forbidding women from doing so were passed in 1934; fortunately, two senior judges managed to push through her approval during the Christmas holidays. Her husband landed in a concentration camp because of his political past; she managed to get him released and then earned the family income as a lawyer, employing him as a clerk in her office.

After the war, both the men and the other women in the Constitutional Council were opposed to unconditional equal rights, fearing legal complications. With the full support of her husband, a true fellow traveller, Selbert moved across the country, mobilising support from women's associations and federations, so that huge bags of letters demanding equal rights arrived at Council headquarters. Her opponents then caved in, pretending that they had wanted to give women equal rights all the time.

France: Self-Centered Intellectuals

In terms of male support for women's rights, France is a great disappointment. The country of Fraternité, the third clarion call of the French Revolution, has turned out to be just that, a community of brotherhood in the narrow sense of the term, indifferent or contemptuous towards women claiming rights. This malaise is augmented by the fact that France's prominent women have often been lofty individualists, more interested in their own careers and lifestyles than in the fate and fortune of other members of their sex.

Among the prominent protagonists of this exalted individualism were Germaine de Staël and George Sand. Both lacked close bonds to men or indeed women despite entertaining a broad spectrum of relationships. Mme de Staël (1766–1817) was perhaps the most prominent Frenchwoman of the revolutionary and Napoleonic eras, supremely self-possessed and capable of talking any man into submissive silence.

Her father, Jacques Necker, was a leading Swiss banker and one of Louis XVI's Finance Ministers, her mother Suzanne ran one of Paris's leading salons and the small girl met intellectuals like Diderot and Gibbon at an age when other children were enjoying themselves on playgrounds. Germaine later became both a political and literary figure; she was one of Napoleon's most prominent opponents and wrote a number of novels and essays including a book on Germany, the land of poets and thinkers as she saw it, which became a classic and influenced generations of Frenchmen.

Jacques Necker (1732–1804), a reformer who made many enemies because of his progressive views, certainly influenced her intellectually, but there is little evidence of his direct encouragement of her considerable talents. Instead, he and his wife pressured Germaine to marry at an early age and her husband, the Swedish Baron Erik Staël von Holstein, was not only 17 years her senior but made no secret of the fact that he was after her fortune. The story goes that when courting her, he danced with her at a ball with such constraint that her father thrust himself on the couple, telling Holstein "Listen Sir, I'm going to show you how to dance with a woman whom one loves," and then danced with Germaine so tenderly that she burst into tears and fled from the ballroom.

She later had a succession of lovers, only one of whom was on her own intellectual level. Benjamin Constant (1767–1830) and Germaine de Staël enjoyed a marriage of minds. He was one of France's great liberal thinkers and spent 17 years in close contact with Germaine, though their relationship ended dramatically and he subsequently refused to take responsibility for their child. Their letters illustrate the close bond between them and the historian Sismondi pointed out: "By means of a mind equal to hers, he alone had the power to put all her intelligence into play, to make her grow greater through their combat..."

Benjamin, of Huguenot origin and well educated, having studied both in Erlangen and Edinburgh, introduced her to German philosophy and accompanied her on her journey through the country, though he was never her mentor. He was considered conspicuously ugly and Germaine, herself the opposite of a beauty, once wrote to the famous salonière Madame Récamier that she would willingly sacrifice half her wit for half of Récamier's beauty. She refused several times to marry Benjamin and he had affairs with other women while under Germaine's sway, secretly marrying Charlotte von Hardenberg while continuing his relationship with de Staël. Constant was more a sounding board for her ideas, a sparring partner who however lacked her rhetorical flourish and suffered under her omnipresence.

Mme de Staël was wont to deal with men of lower social status disrespectfully: there are reports that she treated the well-known literary figure August Schlegel, who piloted her around Germany and served as tutor to her children, like a dog. Germaine criticised the lack of respect with which intelligent women were treated, but, self-centred as she was, can hardly be seen as a real feminist.

George Sand, nom de plume of Aurore Dupin, equally so. Famous for her unconventional life – she dressed in men's clothes, though not on social occasions, smoked cigars and had affairs with a large number of writers and musicians including de Musset, Chopin and Liszt – Sand wrote daring novels, but was surprisingly conventional in other ways. Her feud with France's leading feminist Flora Tristan illustrates this disparity. Sand refused to support suffrage and other issues while attacking Tristan for having neglected the upbringing of her daughter.

Sand (1804–76), like de Staël, married at an early age and soon came to an arrangement with her husband, whereby she received an allowance and brought up their two children, while he gained possession of her estate. Her relationships with other men were intense and, by all accounts, she dominated. In *Indiana*, the first work that Dupin wrote under her pseudonym Sand, the heroine tells her husband that the law of the land has made him her lord and that society confirms this classification, but that he is powerless when confronted with her will. This certainly makes Sand a pioneer crusader for female self-assertion. However, while Tristan devoted her life to the woman's movement, Sand was against female activism of any kind.

This became apparent when the feminist newspaper *Voix des femmes* recommended Sand as a parliamentary candidate. Eugénie Niboyet, the newspaper's founder, was a Protestant reformer with strong moral principles. She had worked for prison reform and the abolition of slavery before imbibing Fourier's ideas of a feminist society. Beyond publishing the newspaper, Niboyet (1796–1883) ran a woman's club open to men that included prominent feminists like Flora Tristan.

In terms of political affiliation, Niboyet was a middle-class moderate; her radical collaborators Jeanne Deroin and Désirée Gay later separated and founded radical publications. Sand not only repudiated the suggestion that she stand for election; she also distanced herself in cutting terms from the newspaper, which canvassed for the reform of women's education and working conditions. Sand rejected the proposition that women should intervene in public affairs, pointing out that the social conditions were such that women could not honourably take on a political function. Evidently, her personal freedom weighed far more than the social issues at stake. One is encouraged to add: more than the social and more than the legal issues at stake.

Lonely Activists

Maria Deraismes (1828–94) struggled together with her ally Léon Richer for reform of the Napeolonic Civil Code. The Association for Women's Rights founded by them in 1869 received no support from the country's prominent women. Her allies derived from the Masonic lodges, including the world's first lodge to accept women. Deraismes became the first female freemason in the Free

Thinkers, from which lodge the International Order of Co-Masonry derived, fittingly called Human Rights (Le droit humain). The Lodge's Grand Master Richer (1824–1911) fought for her admission; however, six months later, the Lodge's members voted to evict her.

Deraismes and Richer were clearly moderates; both refrained from demanding women's suffrage and banned the issue from the International Congress for Women's Rights that they organised in 1878. Despite this, there is no record of any prominent citizens supporting the pair.

The same applies to pioneer suffragist Hubertine Auclert, who, after her introduction to the women's cause by Deraismes-Richer, served as librarian in their association. Later, she founded a rival organisation exclusively devoted to suffrage. Auclert (1848–1914) was distinctly more militant, making no secret of her anticlericalism. Parallel to her agitation for suffrage, she started a tax strike, rather on the lines of the 18th-century American revolutionaries: no taxation without representation. Auclert had stronger contacts with other feminists like Madeleine Pelletier. However, suffrage remained a fringe issue in France and public support for women's votes was lukewarm at best. Moreover, Auclert's abrasive personality apparently alienated potential collaborators.

Madeleine Pelletier (1874–1939) was remarkably versatile, both in her professional life and in her political affiliations. Originally trained as an anthropologist, she later became France's first woman psychiatrist and worked in mental asylums. Parallel to this, she was a cofounder of the new Socialist Party in France, later becoming a Communist Party member and, finally, an anarchist. Pelletier founded the Women's Solidarity Association and participated in suffrage demonstrations at Hyde Park. She also published a suffragist magazine and was an active supporter of both birth control and abortion.

During her socialist phase, she led a delegation of feminists to the French parliament, where the renowned communist leader Jean Jaurès, tragically assassinated in 1914, received them. Jaurès expressed sympathy for the suffrage cause and held a speech supporting it in 1906. He also supervised a parliamentary resolution. However, it was a secondary issue for him; here he strongly differed from the German socialist leader August Bebel or in fact the classic liberal John Stuart Mill.

Outwardly, Pelletier appeared to be a lesbian; with her masculine suit and bowler hat, she looked remarkably like the comedian Oliver Hardy. However, she was celibate; her autobiography was fittingly entitled *The Virgin Woman*. Despite this, she rarely hesitated to call a spade a bloody shovel, once quipping that she would show her breasts if men would respond by wearing trousers that displayed their private parts.

Common Ground: Liberalising Divorce

Divorce was one issue on which male and female reformers could agree. The French Revolution had liberalised and secularised divorce; the Napoleonic Civil Code had however limited the grounds for divorce and manifestly discriminated against women seeking separation from their husbands. While women could be divorced because of adultery, they could only seek divorce if their husbands literally brought their mistresses home. The royalist regime of Louis XVIII later formally abolished divorce.

Divorce's suppression in 1816 was a manifestly religious decision; it was considered incompatible with Catholicism. Those campaigning for its reinstatement were secularists, who profited from the climate of upheaval during the 1848 revolution. A women's club led by Eugénie Niboyet published articles in its favour in their organ *La Voix des Femmes*, while on the men's side, the prominent politician Adolphe Crémieux presented a divorce bill at the National Assembly.

Crémieux (1796–1880) was a man of many causes. As a lawyer

of Jewish descent, he was well acquainted with religious discrimination, both of the Protestants during the "White Terror" and of the Jews. After becoming the leading lawyer in his hometown Nîmes, Crémieux entered politics as a reformer with close links to France's monarch Louis-Philippe, whom he helped persuade to abdicate in 1848. For a short period, he was Minister of Justice and pursued a series of reforms, including freedom of the press, of association and worship and culminating in the reform of the existing marital laws.

Needless to say, Crémieux failed. Public opinion was strongly opposed to divorce and the National Assembly rejected the issue without debate. Despite this, the prominent lawyer had opened the issue and a delegation of 200 married women congregated at the Place Vendôme to thank him.

Ernest Legouvé had greater success and enjoyed an equal degree of sympathy and support both in France and abroad. Legouvé (1807-1903) was a poet and dramatist who became an expert in women's moral history, their rights and the need for better education. His lectures at the Collège de France in 1848 paralleled Crémieux's political efforts and while the latter retired to the background after Napoleon III's accession to power, Legouvé continued his efforts. He analysed the effects of gender in his lectures, thus emphasising the social construction of disparities between the sexes.

The reformer attacked many aspects of the Napoleonic Civil Code, in particular its discrimination against female divorcees. When the law was finally liberalised in 1884, the number of separations increased dramatically. By 1891, 18 times as many divorces as in England were granted in France. At the turn of the century, the French divorce rate reached 23 per 100,000 population, while the British rate doubled from one to two per 100,000. Divorce by mutual consent came only in 1975, two centuries after revolutionary France liberalised divorce in 1792.

Legouvé's moral support came from radical women and men,

including Olympe Audouard and Léon Richer. Abroad, Mill commended him and leading feminists in Germany like Hedwig Dohm and Lily Braun did so as well. However, his main ally was a politician called Alfred Naquet, who canvassed the country and, after many setbacks and a host of compromises, finally managed to get a bill passed, which allowed divorce on the part of both husbands and wives after three years of separation.

Naquet (1834–1916) played many different roles in the course of his long life. Of Jewish origin like Crémieux, he was far more radical, being imprisoned or forced into exile on several occasions. Originally a professor of medicine and chemistry, he later became a member of the Assembly, which gave him a platform to agitate against the divorce laws. A convinced secularist, his reform proposals faced severe opposition from the Catholic Church. He braved laughter, insults and racist caricatures. Later in life, he surprised society by becoming a deputy for the nationalist, anti-Semitic Boulangists. He remains a man of many contradictions, who however was successful where Crémieux, eminently more respectable and respected, failed.

Twentieth-Century Individualism

In the 20th century, literary women continued to practise their own brand of hedonistic individualism. Colette (1873–1954) called George Sand a "tireless bee" and the metaphor reflects back onto her own life. While Sand mostly consorted with men, with the exception of a controversial relationship with an actress, Colette, very much a child of the 20th century, was openly bisexual with a strong lesbian slant. Both women drew strongly on their lives while composing their works, thus providing society with the dual fascination of risqué fiction and non-fiction.

Sand's grandmother brought her up; Germaine's Calvinist mother pushed her intellectually and introduced her to great minds; Colette's mother Sido was an avowed republican, who settled in Belgium and was hostess to a number of radicals who fled from Napoleon III's dictatorship. Sido was introduced at an early age to Fourier's philosophy of free love by his disciple Victor Considerant. After an unhappy marriage to a wealthy drunkard, she had a relationship with a military hero, Captain Jules-Joseph Colette, marrying him after her husband died.

Colette inherited her mother's ideas of sensuality, duly marrying Henry Gauthier-Villars, a literary figure and a libertine, at the age of 20. Then, she had a series of affairs with women while marrying several times; during her career in Paris's music halls, she kissed her intimate friend Mathilde de Morny on stage, provoking an enormous scandal, with further performances of the pantomime being banned. Later, she became a public heroine, converting her husband's property in St. Malo into a military hospital during the First World War and helping Jewish friends during the Second. Colette had the honour of being the first French woman to receive a state funeral.

During this rich life, women gained various rights including suffrage. Colette was openly sceptical, saying that the suffragettes disgusted her and rejecting suggestions that she was a feminist. She even went to the extent of saying that if French women were to copy their British models, they deserved "the whip and the harem." Shades of Queen Victoria. In addition, despite all her achievements, there is an air of resignation in bonmots like "A woman who thinks she is intelligent, demands the same rights as a man. An intelligent woman gives up."

Marguerite Durand was equally flamboyant while truly committed to the women's cause. Durand (1864–1936), a voluptuous beauty born out of matrimony, soon fled from the Catholic convent where she was brought up to enter the Paris Conservatory at the age of 15. After winning the first prize as a comedienne a year later, she duly joined the famous Comédie Française and enjoyed great success in a variety of roles. Then she married a flashy lawyer close to the anti-Semitic, nationalistic movement of General Boulanger.

For a short time, Durand became the "muse of Boulangism" and started writing pamphlets for the movement. She then separated from her husband and became a journalist at the leading newspaper *Le Figaro*. Her bosses had sent her to write a satirical article on the 1896 International Feminist Congress in Paris. Instead of doing so, she was impressed by the arguments and the seriousness of the discussions, quit her job, converted to the cause and became an avowed feminist.

Leaving *Le Figaro*, she started her own newspaper with the help of benefactors enamoured by her charm. *La Fronde* (*The Rebellion*) endorsed a variety of women's causes: better working conditions, admission to institutions as diverse as the Bar Association and the École des Beaux-Arts. The authors represented the crème of female talent: from suffragettes like Hubertine Auclert and pioneer reporters like Severine to Clémence Royer, the first woman to teach philosophy at the Sorbonne, to Jeanne Chauvin, the first woman admitted to the Bar Association in Paris, and to Blance Gallien, France's first female apothecary. With the exception of a janitor, all personnel at *La Fronde* were women. Durand incurred the wrath of the typesetters' trade union when she insisted on employing women for the job and on paying them the same salaries that men would have received.

By doing so, she exposed the unfair practices of large sections of the workers' movement. She also founded an Office for Female Work in 1907 and financed its first congress. However, these successes were short-lived; the newspaper folded in 1905, being briefly revived in later years, while the Office closed down for lack of public funding.

Durand was perhaps unique in wedding feminism with femininity. She once pointed out: "Feminism owes a great deal to my blond hair. I know it thinks the contrary, but it is wrong." Her famous soirées attracted a large cross-section of the Parisian elite, including Presidents of the Republic like Raymond Poincaré and

Prime Ministers like Georges Clemenceau and René Viviani. She made no secret about the fact that she expected the women attending her evening parties to look sexy, asking them to appear in "toilette de soirée décolleté." Scholars like Mary Louise Roberts have pointed out that the link between "acting" and "acting up" indicated the overcoming of traditional gender identities.

This inevitably alienated other, less privileged feminists, who considered her snobbish and mondaine. Beyond that, her impeccable political convictions, she being a republican, a pacifist and a supporter of Dreyfus, seemed less convincing than they would have been if she had been a plainer woman. However, she was probably right to point out that "a studied sense of elegance" was the best way "to deprive short-sighted men of the argument that feminism is the enemy of beauty and a feminine aesthetic." Her studied eccentricity – she went for walks in Paris with her pet lion, whom she called Tiger "for reasons of paradox" – masked a strong streak of philanthropism. Later in her life, she founded the country's first zoological cemetery.

The Office for Female Work only existed because of Durand's contacts to Clemenceau and Viviani. Similarly, Viviani attended the feminist congress held in 1900 and held a bold speech in favour of women's suffrage. However, Durand's male support, which included like-minded journalists like Henry Bérenger and Victor Charbonnel, was tenuous at best. Despite her pacifist convictions, she supported the war effort and was duly disappointed when France's parliamentarians refused to give women the vote after armistice.

An episode demonstrates the separation of the sexes in France. Together with a large number of fellow women's-rights activists, Durand participated in a demonstration in honour of the famous male feminist Condorcet. The photograph taken on the occasion in 1914 shows a large number of well-dressed women and not a single man.

Like Durand, a number of prominent French women used their status as objects of male desire as a way of becoming powerful. Durand grew up in privileged surroundings; the opposite was the case for the fashion designer Coco Chanel and the actress Arletty. Chanel (1883–1971) was born in a poorhouse and grew up in an orphanage. Becoming a tailor and then a singer at café concerts, she quickly discovered her impact on men and embarked on a career as a kept woman that led her to fame and fortune.

She used men as stepping stones: Étienne Balsan introduced her to a life of luxury, while Captain Arthur Capel financed both her apartment in Paris and her first shops. She soon repaid his investment and became truly independent, dealing with businessmen like the Wertheimer brothers, who financed her perfumes, on equal terms. Colette appropriately called her "a small black bull," which certainly accounts for the less savoury aspects of her character: her anti-Semitism, her homophobic tirades, her collaboration with the Nazi regime in France. Here, her attitudes corresponded with the English bluebloods she consorted with, most prominently the Duke of Westminster.

Chanel was in fact a feminist contre choeur: her fashions liberated women from existing gender stereotypes and made them boyish. She appropriated masculinity and substituted sophistication for the opulent ostentation that characterised the Belle Époque. Coco remained Mademoiselle Chanel until the end of her life, though this was more a sign of independence than of feminist assertion.

Similarly, Arletty, the legendary actress in Marcel Carné's cult film *Les enfants du paradis*, became a stenographer and worked in a factory before becoming the mistress of the Jewish banker Jacques-Georges Lévy, who installed her in a villa and introduced her to high society in Paris. Chanel was one of her neighbours, and like Chanel, Arletty (1898–1992) mastered the knack of charming and occasionally seducing men, who promoted her career first as a mannequin, then as a stage actress and a film star. Like Chanel, she enjoyed life during the occupation of France, having an affair with the German officer Hans Jürgen Soehring, for which she was first interned and then exiled from Paris.

The actress practised what many feminists have preached: full equality in her relationships with men and financial independence. Yet, there is no evidence of Arletty solidarising with other women or reflecting on her gender, though her forthrightness – when questioned about her relationship with Soehring, she is reported to have said, "My heart is French, but my ass is international!" – certainly contrasted with the image of idealised femininity that her major films propagated. Chanel was equally frank: when later questioned about her relationship to the German diplomat Hans Günther von Dincklage during the occupation of France, she responded by saying that "a woman of my age cannot be expected to look at his passport if she has a chance of a lover."

Personal Individualism, Collective Lethargy: The French Paradox

Here then is the French paradox. In terms of personal individualism, both in physical and mental terms, France has traditionally been ahead of other Western societies. Precisely for this reason perhaps, steady social progress has been registered elsewhere. It is no coincidence that women gained suffrage in the U.K., the U.S.A. and Germany, not to speak of many other Western countries, far earlier than in France. The same applies to issues like the liberalisation of birth control.

More than in countries like Britain, the U.S. and Germany, male and female feminists were oddly separate. Even when a common cause was found, like divorce, activists rarely found sustained common ground. Crémieux, Legouvé and Naquet were all in their own ways men of principle. Emotional elements like sympathy and friendship with individual female feminists were virtually non-existent. The kind of steady support that women as different as Caroline Norton, Josephine Butler and Emmeline Pankhurst could count on from a broad cross-section of both men and women was unheard of in France.

Profeminists like Léon Richer, who collaborated closely with Maria Deraismes, were lonely exceptions to the general rule. The same applies to Antonin Lévrier, a loyal partner of the suffragist Hubertine Auclert. Lévrier (1849–92) was first her legal adviser and then became her devoted husband. She accompanied him to Algeria, when he became a judge in the French Colonial Service, and returned to France after his death.

In the 20th century, two grandes dames of French feminism had supportive husbands. Maria Vérone was introduced to political radicalism by her father Gustave, who was strongly anticlerical; at the age of 15, she was appointed secretary of the French Congress for Free Thought that her father had co-founded. Vérone (1874–1938) later worked as an editor of Marguerite Durand's newspaper *La Fronde* and then married fellow journalist Georges Lhermitte. Lhermitte (?–1943), who was active in the French League for the Defence of Human Rights, strongly supported his wife, who was President of the corresponding League for the Rights of Women from 1919 to 1938. After she died, Lhermitte became President of the Women's League until his death in 1943.

In Cécile Brunschvicg's case, her husband introduced her to feminism. The eminent philosopher Léon Brunschvicg (1869–1944) firmly believed that women could only achieve equality through the vote. Like Lhermitte, he was active in the French Human Rights League. Both endorsed a moderate brand of feminism. Cécile (1877–1946) was an important member of the French Women's National Federation, as well as the Suffrage Union, and was indeed its leading representative in the interwar years.

Male profeminists remained rare well into the post-war years. By contrast, l'égalité dans la différence, the clarion call for many French reformers, was often an excuse for condescending attitudes, as in the case of Henri Marion, a 19th-century pedagogue who preached the gospel of equality in difference and wrote an influential book, *Psychologie de la femme.* While in favour of education for girls, Marion (1840–96) reacted condescendingly to demands for civil rights and called them confused.

Vive la différence was and is a state of mind endorsed by many prominent women, as Mona Ozouf demonstrates in her book *Women's Words: Essay on French Singularity.* Ozouf allows a broad cross-section of thinkers and activists to speak for themselves, ranging from Germaine de Staël, George Sand and Hubertine Auclert to 20th-century figures like Colette, Simone Weil and Simone de Beauvoir. The common thread is a sense of what Ozouf calls "the inventive variety of individual paths." Since this kind of individualism is apparently stronger than gender solidarity, collective endeavours like female suffrage inevitably become side issues.

The fact that, during the different waves of feminism, men and women seldom united to pursue sustained social progress has meant that in factual terms, France has lagged behind other Western countries. Behind the sophisticated façade and the revolutionary rhetoric lurks a conservative Catholic country, self-righteous and resistant to change.

Epilogue

Male Feminists: An Eternal Paradox?

Women's antifeminism is a paradox awaiting explanation.
Susan E. Marshall: Splintered Sisterhood

If women's antifeminism is a paradox, men's profeminism is, at least at first sight, equally so. In her analysis of the American women who opposed female suffrage, Susan Marshall concentrates on their economic status and family backgrounds. As we have seen in the last part of Chapter 2, the resistance of a sizeable cross-section of antisuffrage women in other countries ranging from Britain and Germany to Switzerland and Spain indicates that this phenomenon was widespread. The explanation however is remarkably simple: the paradox only exists because gender patriotism is assumed as a given.

In reality, women are as little motivated by "sisterhood" as men by "brotherhood." This applies not only to suffrage, but also to a host of other issues discussed in this book. An analogy of this simplistic reasoning is that all Americans, Britons, Germans etc. should believe in the patriotic trope "My country right or wrong." In reality, a minority of mostly right-wing persons generally thought to lack maturity adheres to this ethnocentric "maxim." Others judge their own country depending on upbringing, political convictions, social background and a host of other variables. Similarly, expectations of "My sex right or wrong" are in the final reckoning an insult to the intelligence of the individual woman or man, because she or he is supposed to march in a genetically defined specific direction.

"Can men be feminists?" asks Andrew Shail in the context of a book called *Third Wave Feminism*, published in 2007, and continues: "Is 'male feminism' even viable? Is it at all politically requisite?" This book has demonstrated in ample detail that men have been at least as authentic and effective in their feminism as women, while displaying the same contradictory behaviour.

In conceptual terms, the expectation that men and women should logically behave in favour of their own respective sexes can well be compared to the one-dimensionality of the homo economicus. Classical economics operated under the premise of rational decisions motivated purely by self-interest. Human beings are however a complex mixture of the rational and irrational, as consumer behaviour demonstrates. In entrepreneurial terms, generosity coexists with greed, with ample evidence provided by robber barons and high-tech entrepreneurs like Andrew Carnegie, John D. Rockefeller, Bill Gates and Mark Zuckerberg.

Biological essentialism has been exposed as shallow and misleading by, among others, Anne Fausto-Sterling in *Myths of Gender* and Cordelia Fine in *Delusions of Gender*. There is no convincing evidence of specifically male or female minds, as the personalities described in Chapter 3 illustrate. Chapter 5 has shown that even when men were supportive to women as companions, mentors or soulmates, their motivations and behaviour varied to a great degree.

Antifeminist Principles, Profeminist Behaviour and the Opposite

This book has presented a kaleidoscope of contradictory personalities. Nietzsche played a prominent role in the Prologue: on the one hand an author of infamous incitements to whip women, on the other hand friends with a large number of highly enlightened women and a supporter of women's education.

The same can be said for Darwin, who gave sexism a supposedly scientific foundation and whose reputation as a misogynist is based on flip comments he made when considering matrimony that a woman was "an object to be beloved and played with… better than a dog anyhow." Darwin was not only a devoted husband and father; recent research has revealed that he greatly supported women scientists and collaborated with them on equal terms.

This list can be extended well into the 20th century. The *Shropshire Lad* poet and Latin scholar A.E. Housman, a furtive homosexual, had a cold, overwhelming presence and was often rude to his female students, though others found him supportive. Housman (1859–1936) had a series of deep friendships with women, while he used his frequent visits to Paris to stock up his pornographic library. This duality is part of his persona, parallel to the duality of romantic poet and arcane scholar.

Equally, this book has presented the opposite. Max Weber was committed to feminist ideals and greatly supported his wife Marianne, who played a prominent role in gender affairs at the time. Simultaneously, he was a Casanova with an odd proclivity for both sadomasochism and paternalistic eroticism. Victor Hugo is very similar, valiantly inviting mockery for demanding suffrage and simultaneously treating his wife and mistresses abominably.

A great number of these figures are historic personalities. There is however no problem in finding contemporary examples of paradoxical profeminists. When Edward Kennedy died in 2009, the National Organization of Women hailed him as "Women's rights strongest champion in Congress" and *Ms. Magazine* proclaimed, "The feminist movement has lost one of its greatest champions." The evidence given of his legislative activities to end sex discrimination, a list including the Education Amendment, Family and Medical Leave, and Violence against Women Acts, seems overwhelming.

Reasons of piety obviously inhibited women feminists from dwelling on Kennedy as a man who, according to *The Guardian,* had both a "voracious sexual appetite" and "bizarre sexual behaviour." The infamous Chappaquiddick incident of 1969, in which a young campaign assistant called Mary Jo Kopechne died after Kennedy's car crashed into a dyke and he left the scene, taking nine hours to report what had happened, is perhaps the best documented. Evidence of instances in which he exploited and humiliated women seems equally overwhelming. *The New York Times* summed up the duality of his character fittingly: "Mr. Kennedy spoke for the downtrodden in his public life while living the heedless private life of a playboy and a rake for many of his years." This verdict would ring true with various profeminist men of former epochs.

Paradoxes of Principle

Feminism is often considered an offshoot of humanism. However, those who defended and advanced women's rights often had other unsavoury convictions. Adolph Stoecker is a good example. The late 19th-century court preacher with excellent contacts to Kaiser Wilhelm II made no secret of his anti-Semitic views. Simultaneously, he annoyed many conservatives by stridently supporting women in the working world and by generally having a strong social conscience. In the 20th century, Joseph Barthélemy belonged to a minority of French politicians who called for the women's vote. He was also responsible for anti-Jewish legislation during the Vichy regime and died awaiting trial.

Racists, imperialists and militarists swell the ranks of feminist men and women. In the U.S., female suffragists like Elizabeth Cady Stanton and Susan B. Anthony, dismayed that black men had attained suffrage while white women were denied it, collaborated with Negro-haters like George Francis Train. When criticised for her behaviour, Anthony responded: "Why should we not accept all in favour of woman suffrage to our platform and association even though they be rabid pro-slavery Democrats?" Even moderate feminists like Lucy Stone and Henry Blackwell, who founded the American Woman Suffrage Association in 1869, parting ways with Cady Stanton and Anthony, were by no means free of white supremacist ideology,

Here too, the same pattern can be discerned in the 20th century. The leading suffragette Alice Paul in later years made a dubious bargain with the veteran legislator Howard W. Smith to add a gender component to civil-rights legislation originally designed to end the discrimination against blacks. Smith was an open racist and tried to sabotage the legislation passed in 1964 by making it apply to women as well as blacks.

In the British Empire, both male and female feminists were often clearly imperialistic in their attitudes. This applied to the great crusading journalist W. T. Stead as much as to the New Zealand suffragist Julius Vogel. Others, including the famous abolitionist Josephine Butler, were not ashamed to make xenophobic statements that mostly denigrated foreign women while exalting English girls. Some of this behaviour was obviously tactical: publicity for abolitionism made better copy if it suggestively invoked the purity of English womanhood being sullied by lechers in Continental Europe, particularly in France. However, the evidence presented in Chapter 4 indicates that ethnocentrism was an inherent part of feminism in Britain, Germany and the U.S.

Militant patriotism characterised the women's movements in all major countries involved in World War One. The British suffragettes are a preeminent example; the Pankhursts discontinued their violent activities abruptly in August 1914 and subscribed to aggressive patriotism, going as far as to rename *The Suffragette,* the movement's periodical, *Britannia.* Sylvia Pankhurst by contrast proved to be a worthy daughter of Richard, remaining both socialist and pacifist. However, feminist peace campaigners were a small isolated minority. In Germany, the leading women's associations stridently supported the war effort until the bitter end.

Chapter 4 has documented the links between reproduction

rights and eugenics. Those fighting for birth control and abortion were often motivated by the perceived need to limit the reproduction rate of undesired persons. Eugenics related to racism, classism and xenophobia, as visible in the attitudes of leading members of the Abortion Law Reform Association as in the convictions of birth control's leading women Marie Stopes and Margaret Sanger.

Feminists could be pro- on one issue and anti- on others. The Liberal Party MP Anthony John Mundella was for Married Women's Property but against equality for women. The same applies to his fellow industrialist and parliamentarian Carl Ferdinand von Stumm-Halberg, a friend of Kaiser Wilhelm. Both were great social reformers with strong authoritarian tendencies. Similarly, Liberal MP George Shaw-Lefevre was for property rights but against suffrage, while his Conservative colleague William Wheelhouse was of exactly the opposite conviction.

Personalities are often described in terms of having one conviction or another: being for or against abortion for instance. In some cases, it would be more accurate to speak of convictions during a particular life phase. Dr Alec Bourne first performed one of the most famous abortions ever carried out in Britain. Later in life, he became a strong pro-life adherent.

His American colleague Bernard Nathanson demonstrated that one could move from pro-choice to pro-life with great panache. Nathanson helped found the preeminent abortion-reform association NARAL and not only campaigned for liberalising abortion, but also claimed to have practised it more than 60,000 times. Later, he controversially campaigned against abortion, calling it an "atrocious Holocaust" and making several films with radical scenes showing foetuses being aborted.

Liberal Feminism's Innate Paradoxes

Most of the feminists described in this book were of liberal persuasions. They demanded equal rights and expected the law to respect and promote the individuality of women. Often, they were rationalists in the sense that they rejected biological explanations of gender roles and exposed male powermongering. In addition, they were radicals, believing that sexism went deeper than other modes of repression such as classism and racism.

All this contrasted positively with the socialists and Marxists. Despite the ideas of thinkers like Engels and the efforts of party leaders like Bebel, women's rights were of secondary importance for the doctrinaire left, subordinate to the interests of the working class. This book has concentrated on male feminism in major countries like the U.S., Britain, France and Germany. Since Western society as a whole has remained persistently liberal, socialist activists were rarely responsible for landmark changes.

However, liberal feminism has had its contradictions. Protestations of absolute rationality varied with bows to "woman's nature." The very foundations of Anglo-Saxon liberalism are incipiently patriarchal, being based on the inviolability of life, liberty and above all property. Property however has traditionally been owned and administered by men. Thus, liberal feminism, to be effective, would have had to undermine its own foundations. Ironically, though the American Declaration of Independence substituted the word "happiness" for "property," this did not improve women's status in any tangible way.

Liberalism's original and enduring sin is its lack of social conscience. The patron saint of profeminism John Stuart Mill provides excellent testimony of the overestimation of individuality. Mill's concept of liberty had close links with German romanticism and to Wilhelm von Humboldt's Bildungsideal. His elitist attitudes regarding suffrage eligibility and corresponding distance to the working-class limited the purview of his feminism. His fellow-suffragist Millicent Fawcett's commitment to the economic status quo became manifest during the famous match-girls strike of 1889. Fawcett was a shareholder of Bryant and May, the company that employed the match girls. Needless to say, she sided with the company during the dispute, not with her fellow women.

"Doing it for ourselves: Can feminism survive class polarization?" This was the title of an essay published by the American author-activist Barbara Ehrenreich in 1999. Ehrenreich focused on how the liberal women's-rights movement was unable to transcend income and wealth disparities. A year later, the black feminist bell hooks expressed in her book *Where We Stand: Class Matters* her conviction that the only reason why Second-Wave feminism achieved media attention was because privileged women rebelled against their own class.

One of Third-Wave feminism's greatest achievements has been to raise consciousness for the intersectionality of class, race, nation, region and other social attributes liable to discrimination. Simultaneously, convictions of "hegemonic masculinity" have lost relevance in the context of gender contradictions and historic ruptures. Standpoint theory has relativised former assumptions of sex-based hierarchies. Judith Butler goes as far as considering gender identity to be an unstable fiction.

Feminism's Janus-Face

Feminism is a form of modernist thought. Despite the pioneers portrayed in Chapter 1 of this book, major progress in women's rights mostly came in the course of the 20th-century. Modernist thinking is incipiently humanistic, since it envisages a universal human nature and equally universal rights.

However, paradoxes, contradictions and ambiguities characterise modernism. Marshall Berman affirms that modernity unites mankind and then points out, "But it is a paradoxical unity, a unity of disunity: it pours us all into a maelstrom of perpetual disintegration and renewal, of struggle and contradiction, of ambiguity and anguish."

In view of this amorphous situation, it seems apposite that profeminism is measured and honoured by what it achieves, after the paradoxes are viewed and accepted. Perhaps the most sublimely prosaic example of paradox in praxis is *Playboy*. The magazine has objectified the female body more profoundly than any other medium of communication. At the same time, both the magazine and the Playboy Foundation have vigorously supported women's rights, as Carrie Pitzulo describes in her book *Bachelors and Bunnies: The Sexual Politics of Playboy*.

Playboy is perhaps the ultimate symbol of feminism's Janus-face. Moralists beware. When the magazine announced in 2015 that it would soon stop printing nude pictures, this was a mercantile, not an ethical decision, just as its earlier support for birth control and abortion facilitated a sexual revolution with vast benefits for both men and women. In the face of Internet pornography, the famous centrefolds seemed tame and indeed irrelevant. The magazine's circulation had dropped accordingly. Seductive photos will remain; it remains to be seen if the enlightened attitude to women's rights persists as well.

Virginia Woolf famously remarked that the history of men's opposition to women's emancipation was perhaps more interesting than the emancipation story as such. This book has turned the Janus-face of men's attitudes around to spotlight support, which is hopefully even more interesting.

Selected Bibliography

Acker, Julia Robertson. *"No woman is the worse for sense and knowledge": Samuel Johnson and Women*. College Park: University of Maryland, 2007.

Aronowsky, Leah Vaughan. *Debating Contraception, Defining Motherhood: Women, Doctors, and the State in the Politics of Birth Control*. Middleton: Wesleyan University, 2010.

Bebel, August. *Die Frau und der Sozialismus*. Stuttgart: Verlag Dietz, 1895.

Berg, Urte von. *Theodor Gottlieb von Hippel*. Göttingen: Wallstein Verlag, 2004.

Bohjalian, Christopher A. *Educating Gentlewomen*, in: *Hayes Historic Journal*, Fall 1984, pp. 48–67.

Brooke, Stephen. *"A New World for Women"? Abortion Law Reform in Britain during the 1930s*, in: *The American Historical Review*, April 2001, pp. 431–59.

Bush, Julia. *Women Against the Vote – Female Anti-Suffragism in Britain*. Oxford: Oxford University Press, 2007.

Caine, Barbara. *Victorian Feminists*. Oxford: Oxford University Press, 1993.

Cathcart, Abby. *Directing Democracy: The Case of the John Lewis Partnership*. Leicester: University of Leicester, 2009.

Chernock, Arianne. *Men and the Making of Modern British Feminism*. Stanford: Stanford University Press, 2010.

Delap, Lucy. *The Woman Question and the Origins of Feminism*, in: *The Cambridge History of Nineteenth-Century Political Thought*. Cambridge: Cambridge University Press, 2011, pp. 319–48

Dickinson, Edward Ross: *The Men's Christian Morality Movement in Germany, 1880-1914: Some Reflections on Sex, Politics, and Sexual Politics*, in: *Journal of Modern History*, 75/2003, pp. 59–110.

Dickmann, Elisabeth. *Die italienische Frauenbewegung im 19.*

Jahrhundert. Frankfurt: Domus Editoria Europaea, 2002.

Digby, Tom (ed.). *Men Doing Feminism*. New York: Routledge, 1998.

Forth, Christopher E. and Elinor Accampo. *Confronting Modernity in Fin-de-Siècle France – Bodies, Minds and Gender*. New York: Palgrave Macmillan, 2009.

Fout, John C. *Sexual Politics in Wilhelmine Germany - The Male Gender Crisis, Moral Purity, and Homophobia*, in: *Journal of the History of Sexuality*, 3/1992, pp. 388–421.

Furter, Daniel A. *"Die umgekehrten Suffragetten" – Die Gegnerinnen des Frauenstimmrechts in der Schweiz von 1958 bis 1971*. Berne: Universität Bern, 2003.

Gillis, Stacy et al (eds.). *Third Wave Feminism*. New York: Palgrave Macmillan, 2007.

Gilmore, David D. *Misogyny: The Male Malady*. Philadelphia: University of Pennsylvania Press, 2001.

Gleadle, Kathryn. *The Early Feminists: Radical Unitarians and the Emergence of the Women's Rights Movement, 1831-5*. London: St. Martin's Press, 1995.

Gleeson, Kate. *Persuading Parliament: Abortion law reform in the UK*, in: *Australasian Parliamentary Review*, Spring 2007, pp. 23–42.

Goodlad, Lauren M.E. *"Character worth speaking of": Individuality, John Stuart Mill, and the Critique of Liberalism*, in: *Victorians Institute Journal*, 36/2008, pp. 7–46.

Graham, Sally Hunter. *Woodrow Wilson, Alice Paul, and the Woman Suffrage Movement*, in: *Political Science Quarterly*, Winter 1983–84, pp. 665–79.

Groult, Benoîte. *Gleiche unter Gleichen: Männer zur Frauenfrage*. Munich: Knaur, 1995.

Hall, Donald E. *Fixing Patriarchy – Feminism and Mid-Victorian Male Novelists*. New York: New York University Press, 1997.

Harrison, Brian. *Bertrand Russell: The False Consciousness of a Feminist*, in: *Russell – The Journal of Bertrand Russell Studies*,

4/1984, pp. 157–99.

Hassoun, Danièle. *Histoire de la légalisation de la contraception et de l'avortement en France*. Association Nationale des Centres d'IVG et de Contraception, undated.

Hennigan, Peter C. *Property War: Prostitution, Red-Light Districts, and the Transformation of Public Nuisance Law in the Progressive Era*, in: *Yale Journal of Law & the Humanities*, 1/2004, pp. 1-76.

Holland, Jack. *Misogyny – The World's Oldest Prejudice*. Philadelphia: Running Press, 2006.

hooks, bell. *Where We Stand: Class Matters*. London: Routledge, 2000.

Jacquemart, Alban. *Les hommes dans les mouvements féministes – Socio-histoire d'un engagement improbable*. Rennes: Presse Universitaire de Rennes, 2015.

Jardine, Alice and Paul Smith. *Men in Feminism*. London: Routledge, 1987.

Kiberd, Declan. *Men and Feminism in Modern Literature*. London: Macmillan, 1985.

Kimmel, Michael S. and Thomas E. Mosmiller (eds.). *Against the Tide – Pro-Feminist Men in the United States, 1776-1990*. Boston: Beacon Press, 1992.

Macdonald, Charlotte. *Suffrage, Gender and Sovereignty in New Zealand*, in: Sulkunen, Irma et al (eds.). *Suffrage Gender and Citizenship: International Perspectives on Parliamentary Reforms*. Newcastle upon Tyne: Cambridge Scholars, 2009. pp. 14–33.

Marshall, Susan E. *Splintered Sisterhood – Gender and Class in the Campaign against Woman Suffrage*. Wisconsin: University of Wisconsin Press, 1997.

Meder, Stephan et al (eds.). *Frauenrecht und Rechtsgeschichte*. Weimar: Böhlau Verlag, 2006.

Mesinger, Judith. *The Feminist Movement As Reflected in the Gerrit Smith Papers*, in: *The Courier*, 10/1973, pp. 45–54.

Mill, John Stuart. *Three Essays*. London: Oxford University Press, 1975.

Mosconi, Nicole. *Henri Marion et "l'égalité dans la différence"*, in: *Le Télèmaque*, 1/2012, pp. 133–50.

Murphy, Catherine. *"On an Equal Footing with Men?" Women and Work at the BBC 1923-1939*. London: University of London, 2011.

Murphy, Peter F. (ed.). *Feminism and Masculinities*. Oxford: Oxford University Press, 2004.

Nall, Jeff. *Condorcet – Male Prophet of Feminism*. www.condorcet.info.

Odorisio, Ginevra Conti. *Salvatore Morelli – L'esprit européen de l'émancipation*, in: *Les cahiers du GRIF*, 1/1994, pp. 151–63.

Offen, Karen. *Women, Citizenship and Suffrage with a French Twist, 1789-1993*, in: Caroline Daley and Melanie Nolan (eds.). *Suffrage and Beyond – International Feminist Perspectives*. New York: New York University Press, 1994. pp. 151–70.

Offen, Karen. *European Feminisms, 1700-1950*. Stanford: Stanford University Press, 2000.

Oliver, Kelly and Marilyn Pearsall (eds.). *Feminist Interpretations of Friedrich Nietzsche*. University Park: Pennsylvania State University Press, 1998.

Passmore, Kevin. *Women, Gender and Fascism in Europe, 1919-45*. New Brunswick: Rutgers University Press, 2003.

Pyke, Margaret. *Family Planning: an Assessment*, in: *The Eugenic Review*, July 1963, pp. 71–79.

Pyle, Andrew (ed.). *The Subjection of Women – Contemporary Responses to John Stuart Mill*. Bristol: Thoemmes Press, 1995.

Régnier-Loilier, Arnaud and Henri Leridon. *After Forty Years of Contraceptive Freedom, Why So Many Unplanned Pregnancies in France?* in: *Population & Societies*, November 2007, pp. 1–8.

Riedel, Tanja-Carina. *Gleiches Recht für Frau und Mann – Die bürgerliche Frauenbewegung und die Entstehung des BGB*. Cologne: Böhlau Verlag, 2008.

Rochefort, Florence and Élaine Viennot (eds.). *L'Engagement des hommes pour l'égalité des sexes*. Saint-Etienne: Publications de l'Université, 2013.

Roper, Michael and John Tosh (eds.). *Manful Assertions: Masculinities in Britain since 1800.* London: Routledge, 1991.

Rosenbusch, Ute. *Der Weg zum Frauenwahlrecht in Deutschland.* Baden-Baden: Nomos Verlagsgesellschaft, 1998.

Sanders, Valerie. *Eve's Renegades – Victorian Anti-Feminist Women Novelists.* New York: Palgrave Macmillan, 1996.

Shelton, Jacqueline. *Evil Becomes Her: Prostitution's Transition from Necessary to Social Evil in 19th Century America.* Jackson City: East Tennessee State University, 2013.

Smith, Angela K. *The Pankhursts and the War: Suffrage Magazines and First World War Propaganda,* in: *Women's History Review,* 1/2003, pp. 103–18.

Smith, Paul. *Feminism and the Third Republic: Women's Political and Civil Rights in France, 1918-1945.* Oxford: Clarendon Press, 1996.

Sotelo, Elisabeth de. *Feminist Theory and Feminist Movement in Spain,* in: *Gender…Politik…Online,* January 2006.

Strauss, Sylvia. *"Traitors to the Masculine Cause" – The Men's Campaigns for Women's Rights.* London: Greenwood Press, 1982.

Stites, Richard. *The Women's Liberation Movement in Russia – Feminism, Nihilism and Bolshevism 1860-1930.* Princeton: Princeton University Press, 1978.

Symonds, Richard. *Inside the Citadel – Men and the Emancipation of Women, 1850-1920.* London: Palgrave Macmillan, 1999.

Taylor, Barbara. *Lords of Creation – Marxism, Feminism and "Utopian" Socialism,* in: *The New Statesman,* March 7, 1980.

Telman, Jeremy. *Abortion and Women's Legal Personhood in Germany: A Contribution to the Feminist Theory of the State,* in: *Review of Law & Social Change,* 91/1998, pp. 91–148.

Vickers, Anita M. *"Pray, Madam, are you a federalist?": Women's Rights and the Republican Utopia of Alcuin,* in: *American Studies,* Fall 1998, pp. 89–104.

Walkowitz, Judith R. *Male Vice and Feminist Virtue: Feminism and the Politics of Prostitution in Nineteenth-Century Britain,* in: Snitow, Anne et al (eds.). *Powers of Desire: The Politics of Sexuality*. New York: The Monthly Review Press, 1983, pp. 419–38.

Young, Homer H. *The Founding Fathers on the Education of Women,* in: *Rice University Studies,* 43.1/1956, pp. 48–62.

Acknowledgements

This book developed over a period of several years and I am greatly indebted to institutions and individuals who helped me with my research, as also to those who were willing to enter into a dialogue about male feminists.

This is specifically the case with the Women's Library in London. It has proved a rich source of materials of various kinds. I am particularly grateful to Inderbir Bhullar, whom I have consulted over a number of years. Indy has been of great help during my research; he also read the entire manuscript, making some very relevant comments that I have integrated into the final text.

The Archive of the German Women's Movement in Kassel has been another great source of support for this project. Here too, a well-catalogued array of books, magazines and documents of different kinds was made available. I am very obliged to Dr Kerstin Wolff, who has given both cogent advice and great moral support to the project. Like Indy, she read through the manuscript and corrected some inaccuracies.

Among the researchers and experts I consulted, I would like to highlight the support given by Professor Mary Evans of the London School of Economics. After reading through the manuscript, she sharpened my awareness of redundancies deriving from the book's structure. This was of great help during the final revision of the text.

Dr Lucy Delap of the University of Cambridge made some useful comments on focusing the book and was of particular help in retitling it. The work of other researchers like Professor Arianne Chernock of Boston University and Professor Michael Kimmel of the State University of New York has proved extremely useful and both reacted very positively to the project. Needless to say, mistakes and discrepancies are solely my responsibility.

Index of Names

This list concentrates on men and women with a tangible impact on gender affairs.

Contemporary culture has eliminated both the concept of the public and the figure of the intellectual. Former public spaces – both physical and cultural – are now either derelict or colonized by advertising. A cretinous anti-intellectualism presides, cheerled by expensively educated hacks in the pay of multinational corporations who reassure their bored readers that there is no need to rouse themselves from their interpassive stupor. The informal censorship internalized and propagated by the cultural workers of late capitalism generates a banal conformity that the propaganda chiefs of Stalinism could only ever have dreamt of imposing. Zer0 Books knows that another kind of discourse – intellectual without being academic, popular without being populist – is not only possible: it is already flourishing, in the regions beyond the striplit malls of so-called mass media and the neurotically bureaucratic halls of the academy. Zer0 is committed to the idea of publishing as a making public of the intellectual. It is convinced that in the unthinking, blandly consensual culture in which we live, critical and engaged theoretical reflection is more important than ever before.